D0948586

JOURNAL FOR THE STUDY OF THE OLD TESTAMENT
SUPPLEMENT SERIES
309

Sheffield Academic Press

Culture, Entertainment and the Bible

edited by
George Aichele

Journal for the Study of the Old Testament
Supplement Series 309

Published by
Sheffield Academic Press Ltd
Mansion House
19 Kingfield Road
Sheffield S11 9AS
England

Typeset by Sheffield Academic Press
and
Printed on acid-free paper in Great Britain
by Bookcraft Ltd
Midsomer Norton, Bath

British Library Cataloguing in Publication Data

A catalogue record for this book is available
from the British Library

ISBN 1-84127-075-X

CONTENTS

Part II
ART, LITERATURE, MUSIC

Part III
ON IDEOLOGY

FOREWORD

Athalya Brenner

To be personal: I love this book. All articles. The opportunity to have fun with biblical texts and 'culture' by juxtaposing them. And the remarks I'm going to offer by way of a Foreword, although critical, are in the spirit of love.

One of the things I learnt from Roland Boer, in his response to the Ruth articles of 1997,[1] is to classify articles and group them into coherent units, before discussing them within the space limit available. And so, immediately upon reading the articles here collected, I run into difficulties. Should they be classified by the biblical texts referred to? That would have made two groups. The first would contain articles referring to Hebrew Bible texts, a majority here—either to the Hebrew Bible in general (Walsh and Black, for instance) or to specific texts in it (like Kramer and Rowlett on Raḥab, Joshua 2 and 6). The second group would contain articles referring to New Testament texts (Graham, Pippin and Aichele, Vander Stichele). All these biblical texts, be they from the Hebrew Bible or the New Testament, are read together with extra-biblical intertexts, intertexts from 'culture'. Such an arrangement, foregrounding the Bible, would have made for a more traditional, conservative book: a collection of reflections on/reflexions of biblical texts, proceeding from the canon outward into various instances of its manifestations and reinterpretations in contemporary western life.

In this project, however, another principle of classification was followed. The articles presented are organized not in accordance with divisions of the Bible, but along divisions of 'cultural types'. 'Lowbrow' culture (popular media, especially films but also press and books),

---

1. At the Semiotics and Exegesis section, Society of Biblical Literature Annual Meeting. The papers as well as Boer's response are reproduced in Brenner 1998: 130-70.

'highbrow' culture (literature, visual art, music and education), and ideology are the organizing principles. This choice turns the tables around. The point of departure is now external to the Bible, not internal to it. The basic criteria, the focus, move away from the Bible (be it Hebrew Bible or New Testament) to its presentation, representation and materialization.

The materials here presented are too varied to discuss *en bloc*, which is highly satisfactory. On the other hand, detailed argumentations are left for the authors themselves to perform. This Foreword is *not* going to present the contents of individual articles. So here we go—some personal reflections on some of the points raised, mostly in the form of a series of critical, overlapping questions.

The genesis of this book was, again, in a session of the Society of Biblical Literature Annual Meeting,[2] although several of the essays here included were not presented in that session.[3] I was the respondent to the papers of that session, and would like to pose the same questions I posed then to the authors in this collection. After all, if Bible scholars are to go beyond their traditional pursuit into the 'Bible and/in Culture' dangerous arena, a minor and less rarified place no doubt, some problematization seems to be in order. Although the questions are directed at the authors (whose works presumably contain the answers), they are also directed at the implied readerly audience of this volume. And although 'low culture', that is, entertainment, is possibly more of a hazard for the serious-minded Bible critic, problematization of reading the Bible with fine art intertexts seems worthwhile as well.

Question One to each of the participants in this project (and to their readers) is as follows. Why did you choose god, Yhwh or the Christian god, or Rahab the prostitute or Babylon the whore, or a prophet like Elijah, or a 'good Christian', and so on, as the focus of your articles? Putting aside the simple condition of availability—our children bring in a cartoon film; or we happen to watch television when a certain movie is shown; or a friend recommends a book; or an art piece is viewed at a museum by chance, etc.—what sparked your interest in the particular analogic and dialogic process you have presented to us? Why did you,

2. Again a session of the Semiotics and Exegesis section, in San Francisco, November 1998.
3. The essays by Leneman, Vander Stichele, Tarlin, Runions, Pippin and Aichele.

why should we, go outside the Bible for reading a certain passage? What can we gain by it? What pleasure, of any kind, did/can we achieve this way?

Question Two. Some general concerns are apparent in most articles—about God, about sacred texts, about the millennium, about science fiction and film and education of the young and inexperienced and the ignorant and the existential issues of reality vs fantasy. I understand that you, each of our authors, have a serious reading agenda, over and apart from the simple basic wish to understand, enjoy and also play with the biblical material. May I ask you what your agenda, as a Bible scholar and an individual with personal convictions and tastes, is? This would help me to understand your rich paper. You made a choice of reading culture in/about serious religious/textual issues. I presume that the subject matter attracted you. For instance, therefore, I would like to know whether your readings of the cultural artifacts you chose to juxtapose with the Bible, be they what they may, have enriched your life in any way (before I confess whether they have enriched mine)? And if so, how? And has this exercise made a difference to your work as a Bible scholar? Does the Bible, as I suspect, remain your personal primary text for defining the divine and godly imagery and religious sentiment any time, anywhere? If so, what parts of the Bible? These are not rhetorical questions, far from it.

Question Three. This volume contains social critique of various hues, arrived at through cultural analysis, predominantly directed at contemporary or near contemporary North American socio-cultural phenomena. Is this critique valid or instructive for other times, other places? And if so, to what extent?

Question Four relates to the millennium fever. Several articles have millennial uneasiness and apocalyptic anxieties as underlying strata. For many readers, the millennium change is a scene of deep interest. For me, it provokes only the mildest anthropological interest. This fever is once more a Western European/North American phenomenon, certainly non-Jewish, hence I occupy the position of the new-born squid in the *Men in Black* film here (see Black's article). Would readers of this volume share my stance? Who would, who would not?

Question Five, after a small introduction. I love reading about the Bible in our lives, although 'straight' reflections on the Bible and Bible interpretation interest me profoundly too. Nevertheless, I find the analogy of the Bible to popular, sensational journalism and 'lowbrow' media very apt. I often wonder about the so-called 'original', implied audiences of biblical pieces, about their incredulous reactions to miracle stories for instance (I would), about the historical accidence that meta-morphosed some imaginative canonical fantasies into scriptural revela-tions leading to dogmas. I worry about the absolutism of many biblical passages, about their claims for truth, about their claims on the reader, about their trickery and manipulative character. I worry about my own tendency to listen to that very tiny voice in my thoroughly non-religious being, whispering gently, 'and what if, incredulous as it may seem...' So, where do we go now—does the millennium count in biblical studies, should it? Should we believe, everything or some? What criteria should we employ? Should our attitudes to biblical stories/claims be different from our attitudes to media claims—and how?

Question Six. For most of us, reading the Bible together with literary giants (such as Kafka) or esteemed artists (such as Rembrandt) or influ-ential theorists or philosophers (Freud, Žižek) and musicians (Händel) has been accepted practice for a while. Does the fact that the practice is accepted and acceptable by most make it better and more valuable, say, than examining Bible residues and interpretations in films, children's books, yellow journalism and the like?

Question Seven. Does the Bible-as-popular-entertainment, as it is done in North America and Europe, we've had some examples, get our approval? Is it a 'good thing', even when we dislike a particular per-formance or presentation, or is this approval reserved for when we like it? Do we see the analogies to our guild's practices in the Entertainment practices? Would we join the topical rush and write a children's Bible story, like Alice Bach and Cheryl Exum[4] and Klaas Smelik[5] have done? Or shall we participate in a documentary series, like Carole Fontaine has done?[6] Or shall we do a children's movie like the Israeli serious author Meir Shalev?[7] Or do we dare to bring popular culture into our

---

4. Bach and Exum 1998.
5. Smelik and Naftaniel-Joëls, 1986a, 1986b, 1987, all three in Dutch.
6. In the *Mystery of the Bible* series, also featuring Gale Yee, Jane Schaberg and other Bible scholars.
7. Meir Shalev collaborated on an animated children's movie on the Creation/ Garden (Genesis 1–3). He also wrote a popular book, *The Bible Now* (Shalev 1985), in which he popularizes and updates, in midrashic fashion, several Hebrew Bible narratives. The book was translated into English, Dutch and German, among other languages.

classrooms as exegesis, on the same level as our own belaboured efforts? Or shall we adopt a superior attitude in our dealings with the Bible in/and popular culture, a 'we-know-better' slightly caustic sarcasm, donating a knowing wink and a nod to our cultural environment while retaining our rather sedate equanimity, as befits solemn 'scholars'?

The questions raised here, and by the articles in this book, are serious and go to the core of both biblical studies and the Bible in culture, which are as interconnected as the two heads of the same Janus figure. The Bible has always been an elitist object—produced, consumed, transmitted and studied by elites variously defined by religious praxis, age, gender, class, ethnicity, occupation and status. This applies in different yet also similar ways to the Jewish Bible as well as to the Christian Bible. Although the Bible's democratization was greatly enhanced by its translations into vernaculars, it remained confined in elite secrecy. As scholars, we do of course sustain this legacy of secrecy and perpetuate it, thus hoping to perpetuate—as scholars would—our own influence in the texture of our culture.

But the second half of the last century saw the beginning of changes. The social/normative evaluation of gender, class, ethnicity, patterns of work and even religion have changed. Democratization entails popularization; easy dissemination of information and knowledge requires the abolition of copyright restrictions together with trade secrets. As a secret society, the future survival of the Bible Scholars Guild is in jeopardy.

I wonder, therefore, whether we Bible scholars shall be brave enough to focus on the Bible's heritage in our culture—in the fine arts *and* in the media, among other phenomena. Some of us have already started doing just that, as this book demonstrates, tentatively or with confidence.[8] Others are still afraid of losing the traditional philological/classical base of our art-and-craft. Certainly, a certain loss will be accrued: this is in keeping with the changing modes of education. But the gain of doing cultural/biblical studies so-called, outside organized religion especially, may be enormous. Who knows, this way the Bible may continue to exist as a book for life, an identity cultural marker. Redefining it as a cultural commodity which, yes, also happens to be a

8. See also Exum and Moore 1998.

religious book may save the Bible from popular oblivion. And it may save us Bible scholars from socio-political insignificance too—while allowing for great fun, of the serious and the light-headed types, in the process.

ACKNOWLEDGMENTS

The bibliography at the end of the volume provides details of works cited for all of the articles. Permission to use the following copyrighted material is gratefully acknowledged. All rights are reserved by the respective copyright holders.

Fiona Black's article was previously published in *Semeia* 82 (1999 Society of Biblical Literature) and is reprinted by permission.

Illustration from *L'Apocalypse de Jean* vue par Charles Sahuguet (Saint Maurice [CH]: Editions Saint Augustin, 1998) used by permission of the publisher.

Image from *Bible Stories for Jewish Children from Joshua to Queen Esther* © 1973 Ktav Publishing House, Hoboken, NJ.

Image of 'The Great Whore' (1993) by Phil Vermeer used by permission of the artist.

Images from *The Beginner's Bible* © by James Levinger 1997, used by permission of Performance Unlimited, Inc., Brentwood, TN.

Images from *Weekly World News* © 1997, 1998, used by permission of Weekly World News, Inc., Lantana, FL.

Stills from the videotape, *Above the Law: Part 1, Deception Gustafsen Lake* © 1997 Mervyn Brown, used by permission of John Splitting the Sky Hill.

George Aichele is Professor of Philosophy and Religion at Adrian College, Adrian, Michigan. With Tina Pippin, he has co-edited issues of *Semeia* and the *Journal for the Fantastic in the Arts* on fantasy and the Bible, as well as *The Monstrous and the Unspeakable* and *Violence, Utopia, and the Kingdom of God*.

Fiona C. Black is Killam Postdoctoral Fellow at the University of Alberta. She wrote her PhD thesis for the University of Sheffield on the grotesque body in the Song of Songs. She has published several articles on the Song of Songs and is presently researching erotic and pornographic texts of the Bible. She has recently edited a volume of *Semeia* on autobiographical criticism and cultural studies.

Athalya Brenner is Professor of Hebrew Bible/Old Testament and Chair in the Department of Theology and Religious Studies, Faculty of the Humanities, University of Amsterdam. She is the editor of the *Feminist Companion to the Bible*, first and second series (14 volumes and 5 to come), and lives in Haifa, Israel, and Amsterdam, the Netherlands.

Susan Lochrie Graham teaches in an ecumenical theological course affiliated with the University of Exeter in England. She has just completed *The Flesh Was Made Word: A Metahistorical Critique of the Contemporary Quest of the Historical Jesus* and is working on a textbook for film and theology studies.

R. Christopher Heard is Assistant Professor of Bible at Milligan College. He recently published 'Hearing the Children's Cries: Commentary, Deconstruction, Ethics, and the Book of Habakkuk', in *Semeia* 77. He serves as a consultant for the World Bible Translation Center headquartered in Ft Worth, Texas.

Phyllis Silverman Kramer is a faculty member at The Melton Center for Jewish Education in the Diaspora. She has authored 'The Dismissal of Hagar in Five Art Works of the Sixteenth and Seventeenth Centuries' and 'Biblical Women that Come in Pairs: The Use of Female Pairs as a Literary Device in the Hebrew Bible', in *Genesis: A Feminist Companion to the Bible* (second series).

Helen Leneman completed her cantorial training and Masters in Judaic Studies at Hebrew Union College in Los Angeles. She worked as a cantor for several congregations prior to writing and editing two books on Bar and Bat Mitzvah education. Cantor Leneman has lectured and written widely as part of her concert/lecture series 'Musical Illuminations of Biblical Women', a unique approach to biblical women through scholarship and song. She is currently a PhD student at Baltimore Hebrew University.

Lori L. Rowlett is Assistant Professor of Religious Studies at the University of Wisconsin, Eau Claire. Before earning her PhD in Hebrew Bible at Cambridge University, she studied languages and literary theory. She is best known for her book *Joshua and the Rhetoric of Violence: A New Historicist Analysis*, and her anthologized article ' "All Israel" as Literary Trope: Inclusion, Exclusion and Marginality in the Book of Joshua', both published by Sheffield Academic Press.

Erin Runions is a PhD candidate at McGill University, part-time faculty at the Department of Religion, Concordia University, and an anarchist anti-capitalism/(neo-)colonization activist. She is currently working on a dissertation which reads Micah and Homi Bhabha together, and this work has produced articles in *Semeia*, *Postmodern Interpretations of the Bible*, and *The Labour of Reading*.

Jan William Tarlin is a doctoral candidate in the Graduate Division of Religion Hebrew Bible Program at Emory University, Atlanta, Georgia. He has taught at Emory College, Candler School of Theology, The Atlanta College of Art, and Montana State University-Bozeman. His work has appeared in *Reading Bibles,Writing Bodies* and *A Feminist Companion to Samuel and Kings* among other volumes.

Tina Pippin teaches Religious Studies and Women's Studies at Agnes Scott College in Decatur, Georgia. She is the author of *Death and Desire: The Rhetoric of Gender in the Apocalypse of John* and *Apocalyptic Bodies: The Biblical End of the World in Text and Image*.

Richard G. Walsh is head of the Philosophy and Religion Department, director of the Honors Program, and assistant academic dean at Methodist College. He is the author of *Reading the Bible: An Introduc-*

tion, a literary-critical textbook for beginning biblical students emphasizing diverse readings, and is at work on another book for Sheffield Academic Press tentatively titled *The Myth of Biblical Interpretation*.

Caroline Vander Stichele teaches New Testament at the University of Amsterdam. She is currently doing research on the cultural reception of biblical women.

Part I
POPULAR ENTERTAINMENT

LOST PROPHECIES! SCHOLARS AMAZED!
WEEKLY WORLD NEWS AND THE BIBLE

Fiona C. Black

I intended a study of tabloid use of biblical material long before I saw *Men in Black*. Bored with the choices on the video-store shelves one day, I grudgingly checked out this last-year sci-fi blockbuster comedy.[1] To my surprise, I was *converted* upon viewing it. The conversion was not to the realities of *Men in Black*, with its cast of slimy creatures (though I could be more open to their existence now), but to willingly suspending my disbelief as a viewer and a reader.

The scene that made all the difference is one where the film engages that titanic of truth, the supermarket tabloid, for a major propulsion of plot. Though the film's flirtation with tabloids is brief and somewhat serendipitous, it is illuminating. In the scene in question, MIB Agents J (Will Smith) and K (Tommy Lee Jones) have just sped through Manhattan to intercept the getaway car of an alien, Redgick, who is attempting to leave the planet, but is haplessly stalled at the side of the road while his wife gives birth to their first…squid.

> K: Anything about that seem unusual to you? What would scare Redgick so badly that he'd risk a warp jump with a newborn? Let me check the hotsheets.
> J: *These* are the hotsheets?
> K: Best investigative reporting on the planet. Go ahead, read the *New York Times* if you want to. They get lucky sometimes.
> J: I cannot believe you are looking for tips in the supermarket tabloids.
> K: Not looking for. Found.

---

1. I am grateful to my colleague, W. John Lyons, for suggesting I use the film in my planned study of tabloid use of biblical material. He has been an invaluable conversation partner throughout my journey towards the Truth.

The camera pans over a table laid out with four supermarket week-lies. The tabs appear to be movie-world fakes, but playfully, display titles that have all featured in 'real life' in the *Weekly World News* (*WWN*): *The Eye* blinks out in disbelief, 'Medical Miracle! Pope a Father!' (complete with picture of expecting mother—or Sister, rather—weeping); *The Examiner* announces, 'Top Doctors Baffled: Baby Born Pregnant!'; and 'Man Eats Own House' is unearthed by *The Snooper*. All are recycled stories from the *WWN*, that is, except for the fourth one. It provides the information for which K searches and which pro-pels the film's plot onward: *The World* reads, 'Farm Wife Says, "Alien Stole My Husband's Skin!" ' Armed with this knowledge, K and J are able to interview the first earthly contact of an illegal alien, 'Edgar,' and begin their quest to apprehend it.

Post-viewing, it proved hard not to read certain biblical scenes as fodder for the movie's plot. Acts 9, for example:

> Now as [Saul] was going along and approaching Damascus, suddenly a light from heaven flashed around him. He fell to the ground…[and when] he got up…though his eyes were open, he could see nothing; so they led him by the hand and brought him into Damascus. For three days he was without sight, and neither ate nor drank…
>
> [Then] Ananias…laid his hands on him and said, 'Brother Saul, the Lord Jesus, who appeared to you on your way here, has sent me so that you may regain your sight and be filled with the Holy Spirit.' And imme-diately something like scales fell from his eyes and his sight was restored. Then he got up and was baptized, and after taking some food, he re-gained his strength (Acts 9.3-4, 8-9, 17-19; with apologies to the NRSV).

Saul's conversion reads like an alien visitation, I thought: the 'visi-tor' manifests itself surrounded by bright lights; the subject is rendered motionless, hears voices (someone or something communicates with him), and suffers short-term physical side-effects (Randles 1997: *pas-sim*). There is even a moment in Saul's story when an outsider contacts him to interpret the event and remove its temporary effects, sort of like a biblical Man in Black. And, from that fiery point, Saul's life is irreversibly altered.

I read with disappointment how Saul's extra-terrestrial episode (some would call it a theophany) has been treated in mainstream NT scholar-ship. Here, for example, are some rather unspectacular facts about Saul's close encounter, courtesy of C.K. Barrett's magnum opus on Acts:

- [Luke] chooses to write here in biblical style because he is describing a theophany (Christophany) and an event comparable with the call of the prophets (1994: 448).

- Light is a common feature of theophanies, e.g. Ps. 27.1; 78.14; Isa. 9.2; 42.16; 60.1, 20; Mic. 7.8... (1994: 449).

- Paul himself understood the event as revelation (Gal. 1.12, 15), but not in a gnostic sense. Nor does light mean for Luke illumination of a gnostic kind; it is a physical representation or accompaniment of the divine glory of Christ (1994: 449).

- Paul fell to the ground; another feature of theophanies (1994: 449).

- In the present verse it is both clear that Paul both perceived a sound and distinguished the words that were spoken; according to Delebecque the accusative means that Saul did not *see* the speaker (1994: 449).

- Saul is aware that he is confronted by a superhuman being (1994: 450).

- Luke, without too much concern for rigid consistency, wished in each narrative to express the thought that all recognized a supernatural event but only one understood its meaning (1994: 451).

I recognized my scholarly upbringing in this commentator's work, particularly the propensity to disregard the fantastic in the Bible by translating it into the familiar. Sure, Saul's 'conversion' was remarkable, but we can rest easy that the deity exhibits some habitual behaviour in making appearances and that this pericope brings Saul into line with what we expect of him, from the rest of his biblical legacy.

Before my own film-induced conversion, in an earlier draft of this article, I wrote about tabloids and the Bible in a manner similar to Barrett's analysis of Saul's experiences:

> Biblical material as it appears in my year-long sampling of two tabloids is limited to three kinds of areas. The first and most used are the stories that treat the end of the world. These usually involve claims about biblical prophecies (or lost prophecies of a biblical figure, now found) about Armageddon or Jesus' second coming. Various natural events and disasters are often cited as support for claims about our impending doom (Revelation is very creatively read here). The second group are what I have loosely termed 'archaeological'. These involve the locating of certain key biblical 'props', such as the Tower of Babel or Noah's Ark, and the like. Finally, in a looser grouping, we find what can best be termed

biblical culture—often pietistic stories about the appearance of biblical figures (Mary, Jesus) or phenomena associated with them (the Shroud of Turin). It is immediately clear, then, that not all biblical material is prime for the taking.[2] Tabloid editors are clearly looking for and using material that will be familiar to the popular memory—even if the dim, distant memory from Sunday School long ago. They are also looking to feed popular interest in the end times (there are a similar number of stories on the end of the world that are scientific and not biblical), and use the Bible not so much to increase biblical knowledge, or to show off fancy hermeneutics, but to give credibility to their story. It matters not so much what the Bible says, or how it is being read, just that it says something.

I certainly mastered the ability to catalogue.[3] But there I was the embarrassed reader, putting on the disguise of the cold, objective student of tabloid culture. I failed miserably to see the significance of what hard-working reporters try to bring to our attention each week.[4] I also failed to let myself enjoy what was there for the taking. So what was I missing?

Within the counter-culture of the *Men in Black*, the premise on which the story operates is that there is something going on behind the scenes, perhaps somewhat sinister, which is actually reality; moreover, it is a reality that is so threatening to us that we must either deny its existence, or be protected from it by those who have our best interests at heart (the MIB).[5] Tabloids exist as the best, most accurate source of truth. K does

---

2.   Some of it begs to be included, but has, however, strangely been omitted. I am considering offering a mock up of the woman in the Song of Songs with the caption: 'Woman Has Pet Gazelles: Growing on her Breasts!! "I feed and water them daily," she says!'

3.   The source material used for this paper comprises copies of the *Sun* and the *Weekly World News*, spanning November 1997 to August 1998. My research is thus necessarily limited.

4.   In a self-promoting article (7 April 1998: 18), the *WWN* claims that the reason it is 'No. 1' is by virtue of hard work. To give just one example, a reporter apparently rode three days on a mule to interview a man in Nicaragua who lived for 67 years with a knife embedded in his head (7 April 1998: 18). Would a reporter put himself at such risk and under such hardship for fiction?

5.   The theme is perpetuated through the movie by the character of Laurel Weaver, the city coroner, who keeps discovering evidence of alien existence, but is repeatedly 'neuralyzed' (her memory is obliterated) by J and K, even though she wants to believe. In another predictable ending to a movie, Weaver becomes the latest employee of the MIB, once K retires.

not verbally claim total accuracy and objectivity for them, but this is implied, since whenever he consults them, they happen to be right.[6] Moreover, their accuracy actually saves the world. This same exactitude is manifested when the tabs are used again in the film to grant us our happy, Hollywood ending. The truth of the cover stories can be verified from the plot of the movie. The tabloid J picks up provides us with a way to tie up a loose end (what happens to K?). Thus, the contents of the tabloids are privileged, at least if you know how to interpret them. The MIB have alerted us to the fact that they may be taken literally.

The Bible, as it appears in this tabloid context, takes on a refreshing new shape. One grows weary of postmodernism as biblical critics see it, of textual indeterminacy, of variable authority. Why must we take ourselves so seriously? What if, I wondered, we succumbed to the enticements of tabloid reporting, the invitations to believe the incredible, the assertions of truth against the odds, the insistence on univocal readings? This would be postmodernism with a difference. But, *caveat lector*: tabloids are proselytizing creatures. My T-shirt with a 500-foot picture of Jesus caressing the cupola of the Capital Building (Victoria 1998: 1, 46-47) is wending its way through the post to me as I write.

I worry. Will biblical scholars miss the significance of *Men in Black* and what it suggests for our interpretation of the Bible? Will we miss out on tabloid truth? Agent J (who represents, no doubt, the majority of the film's viewers) is incredulous at K's insistence that the hotsheets are the 'best investigative reporting on the planet'. Pre-conversion, so was I. After all, there is much to dissuade us 'educated' folk from taking them seriously: social stigma, the vulgar tabloid format, their reputation as junk. Even the papers themselves, though their contents flatly deny it, give us an excuse to discredit them. The front matter of the *WWN* reveals a disclaimer, 'Weekly World News is a journal of opinion and information'. The *Sun* is a bit more frank: 'SUN stories seek to entertain and are about the fantastic, the bizarre, and paranormal. Articles are written by and obtained from the SUN staff, the World Press, freelance correspondents and the general public. *The reader should suspend belief for the sake of enjoyment*' (my italics).

---

6.   In the novel by Steve Perry which accompanies the film, K states it a little more clearly. In response to J's incredulity ('You're pulling my chain again, aren't you?') he replies: 'You think so? You know what we do for a living. When was the last time you read about aliens in the *New York Times*?... Those guys don't have a clue. Now *these* guys...these guys are at least on the right track' (Perry 1997: 98).

But such provisos are intended for America's litigious culture. And, they are intended for those who buy these papers with compulsion, but embarrassment,[7] the literary equivalent to the box of Trojan, Ribbed-For-Your-Pleasure, hidden between leafy lettuce and paper towel on the supermarket conveyor belt. Our little secret: the store employee's and mine. Though nothing of what follows these cautionary words intends for one minute to uphold them ('True!' 'Believe!' 'Revealed!'), they exist for people who are too afraid to consider the alternatives. Here lies permission from the papers (if we require it) to avoid what really hits home to us. Here also lies a foil, for the truth is not for everyone to handle. The publishing provisos fit the same role as plush chairs and theatre screen. Viewers can depart, all the better for their popcorn-induced fantasy, and reassure themselves—if they have any doubts—that it's only a movie. Such provisos are for biblical scholars, too, who can pick apart biblical texts with gleeful violence, condemning them for all they are worth, this patriarchal, colonial, monstrous collection. It's only a text, they can tell themselves.

Men in Black can capably deal with the fantastic and the incredible because it is played straight, as the actors themselves note, 'like this stuff is completely normal' (Will Smith in Herzog 1997). The film plays with 'tricks that invite the audience to gleefully suspend their disbelief, not just willingly' (Tommy Lee Jones in Herzog 1997). The Bible also shoots straight from the hip. Naturally, it makes no stipulations in its introductory pages: 'In the beginning… [footnote: 'God makes no claims for veracity in the stories that follow. Readers should suspend belief for the sake of enjoyment and thrilling frights'].' Quite the contrary, those first three words launch stories that demand full concentration from the reader (even in the boring bits) and one hundred percent assent to their veracity, again, a gleeful suspension of disbelief. Rows 1 through 10 are *not* reserved for 'Resistant Readers'.

---

7.   At this point, I must offer a word of thanks to my mother, who painstakingly bought me a copy of the *Sun* and the *WWN* for almost a year and shipped them out to England for me, where they are not available. I was amused to learn of her initial embarrassment at the purchase, explaining to the probably oblivious check-out clerk that she was buying them for her daughter who was writing an article on them. What, I wondered, is more embarrassing and unbelievable? Someone who reads these papers, or someone who is crazy enough to drag them into the hallowed halls of the ivory tower, and link them with, of all things, the Bible?!

For *Men in Black*'s director Barry Sonnenfeld, there is also some-thing more consequential at hand:

> I love the fact that I could make a movie and play it totally for the reality of the situation, with aliens in it, and let the world know that we truly don't know. I mean, I truly believe that we don't have a clue what's *really going on*.[8]

Tommy Lee Jones echoes the sentiment: 'the universe is a large and varied place and we're not living at the centre of it' (Herzog 1997; is Jones speaking of the movie's world here, or his own?). And, in a characteristic move, this notion also finds its way into the plot of the movie:

> K: All right kid, here's the deal. At any given time there are around 1500 aliens on the planet, most of them right here in Manhattan. And most of them are decent enough. They're just trying to make a living.
>
> J: Cab drivers.
>
> K: No, not as many as you'd think. Humans for the most part don't have a clue. They don't want one or need one either. They're happy. They think they have a good bead on things.
>
> J: But why the big secret? People are smart, they could handle it.
>
> K: A person is smart. People are dumb, panicky, dangerous animals and you know it. 1500 years ago, everybody knew the earth was the centre of the universe. 500 years ago, everybody knew the earth was flat, and 15 minutes ago, you knew that people were alone on this planet. Imagine what you'll know tomorrow.[9]

---

8. Herzog 1997. Further to this, Sonnenfeld adds in a foreword to the *Men in Black: The Script and the Story behind the Film*, 'I once took a college course where I learned that every single thing 'experts' on the planet have ever claimed about the truth has turned out not to be true… So for us to talk as if we have firm knowledge of anything is ridiculous… I wanted to make a movie that in a light and fun way shows us that perhaps we are clueless… Even though this story is a fan-tasy, working on this movie has made me stop and wonder if it's closer to reality than we think' (Solomon 1997: 6-7).

9. Perry's novel adds the following onto the discussion. K: 'Yeah. A hundred years from now, whoever is here will probably pee themselves laughing at what we believe. Thing is, we don't live in the future, we live in the now. And *now*, the truth is, we have aliens walking around on our planet. Only a handful of people know this, and at the moment, you are one of them. You're like the guy who knew the world was round when nobody else believed it… You have access to a piece of truth that most people don't. The truth isn't always popular or pretty, but it is the truth' (Perry 1997: 66). J rather likes the power behind this sentiment. Again in the

In his direction, Sonnenfeld is clearly not intending a serious inquiry into the possibilities of an alien presence. Ultimately, he is out to tell an entertaining story and to direct a successful movie: 'We have a really great story and really great actors. And that is really why people go to the movies' (Herzog 1997). And, why, really, do people read the Bible? Why read it for a living, especially if one happens to be a proud disbeliever and an avid antagonist of biblical myth?[10] Perhaps a better way of asking these questions is to consider why the Bible is still a good sell, in popular and academic culture. The Bible has its share of oddities and it thrives on nothing being what it seems. World-floods and dividing seas, near-disaster, grotesqueries, resurrecting gods, sparkling, brave new worlds: are these perhaps what attract us? Take a look at what is on the 'growing edge' in biblical studies these days—the 'juicy' stuff. Gender, horror, bodies, sex, porn, shit. Of course, we perform the necessary theoretical prestidigitation to assure ourselves that we have brainy, just intentions for the text. But maybe we immerse ourselves in these stories because we are fascinated, titillated, and because we are considering the possibility—fearfully perhaps?—that they are true. The greater our credibility is taxed, the better our chances for diversion: the weirder it is, the better, the truer, the read. And who can deny that he or she is out for a good read? Bible-as-tabloid provides a perfect alternative to scholarly anxiety and ennui.

After the editorial words that excuse and disguise, the tabloids tell an altogether different story. The papers resemble the world of the *Men in Black* in their fantastical subject matter.[11] Not surprisingly, the fantastic

novel, he ruminates over his new job offer: 'Thing was, Edwards [J] kind of felt like a guy who'd been issued a dip net and sent to clear minnows out of a reservoir. Nothing wrong with that—unless you looked up one day and saw a couple of sharks glide past. How could you concentrate on the minnows once you knew about the bigger game swimming past?' (Perry 1997: 69).

10. Readers should not be mistaken. I am not privileging biblical interpretation by theologians or people in particular relationships with faith communities. I am merely curious about what attracts a certain kind of biblical scholar to this text in the first place.

11. It is not at all remarkable (to the converted) that the tabloids reinforce the connection the film makes with them. On December 30, 1997, the *Sun* printed the article, 'Fear Silences Ham Radio Witness: "Men in Black" Riddle of US Jet Buzzed by UFO'. In the top left hand corner is a snapshot of Will Smith and Tommy Lee Jones, as Agents J and K. The caption underneath reads, 'Men in Black: More than a Movie' (Balfour 1997).

is a prerequisite for tabloid reporting. I was fortunate enough to see an interview with *WWN* Editor Eddie Clontz on NBC's *Entertainment Tonight* (12 March 1998). Clontz says proudly: 'the wildest stories of the week? Those are the ones we go after. A story too weird for the *WWN* to run? Not in the sixteen years I've been here, no.' 'Weird' and 'wild': these, then, are the criteria for what constitutes the news. At every available opportunity reporters insist on the validity of their stories—by sensationalistic headlines, by consulting 'experts', by claiming their truthful, prophetic quality. One could not, of course, verify all the stories one reads, but occasionally one sees events reported that have taken place in one's own neighbourhood. For example, the *WWN* recorded the cases of Simon Weston, the Falklands War hero who advertised for a woman to marry him, despite his terribly burned and scarred face (Lind 1997); of Alison Kennedy, who was stabbed in the head with an 18-inch hunting knife on a London train, and lived (Morgan 1998); and of Nigel Wesson, whose hungry tiger bit off his arm up to the elbow in Oxford (Berger 1998). All true. It is just that 'truth' is stranger than 'fiction'.

Interestingly, this same hermeneutic influenced the making of *Men in Black*. The film's own origins stem from a 1990s comic of the same name created by Lowell Cunningham. The comic playfully engages the possibility that there were mysterious Men in Black who tried to suppress all knowledge and rumour of alien activity. It is based on an urban legend that can be traced to the 1950s, when the world was rocked by the outrageous claims of Albert K. Bender and others like him, who wrote of their first-hand experiences of aliens and then subsequently, attempts by mysterious Men in Black to prevent them from speaking about their experiences. Cunningham's remarks about his work in an interview which appeared in the first comic are telling:

LC: Maybe we need an organization like the MIB.
Q: Because so many weird things are going on?
LC: Sure, I mean, look at some of the things reported in the media. There's the Gator Man over in South Carolina. In Europe there's a 'ghost crossing' on one highway. In big cities, convenience stores are being held up by nude men who steal clothes… Here in Tennessee there's a musician who claims to be artistically inspired by aliens. And that's just what makes it into the news. Who knows what else is going on?
Q: You must really keep up with the news.

> LC: I think truth really can be stranger than fiction. A lot of what I've
> written for this series was inspired by news stories… Whenever I hear
> about something which is dismissed as hysteria or sensation, I imme-
> diately think, 'But what if it really did happen?' (Solomon 1997: 18).

Cunningham's criterion for something newsworthy is something that is
dismissed as hysteria or sensation. Furthermore, as *WWN* fans and non-
fans alike will notice, the stories are not what we might call mainstream
news: the Gator Man has become a *WWN* cult object, soon to rival even
the notorious Bat Boy.[12] It seems fairly clear to what branch of the
media Cunningham subscribes.

The right branch? *Men in Black* and Cunningham in his comic both
argue for the privileging of the tabloid media as an inspired source of
truth. By no coincidence, the same is claimed for the Bible by many
interpretive communities, and, implicitly (or sometimes not), by some
academic traditions of reading it as well. And when these two worlds
collide, we are left with an extremely entertaining and enticing proposition: if the Bible appears in the tabloids, and the tabloids have a special
avenue to the Truth, it follows that the way the Bible is used and interpreted in the tabloids must be the 'right' way. And why not?

Like many in my generation of biblical critics, I was preliminarily
'trained' to do historical criticism, but I learned early not to expect historical accuracy—as I uncritically understood it as a young undergradu-
ate—from the biblical text. Noah's ark probably did not exist and the
burning bush did not really burn (there may have been a bush, but in all
likelihood it just looked bright in the midday sun). The *WWN* and the
Sun, however, provide scientific evidence for these unscientific phenomena. The bush certainly burned—and it is still burning: it was found
on 27 February 1998 in the Holy Land and photographed by scientist/
clergyman Ira Roget (Cunningham 1998; see Figure 1). Roget's conclusions that something 'genuinely odd is going on' (we are frequently
afraid to admit this, I find) and that God might be preparing to speak
again certainly fill out my previously deprived experience of this story.
Moreover, they make it extraordinarily relevant for our current, tumul-
tuous times.

12. Batboy was discovered by the *Weekly World News* in 1992. Visit
http://www.weeklyworldnews.com/batboy/batboy.html for more information.

BIBLE'S BURNING BUSH FOUND IN HOLY LAND!

By ROBERT CUNNINGHAM / *Weekly World News*

JERUSALEM — The discovery of a burning bush has stunned scientists who say that flames reaching temperatures of 2,000 degrees leap from the tender branches and leaves of the shrub 24 hours a day — but cause no damage whatsoever!

Clergymen are also excited by the find. And at least one has gone so far as to speculate that God might be preparing to speak through the burning bush — just as the Bible says He spoke to Moses in Old Testament times.

"I don't know what else to say — it's a miracle," declared Dr. Ira Roget, one of dozens of clergymen and scientists who have been studying the bush since it was found.

"This little shrub defies the laws of physics. And short of having faith in a Supreme Being who has the power to make a bush burn like a torch without turning to ash, there is absolutely no way to explain it."

The Los Angeles-based physicist jetted to the Holy Land after a col-

Dr. Ira Roget photographed the bush.

2,000-degree flames burn 24 hours a day — but never harm the miraculous plant!

Figure 1. From *Weekly World News*, 10 March 1998. Used with permission.

Perhaps even more significant than the recovered burning bush is the stunning news that the Tower of Babel has just been located on Mars (readers might recall NASA's recent Pathfinder Mission there with the Sojourner).[13] It is said to be almost definitely identical to Earth's Tower of Babel, the remains of which were recently discovered by archaeologists (the *WWN* does not say when; Foster 1998b). The biblical text is cited in the *WWN* article as evidence for both archaeological finds, which presents us with an intriguing state of affairs: media, history, and Bible are now apparently unanimous in their conclusions about this structure. Bible supports history and history supports Bible. We need no longer to assert that the truth is 'out there'; this chapter is at least closed, since the truth is *in fact* right before our eyes. And in an interesting twist, the article also has important implications for the history of art. The photo included in the article bears a remarkable resemblance to Pieter Breughel the Elder's painting of the Tower (1563), which raises some curious questions (see Figure 2). Could Breughel have seen Earth's Tower, or, was there in fact, extant documentation of it,

13. For more information, consult the Center for Mars Exploration web page, http://cmex-www.arc.nasa.gov/.

available to Breughel, but since lost? It would do well for archaeologists to begin looking (perhaps the Dead Sea Scrolls might offer some assistance, now that they are all available for study). Or, what might be more to the point, do we now have evidence for alien (Martian) presence on Earth from the late Renaissance period? In all, though it is not argued in the *WWN* that life presently exists on Mars, the fact that the Tower was discovered there presents stimulating questions for further study, not to mention exciting possibilities for future colonization of the planet.

Figure 2. From *Weekly World News*, 19 May 1998. Used with permission.

Two further *WWN* archaeological articles are possibly the most exciting for NT scholarship and Christian theology. On 23 December 1997,
the *WWN* published a Christmas-time 'double whammy'. The headlines
read: 'Virgin Mary's Toothbrush and Sandals Found...Buried Near
Rock Where She Rested on the Way to Bethlehem' (Creed 1997a) and
'Star of Bethlehem Was Really a UFO...Sent to Earth by God Himself,
Says Expert' (Jeffries 1997c). Though the paper makes no claim that
the stories are connected, they obviously are (no need to be coy and say
we're reading intertextually) and, in turn, provide vital new insight to
our understanding of Jesus' birth. The first story refers to an excavation
of the Byzantine Kathisma Monastery on the outskirts of Jerusalem (see
Figure 3).

Figure 3. From *Weekly World News*, 23 December 1997. Used with permission.

According to an online news source,[14] the church and monastery were
built in the mid-fifth century CE on the rock or seat (*Kathisma*) where
Mary is said to have rested on her journey to Bethlehem. The *WWN*
claims that it is under the *Kathisma* that a reliquary containing the
artifacts was found (Creed 1997a: 37). A short time after Mary took her

14. Jerusalem Observer Online (www.atcom.co.il/jeronline/jol2.htm [Mother of
Jesus Find]).

rest, she reached Bethlehem, where the baby Jesus was born,[15] and, according to the Gospel of Matthew, Magi followed a 'star' to the birth place in order to worship him. The *WWN* points out, however, that the star does not behave like a star, and was most likely a UFO—Matthew was unable to describe it as such because he did not have experience of such phenomena (Jeffries 1997c: 7).

Biblical scholars concur that the information given about Jesus' birth and childhood in the Gospels is sparse. We know from Luke that Jesus was born in Bethlehem, and that Mary and Joseph had to travel there because of a census (Lk. 2.1-7). Later, they were visited by shepherds (Lk. 2.8-20) and by Magi (Mt. 2.1-12). What is not known, however, are the particular details of the stories and how they fit together. Moreover, we have not had, until now, any archaeological evidence of the texts' account, and so the less believable aspects have heretofore been viewed skeptically. The Anchor Bible Commentary on Matthew will suffice as an example: 'This account of the visit of the Magi to Bethlehem has on the face of it all the elements of historical probability, and yet at the same time elements which appear to belong more plausibly to parable' (Albright and Mann 1971: 13). These conclusions are true enough for much of the infancy narrative.[16] Luke's version doesn't even take us through the pregnancy and birth—and the conception is explicated in a rather scientific, unexciting manner. Matthew does not describe how the couple traveled, but whisks them from A to B without so much as a by-your-leave (Mary's pregnancy was almost to term; popular reconstructions of the story have her sitting on a donkey, but no donkey is mentioned in the text). Once they reached Bethlehem, we might ask how they found the place where they stayed, if, as the Gospel implies, the town was completely inundated with visitors. Would the stables not also be full with the animals that all the visitors had brought with them? Did God show them? How?

The Gospels are reticent on these vital details, but the *WWN* stories provide us with more information. Mary did not walk to Bethlehem— how could she? She was transported via star/ship, and clearly, shown

15. For the skeptical, the *WWN* recently released evidence that virgin birth is, in fact, possible (23 June: 26). In a virgin birth, where an embryo spontaneously develops, a baby girl would be an exact genetic copy of her mother. And a baby boy...?

16. I use the phrase to refer not to one Gospel's version, but all the information about Jesus' infancy that is available from the (canonical) Gospels.

where to go once she reached her destination. The star/ship remained in orbit until the Magi (Mt. 2.1-10) found the baby Jesus some time later. According to the specialist consulted in the *WWN* article (Dr Clarence Majedo), the angel who appears to the shepherds in Luke was an alien who had been traveling in the ship seen by the Magi (Jeffries 1997c: 7). But the stories raise additional questions: how do we explain the presence of the toothbrush and sandals? It seems clear that these items are obvious plants by the aliens—or Men in Black—to create a more realistic context for the sparse infancy narrative, and to make people believe that Mary and Joseph actually made the journey. The deception is clear enough to the initiated: Mary would *not* leave such vital belongings carelessly behind. Though we have little biographical information on her, we cannot, without evidence to the contrary, accept that the mother of Jesus was anything but meticulously organized. *WWN* not only answers persistent questions about Jesus' birth, it also assists in ameliorating the abiding Synoptic Problem that troubles so many biblical scholars: aliens provide the essential connection between the Lukan and Matthean stories.

Another article printed in the *Sun* (Roller 1998) provides an interesting postscript—really a prophecy—to this story. Billed as an 'Amazing Archaeology Triumph', the *Sun* claims that the whereabouts of Noah's Ark are known to the CIA,[17] and, most importantly, that in the possession of a British solicitor are six tablets, found with the Ark, that were written by Noah at God's command. One of Noah's predictions is that visitors from space (he called them 'Angels of the Lord') will intermarry with Earthlings in our future and create a new species 'of tall, intelligent super-humans who will one day reach the stars' (Roller 1998: 21). The tablets read: 'The sons of the angels will return to the heavens and all the shining stars in the firmament will be taken for dwellings' (Roller 1998: 21). Noah could not have been more accurate, as we now realize from the tabloid accounts of Jesus' birth. It would be tempting to suspect that Noah was referring to a group like the *nephilim*—fallen ones—of Gen. 6.4, but, as is clear from his prophecy, the

17. Interestingly, the ark was reputedly discovered in 1949, which happens to be around the same time when the furor over the MIB phenomenon first came to light (see Randles 1997: 22-50). Considering the alien connection in this story, and the possibility that MIB are really government agents (refuted by the US Air Force in 1967; Randles 1997: 92-94), the *Sun*'s story has important implications for the MIB debate.

outcome of these visitors will be for good, not evil, as in the Genesis account. The 'sons of Angels' are, as the *Sun* reporter has correctly interpreted, children of alien and earthly parents. What is more, the presence of their alien parents was made known long before our time in the travels of Mary and the birth of Jesus.

The *Sun*'s article on these mysterious tablets brings us to what are by far the most consequential aspects of the Tabloid Bible. Though the 'archaeological' stories may be fascinating and entertaining, the world's uncertain fate means that their relevance for our times is somewhat limited. Should we colonize Mars, for instance, how many of us might still be around to see it? Our planet seems to be on a crash course for destruction, and it is clear that this is a weighty preoccupation in popular thought. Indeed, the end of the world is big business. One only has to look to recent Hollywood hits and near misses such as *Independence Day*, *Deep Impact*, or *Armageddon* for evidence.[18] In the tabloid media, a dose of fantastic frighteners about the world's demise is at the ready, where the Bible leads the way, contextualized so that its true eschatological orientation can be brought to the fore.

Noah's prophecy offers some harsh words for humankind's future.[19] Tablets 4 through 6 speak of impending Armageddon, which, warns Noah, could only be avoided through a worldwide effort of prayer, initiated by the government.[20] The alternative is a terrible battle that will 'devastate the earth and render it uninhabitable for a hundred years and fifty' (Roller 1998: 21). But is this a true alternative? Measures for

---

18. It is a wonder that in all of this near destruction of biblical proportions, though, the Bible is not invoked more frequently in the movie industry. With its tell-it-like-it-is ending of doom and gloom for the planet (except, of course, for a chosen few), it is especially ripe for the picking. Will it be long until we see a feature-length version of The Last Days of Revelation? Only, where would America fit itself into the story to save the world? That space, annoyingly, is already occupied by Jesus.

19. But it is delightfully written. For example, the writer's source, a 90-year-old archaeologist, says: 'They stripped the ark bare, then they took the boat itself.' Then we read: 'A match flared in the darkness as the archaeologist fired a cigarette, revealing a face grown old under countless suns on every continent in the world' (Roller 1998: 20). One can almost see his wizened face, smell the sulphur as the match fizzles out.

20. It is fortunate that the leader of one major world power, Bill Clinton, is a churchgoer and avid man of prayer, as recent events in his political and personal life concerning Monica Lewinsky have illustrated.

avoiding it seem highly unlikely. Moreover, the final tablet forecasts a period of peace, if disaster is averted, where health care is free and spending for defense cut drastically. It would be wiser to prepare oneself for the inevitable—or settle down with a nice alien—than to live on false hope.

Other tabloid articles about the end times point to the grim eventuality of the destruction of Earth. Any 'golden age' realized will be solely for the benefit of those who prepare themselves, and it will be heavenly, not earthly. Whereas Noah was not able to be too specific in his prophecy as to when the event would occur, recent texts recovered from an original manuscript of the Gospel of Matthew[21] contain prophecies of Jesus about the end of the world that are more exact (Creed 1997b). The finder, a Dr Frank C. Blagner, projects that the end will be some time before 2005. The recovered text declares, 'a deadly fire 27 times hotter than any before it will rain from the sky because of man's hatred, and the world of sin and wickedness will pass away' (Creed 1997b: 25). There are a number of other prophecies also included, among which are that animals will begin talking; the dead will return; humankind will make links with alien civilizations; a war between two major powers will be declared; a comet will strike Asia, bringing much death. The forecast may sound like a *Simpson*'s Halloween special, but the tabloid really does mean business. In what can only be viewed as a stroke of providence, another article in this issue promises a twelve-point plan to get oneself into heaven (Dexter 1997).

Yet another important artifact, this time found in Jesus' tomb by French archaeologists (Jeffries 1998b), contains prophecies from Jesus. Some of these have already come true (e.g., the destruction of the temple in 70 CE; strife and bloodshed for the Holy Land until the end of the age), while others chillingly refer to the new millennium. In the year 2000, Jesus foretells that a bright light will appear in the sky and many will turn to God because of it. Dr Paul Renoit believes that this refers to one of at least four comets which will be visible from Earth at that time (we should forgive Dr. Renoit for missing the star/ship that he is not looking for). In addition, visitors will come from other worlds to carry people to heaven (Jeffries 1998b: 9). And there is more.

These alien visitors are thus not only important to the infancy stories of Jesus, but will also be recurrent features of the end times. The

21. The article explains that they were removed from their original position after Mt. 24.36, for fear that they would be too disturbing.

significance of alien involvement in our past and for our future cannot be underestimated. People are already making contact with alien races, as many news articles, not to mention movies, have illustrated (e.g. Carlton 1998; Creed 1998; Silva 1998). When we are too misguided to realize what is actually happening from the signs around us, there have been occasions when these helpful folk have ventured to Earth to deliver warnings. On 18 November 1997 (Jeffries 1997a), the *WWN* revealed that a captured alien, after learning English in a single afternoon, disclosed God's displeasure at Earth's ways and God's plan to systematically destroy all that had been created (see Figure 4). And the alien should know. His race has the ability to communicate directly with the deity, and past pleading on behalf of their own world was to no avail: it was recently decimated. God's intention is to destroy our planet on 11 January 2000 (Jeffries 1997a: 3).

Figure 4. From *Weekly World News*, 18 November 1997. Used with permission.

So where is Jesus in all this? There is, as yet, no convincing evidence (or, perhaps I should say, no clear revelation) that he was an alien. But there is obvious communication occurring between the divine world and alien races. It appears that, as per biblical prophecy, Jesus will return to Earth, but just what 'return' means is open for debate. Many of the tabloid stories prophesy Jesus' second coming. However, according to a report leaked from the US government (Sanford 1998c), Jesus is already on Earth, and he has been since his second earthly birth in Los Angeles in 1967. He has been living a quiet life, thanks to the US government, in a secured safe house in Maine. The article points out, however, that in the year 2000, he will be 33 years of age, the age he was when he was crucified, and he is expected to make himself visible shortly by beginning a preaching career. And this re-entry back into the preaching community may well be as the tabloids and the Bible describes ('on the clouds of heaven'; Mt. 24.29). Will he preach on repentance and the kingdom of heaven? Or on alien 'abduction'? Watch the tabloids for the answer.

If anyone suspects it, tabloids do not make bold but unfounded claims about our future. Signs of the coming Apocalypse are supported by various 'top' biblical scholars. In a double-page spread (*Weekly World News* 1997b), REPENT appears in large, fat letters, the insides of which are filled with the photographs and insights of twelve 'clergymen' (see Figure 5). (The *WWN* interviews the world's top twelve Bible scholars: Reverend Roger Cleypoole; Father Vincente Donatello; Father Janos Soltesz; Dr Jonathan Doering; Professor Brian Kingsley; Reverend Edith Rodale; Dr Otto Kahn; Reverend Sandra Wayans; Dr Hamid Said; Professor Joan Merchen; R. Herzl Rosenblum; Professor Hong Tran Hoa, calling them, variously, 'Bible scholars,' 'clergymen' and 'religious thinkers'. We should be chastened that none of the experts are members of the American Academy of Religion or the Society of Biblical Literature). All twelve have independently given the year 2000 as the date when they believe the world will end. One consolation is that the article does make avoidance of the 'fires of hell' (*Weekly World News* 1997b: 9) a possibility, suggesting a six-part plan to secure a place in heaven (repentance, cessation of sin, avoidance of temptation, monetary donation to churches, forgiveness of enemies, and acceptance of Jesus as saviour). For many on the panel consulted, the book of Revelation provides some important clues to the Doomsday details and key players.

Figure 5. From *Weekly World News*, 18 November 1997. Used with permission.

Revelation 8.10 ('and a great star fell from heaven, blazing like a torch') signifies that the planet's destruction will be via comet (or is this star/ship—intergalactic attack?); Rev. 8.1 ('When the lamb opened the seventh seal, there was silence in heaven for about half an hour') points to a silence, apparently experienced in Spain just last year, which reveals that the apocalypse is imminent; the so-called 'Whore of Babylon' in Revelation 17 has been identified with the singer Madonna—who is pictured appropriately in the corner of the article; and, with some ingenious figuring, Hitler is named as the Anti-Christ—he stares devilishly at his accuser (Professor Joan Merchen).

Lest we become smug, the tabloids do not limit their research on the end times to biblical scholars. They support their findings by consulting a wide range of specialists in a variety of fields: physicists, ecologists, anthropologists, philosophers. Of over 1500 such specialists polled (Victoria 1997), 95.14 percent answered yes to the question, 'Are we in the biblical last days?' Those interviewed point out that the ecological chain is irreparably damaged; that we are overpopulated; that we have become 'little more than hate machines'(Victoria 1997: 8) ourselves, and that our planet is threatened by, at the least, 238 comets (five top experts in ecology, history, philosophy and Bible interviewed in the *Weekly World News* come to similar conclusions; Jeffries and Sardi 1998). Though the Christian minister interviewed agrees that the Bible certainly foretells this destruction (Isaiah, Matthew, John, Revelation), he does point out that we have not accounted for God's mercy in this dismal equation. Though he may be right, however, other *WWN* articles (mentioned above) make it clear that mercy, if it is forthcoming, will not alter Earth's course, but perhaps only rescue some of its inhabitants from hellfire.

For those who have not read Revelation, or made themselves aware of recently discovered prophecies of Jesus, there are plenty of other signs to be found in the world around us, if we care to be vigilant (see Mt. 24.36-44). Some of these are particularly remarkable and manifest themselves immediately as signals of impending disaster ('Sky Turns a Strange Shade of Green from Jerusalem to Bethlehem'; Jeffries 1997b). As would be expected, there is biblical support available to back up the tabloids' interpretations of these events as apocalyptic. Bible expert Dr Franz Weinburgh points to Matthew 24, the Dead Sea Scrolls, and a recovered portion of the Gospel of Luke for scriptural evidence. The lost Lukan passage is particularly revealing: 'When you see the sky flashing the colour of grass, know that my return is imminent' (Jeffries 1997b: 9). Closer to home, disastrous winter weather constitutes another sign of Jesus' return (which, through the above-mentioned article, we understand as his self-revelation and the resumption of his preaching). In fact, the latter is so significant that the *WWN* has actually covered the same story twice ('Is Bizarre Christmas Weather a Sign of Christ's Second Coming?'; Sanford 1997; 'Weather Disasters are a Sure Sign Christ Will Return to Earth Soon'; Sanford 1998b). There, Bible prophecy expert Reverend Theodore Brunel uses a sampling of prophetic texts to explain recent weather disasters (Ezek. 1.4; Hag. 1.11; Mt. 24.20-21; Rev. 11.12, 13; 12.15): whirlwinds, droughts, blizzards, earthquakes, floods. All of these are signs that we are living in the end times.

Yet, reading the tabloids by no means necessitates a suspension of one's critical faculties. Consider the article, 'Hitler Was the Anti-Christ and the End Times Are Already Over' (Foster 1998a). Leading Bible scholar Reverend Mitchell Carlowe claims that it 'doesn't exactly take a rocket scientist to see that the Bible was referring to Adolf Hitler [re: the Anti-Christ]...he was the closest the world will ever see to the Devil Incarnate'. Carlowe posits that the so-called mark of the beast (Rev. 13.16) refers to the tattooing of Holocaust victims; the sky folding back on itself (Rev. 6.14) to the bombing of Hiroshima; and the return of the Jews to the Holy Land as the creation of the State of Israel in 1948. Carlowe concludes that we are, in fact, living in post-apocalyptic times. Whereas this 'scholar' could be right in some of his analysis (Hitler *was* the Anti-Christ; see *Weekly World News* 1997b), his overall conclusions cannot be substantiated because they contradict the biblical text (the world was not destroyed in an apocalypse after Hitler), and, most importantly, because they do not jibe with the rest of the record in the Tabloid Bible (destruction of the Earth is imminent). This is clear evidence that even these texts must be read critically: there are aspects of it that are purposely added to trip up and confuse the gullible. To the observant, the ruse is transparent: the Reverend Carlowe is dressed almost entirely in black in the accompanying photograph. Even the tabloids have their Men in Black.

If some find this propensity to mislead somewhat disturbing, they should not. As Agents J and K pointed out in *Men in Black*, the contents of the tabloids are privileged. This was the reason for the cautionary words in the front matter of the papers—to throw people off the trail—and it is the reason that the projections in the tabloids, though ostensibly overt, are in reality sometimes convoluted. Imagine the mayhem that could be caused if every reader was an enlightened reader, if everyone believed. So it was with the Evangelist Mark's depiction of the so-called Messianic Secret. How would it have been if everyone immediately understood and was changed, before the crucifixion? Jesus would have had a share in the family business (quite lucrative, since Joseph was really a successful architect [*Sun* 1997]), and died a happy old man in the arms of Mary Magdalene.

All of this doom and gloom may appear to take the fun out of the Tabloid Bible—but does it really? No tabloid reporter worth his or her salt would dream of denying readers a few last minutes of enjoyment mingled with the first whiffs of smoke from our smoldering planet. One issue of the *WWN*, for example, nicely juxtaposes an article on the end times ('The Great Tribulation Has Begun!…Only the Bible Can Save Us Now, Say Experts!'; Jeffries 1998a) with this one: 'Gal with 36-Inch-Long Fingernails Kills Herself—WHILE PICKING HER NOSE' (*Weekly World News* 1998a). She impaled her brain with her index finger, it appears. How ironic, I thought. Here's one lucky woman who won't have to face what the rest of us might, and she was not even reading the Bible when it happened. The tabloids do offer other means of consolation and diversion, as well. In addition to working on securing a permanent place in heaven, one can gaze at the paper's graphics and enter the Holy Realm for brief, therapeutic visits (Broder 1997); one can hold real crosses, made by God himself (*Weekly World News* 1997b: advertisement); one can take biblical herbs (*Weekly World News* 1997a: advertisement); read interviews with the Anti-Christ (*Weekly World News* 1998b); even buy a 'fig-leaf' swimsuit and take a dip to while away the time (Wills 1998). And, rest assured, if anything can be done by our fearless leaders on earth to make the sticky spot a little less unpleasant, it will be ('Holy Moses! Did President Clinton Meet Jesus?'; Sanford 1998a; see Figure 6).

In a fitting postscript to my study, I have recently discovered that Nick Page (who calls himself a 'believer') has just published *The Tabloid Bible* (1998), a recasting of the best of the Bible's stories in tabloid format. I was, at first, delighted to hear the Good News—until I realized it was just that, a sort of *Good News Bible*, Version Two. Says the author: 'It is not to replace the Bible, but to introduce people to some of what it is about, to break down some barriers… We need to rescue the

Bible from its image as an antiquarian book' (*Church of England Newspaper* 1998). *The Tabloid Bible* is limited to events that actually happened, he notes, because he had to imagine that a reporter was present. What kind of reporter? I wondered. I figure Page's *Bible* will be deceptive, since it uses the right lingo, but merely recycles the usual texts without giving people the real truth.[22] Page has somehow missed the point, hasn't he? Or was this Old Nick's plan all along?!

Figure 6. From *Weekly World News*, 7 April 1998. Used with permission.

22. Of course, there are a few exceptions. I think Page has the right idea on Paul's conversion: 'Chaos on Damascus Road. Did Aliens Cause Multi-Chariot Pile-Up?' (1998: 139).

RECENT FICTIONAL PORTRAYALS OF GOD, OR: DISNEY, SHIRLEY MACLAINE, AND HAMLET

Richard G. Walsh

Introduction

For this old god no longer lives: he is quite dead (Nietzsche 1961: 275).

Popular religion, in short, is that carried on outside the formal structures provided by most societies for such activity. Such religion is usually an expression of the inadequacy of formal structures for the satisfactory ordering of the cosmos for all. For the 'elite'...there have been the alternatives of philosophy...or the founding of new religious groups... For the less sophisticated or less formally educated, however, something more tangible has usually been in order (Williams 1980: 228).

Although he may be the most famous, Nietzsche was not the first to notice God's demise. Many post-Nietzschean biblical scholars have even argued that the biblical God died or, at least, left the scene even before the end of the Hebrew Bible (e.g., Terrien 1978; Patrick 1981; Friedman 1995;[1] Miles 1995). According to Robert Grant (1986), it was the demise of such old gods which made new religions like the mystery cults and Christianity appealing in the Hellenistic era. If God, or one of his agents, made a comeback during this era, he soon left or died anew. Numerous scholars have charted this subsequent departure, although usually calling it secularization rather than the death of God (e.g., Berger 1969; Harrington 1983). In her popular *A History of God* (1994), Karen Armstrong tells a similar story. She prefers to speak, however, of God's objectification, by which she means rational, philosophical discussion of God as opposed to a mystical encounter. For Armstrong, objectification, which is particularly notable in the Western Christian

---

1. Friedman's work traces the demise of God both in the biblical tradition and in the modern Western world with particular attention to Nietzsche.

imagination, leads logically to the death of God, atheism, and fundamentalism.

While Armstrong hopes beyond hope that mystical encounters with
God may yet be forthcoming,[2] the waning of the influence of the established churches provides concrete evidence for Nietzsche's claims. Disenchanted intellectuals have not for the most part returned to the old
Western God but have turned for religious satisfactions to science,
philosophy, self-help movements, or some quasi- or exotic religion.[3]

On the other hand, surveys of popular opinion (e.g. Gallup) continue
to testify to the belief of many moderns in various religious notions
including God. More importantly, contemporary sociologists, like Peter
Williams, find religion alive and well among the populace although in
'popular', rather than in institutionally approved, forms:

> In terms of *symbolism, expression,* and *behavior,* 'official' religion tends
> to take on characteristics consonant with the broad sociological process
> called 'modernization.' It usually is routinized and bureaucratic, and
> views with suspicion expression and behavior disruptive of its routine.
> Among conservative groups, theology tends to harden into scholasti-
> cism—that is, the codification of revelation into specific propositions and
> the working of increasingly detailed commentary upon those proposi-
> tions. Among liberals and the 'Neo-Orthodox', God tends to become
> either very human (such as the Unitarian Jesus, who is not really God at
> all), or else very abstract, and the theological concern is focused largely
> on social ethics.
>
> Popular movements, in contrast, generally look for signs of divine
> intervention or manifestation in the realm of everyday experience. This
> may take the form of possession by the Holy Spirit; of the expectation of
> an imminent millennium; or miraculous healings or other providential
> intervention into the natural or social realm; of new revelation from on
> high; or conversely, of the demonic disruption of everyday life in the
> form of witchcraft (Williams 1980: 17-18).

2. Armstrong (1994: 377-99) believes our 'fast food' world makes mystical
awareness difficult, if not unlikely.

3. Most descriptions of recent religion are fairly similar to this list. See, for
example, Livingston 1998: 177-85; Molloy 1999: 455-89. Similarly, Stephen Toulmin (1985: 262) argues that modern science has ended the dualistic metaphysic of
traditional Western religion and left the field of natural theology to modern versions
of Stoicism and Epicureanism. Interestingly, Robert Bellah's description (1985) of
utilitarian (cf. Stoicism) and expressive (cf. Epicureanism) individualism strongly
resembles Toulmin's analysis (1985).

What, then, are we to make of this contrast between the intellectual and popular world? Is God dead or very much alive in new places? The popularity of recent works by Miles, Morrow, and Ferrucci might suggest the latter. They certainly demonstrate that God still sells. But, are they mythic? Do they truly indicate yet another divine comeback or are they simply contenders in the 'politics at God's funeral' (the title of an intriguing book by Harrington)? To assess the mythic significance of these works, we must locate these authors' books in an intellectual, cultural context, isolate their preferred symbols for God, and attend to the delivery systems that they have chosen for their symbols (including media, genre, and narration).

Modern Fictionalizations of God: Miles, Morrow, and Ferrucci

> If there were no God, it would be necessary to invent him (Voltaire, cited in Bartlett 1951: 1167).

> ...for all gods are poets' images, poets' surreptitiousness! Truly, it draws us ever upward—that is, to cloudland: we set our motley puppets on the clouds and then call them gods and supermen (Nietzsche 1961: 150).

Jack Miles's Hamlet

Of these three recent books, Jack Miles's *God: A Biography* is most at home in the Western intellectual religious tradition. After all, Miles is a scholar trained and proficient in the academic study of the Bible. In *God: A Biography*, however, Miles abandons standard historical-critical readings and strikes out in an innovative fashion. Instead of finding different theological conceptions, religious groups, and historical occasions behind the well-known cracks and seams that constitute the Hebrew Bible, Miles finds the biography of one divine character.

For Miles, the Hebrew Bible's lack of integrity means that God is an amalgamated personality (Miles 1995: 5-7, 22-24). The diversity of this divine person is evident in the 'titles' which Miles employs to describe his hero: creator, destroyer, friend of the family, liberator, lawgiver, liege, conqueror, father, arbiter, executioner, holy one, wife, counselor, guarantor, fiend, sleeper, bystander, recluse, puzzle, absence, ancient of days, scroll, and perpetual round. Amidst this welter of personalities, Miles asserts that the major aspects of the divine character include creator (YHWH + Elohim), cosmic destroyer (of Tiamat), the personal god of the patriarchs, and warrior (Baal). Genesis and Exodus resolve these tensions, create the one God of the Hebrew Bible, and are, thus, the basic sources for the divine biography (Miles 1995: 93, 127). After God reaches this level of maturation and integration, he then becomes a 'stable' part of the 'scenery', rather than an active member of the cast of characters (Miles 1995: 150-53). The covenant failure forces God to go 'international' (1995: 188-89) and to become the distressed, mysterious God of prophecy (1995: 226-36). Finally, after a last hurrah with Job, God grows old and fades away:

> Real lives never end with artistic finality. Either they are rudely interrupted, as Ecclesiastes says, or they end in a slow fade that has none of the rounded perfection of a well-wrought last page. Real lives end, we might say, just as God's life ends: A supreme effort falls slightly short (the Voice from the Whirlwind), a long period opens in which one has progressively less to say and the devotion of one's friends is slowly overtaken by their silence; a final claim is mounted that one's counsel has always mattered more than one's prowess, and the claim helps—but only somewhat. And then the light fails (Miles 1995: 371).
>
> As the Tanakh ends, the mind of God has been objectified in law, the action of God incarnated in leadership, and now, finally, the voice of God transferred to prayer (Miles 1995: 396).

In short, text, cult, and active human leaders have replaced a silenced and objectified God. In fact, the Hebrew Bible has become his rather lengthy epitaph.

In short, then, Miles accounts for God's diversity by describing a developing God. He lives—matures and fades. As he matures, he only gradually discovers his intentions (on the divine self-ignorance, see Miles 1995: 250-51). As Tanakh offers few inside views, Miles turns to God's interactions with humans to trace God's growing self-awareness (e.g., 1995: 85-95). God only gradually discovers that he wants humans to become his image, which for Miles is 'the only real plot that the Bible can be said to have' (1995: 87).

The climactic moment comes with God's interaction with Job (Miles 1995: 303-33). For Miles, Job is God's alter ego, 'the supreme image of God's desire to know God' (1995: 404). At this crucial point, Miles abandons his flowing narrative style and adopts that of a detailed commentary in order to arrive at a 'corrected' translation of Job 42.2-6:

> Then Job answered the Lord:
> 'You know you can do anything.
> Nothing can stop you.
> You ask, "Who is this ignorant muddler?"
> Well, I said more than I knew, wonders quite beyond me.

"You listen, and I'll talk," you say,
"I'll question you, and you tell me."
Word of you had reached my ears,
but now that my eyes have seen you,
I shudder with horror for mortal clay.' (1995: 325)

The translation emphasizes the standoff which Miles believes God and Job have reached. Job speaks at length about justice and demands a response which God refuses. God speaks at length about power and demands a response which Job refuses (1995: 317-18). Job's final speech, then, is ironic. It is not a repentance. Instead, God repents and discovers his own ambiguity, the devil within (1995: 329). Impotent omniscience replaces ignorant omnipotence (1995: 402). Thereafter, God, not Job, is silenced. The whirlwind is the last divine speech (1995: 329). Secularity and active humans replace God (1995: 406).

Humans can replace this God because he is so thoroughly human. Thus, unlike Greek mythology and tragedy, Miles's Tanakh is driven by the character of its protagonist, not a plot in which a character confronts necessity (1995: 397-402).[4] This God is akin to Hamlet, a personality deeply riven by internal conflicts and tensions, wrought by indecision, and ultimately silenced by his own action. Not surprisingly, given the influence of the Bible and monotheism on the Western imagination, this Hamlet-God has become the model for Western humanity (1995: 407-08). All modern Westerners are now Hamlets—composite, lonely selves, 'divided images' of a divine, 'divided original' (1995: 408; cf. 5-7, 23-24).

While this divine characterization is innovative, it is not without precedent. Miles's attempt to write God's biography recalls two centuries of attempts at a 'life of Jesus'. Of those attempts, Miles's work most resembles those works (from the 1860s) which depicted Jesus' psychological development through a now questioned exegesis of the gospel of Mark (see Schweitzer 1961: 193-222). A certain similarity also exists between Miles's God who is revealed in action to himself and the God of the 1960s biblical theology movement who was revealed in history to Israel and the church. Where the biblical theology movement supplied important ideological support for historical criticism, Miles's

4.   As an additional, satirical defense of his proposal, Miles closes his book with another reading of Tanakh starring multiple 'Greek' deities, rather than his amalgamated deity (1995: 398-402). For Miles, the resulting 'Greek' tragedy forms the perfect riposte to those who would challenge his integrated reading.

proposal offers a quasi-religious foundation for modern individualism. Here, of course, Miles is engaging in a familiar apologetic move. This maneuver typically claims that its favored antique—in this case the Hebrew Bible—is in some essential way the ancestor of the reigning world-view—in this case, humanism—no matter how inimical the world-view may appear to the antique. Other apologists have claimed similarly that Christianity paved the way for science or secularity. The result in each case is to claim a 'home' for the antique within modernity.

Not surprisingly, then, while Miles may make God Tanakh's protagonist, God is not Miles's protagonist. Miles' protagonist is Job, the mature human who understands God better than God does himself, or Nehemiah, the mature human who like the early God is actively involved in secular, human life. Of course, Miles is the most understanding of all as he serves as his Hamlet-God's father confessor, analyst, and Horatio. History and theology have become psychology. God has become an analyzed object and the subject of another narrator's report. The real hero is Horatio, the humanist scholar. Miles, however, does not lack respect for his subject. After all, he does find a Hamlet-God, not a Humpty Dumpty-God. Further, he does not write in the ribald style of Jeremy Leven (1982), father confessor and analyst for Satan. Instead, Miles struggles to explain and to maintain the Bible's significance, even outside its ritual home, as a Western classic basic to the Western imagination.

James Morrow's Disneyfication of God
In contrast to Miles's academic background, James Morrow is an award-winning author in the fantasy and science fiction genres. He has also produced a fantastic trilogy featuring God: *Towing Jehovah* (1994), *Blameless in Abaddon* (1996) and *The Eternal Footman* (1999).[5]

In *Towing Jehovah*, an anthropomorphic God literally dies, and his two-mile long body falls into the sea. Thereafter, the story deals with a horrific, yet humorous waste-disposal problem.

Decaying angels assemble the story's cast: Anthony Van Horne, a deposed oil tanker captain, and Thomas Wickliff Ockham, a Jesuit

5. When this essay was written, only a portion of the third volume was available at http://www.sff.net/people/ Jim.Morrow/footman.html. Morrow has also written a fascinating series of short stories with religious themes, *Bible Stories for Adults* (1990), and a modern version of the gospel, *Only Begotten Daughter* (1984).

priest, philosopher, and physicist. The angels charge Van Horne with the job of towing the body to the Arctic for internment and Ockham with explaining the event. The resulting voyage, with appropriate allusions to *Moby Dick*, *The Sea Wolf*, *Lord Jim*, and the *Exxon Valdez* oil spill, becomes a journey for absolution for Van Horne who deals with guilt over a previous oil spill and a scornful father and a journey for theological meaning for Ockham.

Ominous elements soon enter the story:

- The Vatican has not given up hope of resuscitating the body.
- Cassie Fowler—atheist, feminist, and biologist—decides she must destroy the 'too-physical' evidence for Western patriarchy and enlists the aid of her wealthy fiancé, Oliver, and the Central Park West Enlightenment League who hire Pembroke and Flume's World War Two Reenactment Society to attack the corpse.
- Recollections of Nietzsche haunt the priest (Morrow 1994: 118-19).
- The body disturbs atheists because it lends credence to past religious claims.
- More importantly, when the tanker runs aground on an uncharted island, the crew 'goes pagan' and dramatically enacts Ivan Karamazov's fears 'that without God, anything is permitted'.
- Ockham and Sister Miriam's attempts to convince the crew of Kant's moral law within (the categorical imperative) are largely unsuccessful. Ultimately, however, famine ends the bacchanalia, and Van Horne restores order by offering the crew the divine body to eat with the confession that the captain is 'the bread of life'.
- The tanker towing the body is sunk by the Central Park West Enlightenment League.
- The Vatican orders the body burned.

The novel climaxes with God's funeral (in direct disobedience of the Vatican) which Cassie concludes with her paraphrase of Job: 'You were not a very good man, God, but You were a very good wizard...' (Morrow 1994: 353). In the denouement, Ockham learns from the last, dying angel that God did not decree his own burial and tries vainly to convince the others that they must announce the gospel of God's death, the father who died deliberately to set his children free (Morrow 1994: 362).

The second novel, *Blameless in Abaddon* (1996), retells the story of Job with modern characters, plot, and setting. The Job-figure is Martin Candle, Justice of the Peace of Abaddon (hell), PA, a good man who is interested in and active for justice. He meets and marries Corinne Rosewood, but then develops prostate cancer.

First-person soliloquies by Jonathan Sarkos, aka the devil, interrupt this story frequently and provide explanatory comments. Notably, one learns that an earthquake has loosed God's body and sparked a worldwide theological debate. The devil himself believes, as did Thomas Ockham in *Towing Jehovah*, that God died in order to force his creatures to mature. Humorously, the Vatican has sold the body to the American Baptists who have created a life support system for the body[6] and turned it into a vast amusement park—Celestial City USA—in Orlando.

Claims of miracles at the park lead Martin to make a pilgrimage to Orlando, but he is not healed. His misfortunes continue when his wife, Corinne, dies in a traffic accident. Martin falls into a drunken tailspin until he drops in on a performance of Wiesel's *The Trial of God*. There, he remembers Ivan Karamazov's famous attempt to return the ticket to a world of suffering to God and decides to put God on trial at the International Court of Justice at The Hague. He swears, paraphrasing Melville's Ahab, that he'll chase God 'round Good Hope'.

When funds for the project are lacking, G.F. Lovett, professor and author of children's books (profitably made into movies), comes to the rescue and finances the case out of a desire to defend God's innocence publicly.[7] Despite opposition from Baptist capitalists and Sword of

6. Is God dead or not? The issue is not clearly decided in the first two volumes. God's funeral which ends volume one does not prevent volume two from resuscitating God and allowing Martin to murder him. Aichele struggles with this problem in an article in *Paradoxa* entitled 'An Apology for the Madman' (1999). In light of our concerns, it would be convenient to say that Morrow is wrestling in true mythic fashion with God's death and the vitality of popular religion. It seems more likely, if this is not merely a case of hasty writing, that the tension, like Ferrucci's depiction of a God who vanishes and returns, simply depicts the ebb and flow of conceptions of the divine in history. In short, as our introduction notes, God has died and come back before.

7. Aichele observes (1999) that Lovett is a thinly disguised parody of C.S. Lewis. The critical treatment of this character coupled with the comparably

Jehovah terrorists, Van Horne tows the body to The Hague. En route, Martin, Ockham, and two scientists explore the divine brain. All the 'neuronauts' are seeking answers to troubling theological or scientific riddles. Inside the divine brain they encounter a world of Platonic archetypes—including the devil, dinosaurs, Augustine, and biblical characters—who reflect upon the same five theodicies in which Lovett had already instructed Martin (see table below).

Table 1

Theodicy	Biblical story/Characters	Derisive tag
eschatological	Abraham, Isaac, the ram	'Disneyland defense'
disciplinary	Lot, wife, daughters	'Spare the rod, spoil the species'
hidden harmony	Noah and the flood	'Father knows best'
ontological	Job	'Best possible world'
free will	Ape ancestors	

At the trial, Martin brings victim after victim to the stand as well as experts in cataclysm. The defense's cross-examination reiterates several points: historical victims rarely held God responsible; sufferers commonly believed they were punished for sins; tragedy could sometimes be interpreted as serving some greater good; and God has intervened (i.e. in Jesus).

The defense's case consists of three experts who recap the five theodicies and of various victims who are still grateful to what they consider to be a benevolent God. The trial's climax occurs when Lovett calls Martin to the stand and poses the Joban whirlwind's questions to him: 'Where were you when I laid the foundations of the earth?' Not surprisingly, Martin faints and is hospitalized.

In the finale, the judges return a complicated verdict which reduces the trial's crucial question to whether the defendant should have intervened to reduce his creatures' pain. They conclude that he could not without destroying a world where charity, compassion, courage, self-sacrifice, and so forth are possible. God, therefore, is not guilty (Morrow 1996: 366-69). Enraged, Martin leaves the hospital to attack the corpse's cardiovascular machine. The resulting stream of blood sweeps Martin into the divine body where he meets various, now dying arche-

sympathetic treatment of Ockham illustrates one of the targets of Morrow's satire and helps locate Morrow in the intellectual, rather than the popular, religious world. See the section below on summary and comparison.

types. Notably, Martin admits to Job that his attack on God's body was vengeance, not justice, while Job maintains that he never repented (Morrow 1996: 382-83).

The Idea of Lovett and Martin then meet at Yeshua's place. Yeshua finally provides responses to the two theodicies which Martin was unable to refute: (1) versus the ontological theodicy, Yeshua asserts that God should have revealed the world's rules and (2) versus the free will theodicy, Yeshua asserts that there should be more free will. Dramatically, Yeshua, then, morphs into the devil and asserts that dualism is the only possible theodicy. God is both good and evil. On this basis, he offers advice to Lovett:

> 'Theodicy's a sucker's game, Professor. When Yahweh was operational, humanity's obligation was to *worship* Him, for christsakes. It was to celebrate His creativity and stand forevermore opposed to His malice. And anybody such as yourself, anybody who sought to shoehorn an omnibenevolent God into the same universe with Auschwitz…that person, Dr. Gregory Francis Lovett—that person did the Devil's work for him.' (Morrow 1996: 391, Morrow's emphasis)

For Martin, he has simpler advice: 'Cheer up, we're doomed but life goes on' (Morrow 1996: 392). The novel concludes, as it switches eerily back and forth from 'ideas' to reality to drug-induced dreams, with Martin's death and the devil's fading.

In *The Eternal Footman* (1999), the Vatican hires a lapsed Catholic sculptor to create a reliquary for the bones of God. While returning to Orlando from The Hague, God's organs blow up. The bones become the property of the Vatican again. The skull disappears and, then, as the millenium turns, goes 'into geosynchronous orbit directly above Times Square…' The novel's conflict centers around the sculptor's dilemma: will he make the reliquary that God wants (as revealed by Ockham) or that which the Vatican wants? In essence, a creative artist takes God's place.

Like Miles then, Morrow offers a thinly-veiled allegory of Western intellectual history, creates a contradictory God, features Job as a hero, and celebrates humanism.[8] Where Miles writes a serious, scholarly

---

8.   Morrow's novels are replete with references to Western literature as well as to religious issues. Although *Towing Jehovah* utilizes various sea stories, the dominant references are to Nietzsche, Dostoyevsky, Kant, and Job. Volume two rewrites Job, of course, but it also employs *Moby Dick* and *The Brothers Karamazov*. Two refrains from the latter repeatedly punctuate the story: 'if everything

tome (though for a popular audience), however, Morrow offers a delightful entertainment replete with fantasy, satire, and morbid humor.

Like Miles, Morrow also objectifies God. In fact, Morrow goes further in this regard than did Miles. Where Miles depicts God as an object for psychological analysis, Morrow presents God as a corpse, and, then, to add insult to injury, the body is 'exhumed' for trial. Further, this God is a political football with one group after another striving to make it a means to their success. Most humorously, or most pitifully, the body becomes a Baptist Disneyland in *Blameless in Abaddon* and an additional moon in *The Eternal Footman*. In a sense, then, Morrow begins where Miles ends with a silenced God who has become mere scenery, rather than a significant character. God, then, is more a figure from the past for Morrow than it was for Miles. His body remains, but not his imaginative influence. Beyond God, for Morrow as for Miles, are mature humans modeled on their unrepentant Jobs.

Not surprisingly, then, Morrow's God is thoroughly Western. Thus, Morrow's God is entirely anthropomorphic. Further, Western religious problems dominate the novels. The death of God, human suffering, and theodicy fascinate; the continuing influence of Western religion bemuses; and fundamentalism appalls Morrow. In fact, one might describe these novels as lecture notes for Western religion classes set to a fantastic, humorous music. The humor is, of course, black and sharp. If not God, at least, religion and its institutions come under heavy critique and mockery. Nonetheless, and despite the outright fun of it all, something serious lurks in Morrow.

About these novels there is more than a touch of *adversus haereses*. *Towing Jehovah* debunks gnosticism. *Blameless in Abaddon* refutes polytheism. Even the dualism with which that work concludes savors more of Isaiah's 'strange works' of God (Isa. 28.21) and less of the Manicheanism with which it flirts. In fact, the devil—exposed as a divine archetype—with which *Blameless in Abaddon* ends differs little from Miles's amalgamated God.

Perhaps, more importantly, *Towing Jehovah* seems to 'christianize' Nietzsche. Where Nietzsche envisions the overcoming of God (his murder) by his children, Morrow reflects on God's sacrifice of himself for his children (but see n. 6). Not surprisingly, then, despite the pyrotechnics of *The Eternal Footman* (1999), nothing really seems different

were rational, nothing would happen'; and 'I respectfully return my ticket'. The references indicate Morrow's overwhelming concern for order.

about the world after God's repeated deaths (cf. Aichele 1999). The way is either carefully prepared for secularization by God himself or God never had much to do with the order of the world anyway.

Morrow's basic ideology is clearer if we compare his trilogy to a more recent novel by Laurence Cossé, *A Corner of the Veil* (1999). In that novel, God never appears, but an irrefutable proof for his existence falls into the hands of the Jesuits. The novel, then, portends the earth-shaking consequences of the death of secularization. In particular, the terror with which political, religious, and economic leaders greet the proof is strongly reminiscent of Dostoyevsky's 'The Grand Inquisitor'. The contrast with Morrow's trilogy in which no great changes follow the publication of the death of God is obvious. Although Morrow seems to christianize Nietzsche, then, he is actually and ironically supporting modern secularity.

Franco Ferrucci's Shirley MacLaine
In striking contrast to the third-person divine presentations of Miles and Morrow, Franco Ferrucci dares a first-person divine autobiography in *The Life of God (As Told by Himself)*.[9] Appropriately, then, Ferrucci arranges the story according to the parts of God's life—childhood, adolescence, adulthood, and old age. More importantly, inside views of the divine mind dominate the story. Thus, the novel begins:

> For long stretches of time I forget that I am God. But then, memory isn't
> my strong suit. It comes and goes with a will of its own.

Ferrucci's depressed, forgetful God vaguely recalls his dynamic, histrionic childhood in which he created the world out of loneliness. The resulting creation, God's 'improvised theater', mirrors both God's nature and his quest for identity. In fact, both God and the world evolve together through plant, aquatic, amphibian, reptilian, and ultimately mammalian stages. As God is not responsible for the birds or for man's evolution from God's comic monkey, he worries that another, more superior divine being exists (1996: 8).

A prolonged divine absence, during which humans evolve, marks the end of the divine childhood. God, then, enters a period of adolescent

---

9. Ferrucci's book was originally written in Italian as *Il Mondo Creato* (Milan: Arnoldo Mondadori Editore S.p.A., 1986). The English translation is admittedly a free adaptation (Ferrucci 1996: 283). All remarks here concern the English translation.

infatuation with prophets, notably Moses, who God hopes will finally enable him to understand himself. Tragically, Moses rejects God's autobiography and writes his own story about God in order to obtain power over the crowd (Ferrucci 1996: 62-69, 85-88). Against the growing powers of religion, Ferrucci's gullible God has little success:

> That is the way I have always been: hypersensitive and moody, but also credulous enough to take the words of my followers as sincere. Every time I realize my mistake, however, my reaction is not one of revenge, but of detachment. I concede that God should not have such a profound need for affection that he immediately trusts whoever compliments him. But it is not his fault that he was born an orphan, that he spent his childhood alone and starved for affection. I'm being defensive, I suppose, so it comes naturally to fall into the third person (1996: 67).

A disenchanted God turns, then, from prophets to philosophers. They, too, disappoint, for they mistakenly think God to be eternal, omnipotent, omniscient, and apathetic. Of them all, God finds only Heraclitus and Buddha promising. Their respective concerns for creative opposition and quietude seem to encapsulate the central tensions in both God and the universe.

Reinvigorated, God returns to Palestine where a tryst with a young prostitute leaves him unsure about Jesus' parentage. Ultimately, God, disguised as a Greek philosopher, does recognize Jesus as his son, but only one among others. More importantly, God realizes that

> the splendid things that he said mixed truth with lies. It certainly was true that I wanted men to love one another. That was why I had created them, to remedy the evil that flooded the world; but this evil had not been caused by mankind, as people stubbornly insisted on believing. Evil was due to the imperfection of the world, to my own lack of skill (Ferrucci 1996: 123).

Despite God's counsel, Jesus persists in a suicidal program designed to found yet another institutional religion. Disheartened, a drunken God wiles away time with a prostitute as Jesus dies.

Jesus' death ends God's adolescence. Thereafter, God moves toward adulthood in a Janus-like effort to understand simultaneously his inner self and the external world. Like the prophets and the philosophers, the theologians frustrate God's search for self-understanding. They, too, imagine a God who suits their own lust for power.

Although initially agnostic about the devil, God finds Satan by becoming an exorcist. Through various encounters, God ultimately learns that Satan is a human creation and that men disavow God because they know they have failed their divinely implanted mission (Ferrucci 1996: 175-77). Humanity's immature desire for a choleric, divine father drives God mad. Of God's various incarnations during this period, the most notable are a cartographer (reflecting the divine desire to recreate a muddled world) and a mediocre artist (reflecting the divine discovery that failure is part of God).

Modernity is God's old age. Therein, he meets various humans who resent the fact that they are not God and watches as humans, failing to transform themselves and to fulfill their divine mission, turn to the invention of machines (Ferrucci 1996: 230). Finally, he realizes in modern science both the human desire to 'kick him out' and the means by which he may leave home. Nostalgia for love, however, holds God back, and he goes through various 'incarnations'. Finally, a tiring, old God falls asleep in a lizard and is torn apart by child torturers. Still, God invades those torturers and hopes

> that someone would find a bit of me in a corner of the world, so that I would be able to recognize myself again after my innumerable oblivions (Ferrucci 1996: 273).

God prays to be better than he is but excuses himself by reflecting that

> beauty and knowledge were supposed to be remedies against the pain of existence. What would they do in a world that does not suffer? I am now and forever the artificer of the world's imperfections (Ferrucci 1996: 279).

Finally, God reaches a senile inactivity barely aware of the words of confused prayers.

In sum, Ferrucci's first-person narration renders a distinctive portrait of God. Unlike Miles and Morrow, Ferrucci does not objectify God. Instead, Ferrucci has a highly subjective depiction of the divine. Thus, despite sections of dialogue, the bulk of the book consists of divine confessions and ruminations. This God thinks out loud (or in print). That which this God knows best is his own mind. Comparatively, he understands his human creation (and the world at large) not at all. He depends upon the devil to explain humans to him and, more importantly, waits in vain throughout his life for a human interpreter who can provide him with self-understanding.

The divine mind of these confessions lacks coherence. Like the God of Miles, Ferrucci's God is a contradictory character beset by opposing impulses. Like his human creation, he has a need for security and a craving for freedom. He is both Heraclitus and Buddha. Not surprisingly, this God is a puzzle even to himself. Even less surprisingly, he has an animus toward those who claim to know him too securely, that is, toward prophets, philosophers, and theologians.

Not only is this complex, contradictory God not eternal, omniscient, and omnipotent, he is also nervous, forgetful, anxious, guilty, and lonely. Ferrucci's God desperately desires to fly like the birds. Further, he is given to bouts of amnesia, to spasmodic recollections of his past, and to fits of depression leading to attempted suicides and periods of unconsciousness. To compound matters, God is wraught with anxiety about the presence of superior divine beings. He is not sure that he is alone, nor that he is the most supreme being. Like his human creation, however, he has the ability to repress these doubts and anxieties. Perhaps, most importantly, this God is wracked with guilt. He knows his creation to be imperfect and realizes his culpability for evil and suffering. In short, he is 'the artificer of the world's imperfections'.

In keeping with the Western cultural tradition, Ferrucci's God is personal. In fact, like Miles's God, this God is a person written large with all the foibles and failings appertaining thereto. Further, as a self-made being and an orphan, he is easily flattered and duped. He is constantly looking for love. Creation itself, then, springs from the divine loneliness.

Unlike Miles's outmoded model and Morrow's decaying scenery, Ferrucci's God is the hero of the story. In fact, Ferrucci's God so dominates the story that one begins to wonder if there is another story. For this reason, Ferrucci's anxious, quite 'human' deity constantly borders on pantheism:

> I immersed myself in whatever I did. I was and I was not my world. I was the impulse that lived in it; and the world, inhabited by my soul, went its own way (1996: 12).

In fact, other than the first-person narration, pantheism is the distinctive element of Ferrucci's divine character. God, the world, and humans are such closely connected images of each other that they lack meaningful difference. God, then, identifies himself with the world's evolution, with meaningful and meaningless moments in human history, and with various random incarnations. In short, Ferrucci's God is a new age deity remarkably like Shirley MacLaine.[10]

---

10. If one rewrote Ovid's *Metamorphoses* with a single hero-narrator reappearing in scene after scene, one would have something like Ferrucci's god.

Summary and Comparison with Traditional
Western Conceptions of God

Fire God of Abraham, God of Isaac, God of Jacob, not of the philosophers and the scholars (Pascal, 'Memorial' [Mesnard 1969: 116]).

But if oxen (and horses) and lions had hands or could draw with hands and create works of art like those made by men, horses would draw pictures of gods like horses, and oxen gods like oxen, and they would make bodies (of their gods) in accordance with the form that each species possesses (Xenophanes [Hyland 1973: 92]).

Gods are cultural locations of power and meaning. The most common divine locations are the world, being (life, force, etc.), person, or some shadow complement/opposite thereof. Polytheism, nationalism, and animism locate the divine in the world. Pantheism and monism locate the divine in ontology. Monotheism, henotheism, polytheism, and humanism locate the divine in person(s). The historical religions typically employ 'shadow' locations creating their well-known dualistic metaphysics (e.g. this world and another). Put differently, the historic religions 'disenchant the world' (Max Weber [Berger 1969: 110-12]).

The dominant Western religious tradition locates power in a person. As a historic religion, however, it also 'absents' that deity. Not only is the divine person not present, God is also person, yet not. He is person 'xed-out'. Not surprisingly, then, the Western religious tradition has in the modern world both a tendency to deny the divine person (deism, atheism) and a contrary tendency toward the continuing personification of God, either as dead (death of God) or human (humanism) (cf. Armstrong 1994: 293-399).

The traditional delivery system for the traditional Western God is a myth-ritual performance which allows the worshipers to engage and await their God. In that context, God is the sacred subject who dominates religious life and whom the worshiper fearfully approaches. In a living myth, a myth enacted in its ritual medium, God is never truly absent. Even if God is not present as a story character, context and genre expectations make the divine absence a palpable presence (cf. Miles 1995: 253). Further, the traditional voice (narrator and perspective) of myth is no less than God or his representative (cf. Walsh 1997b: 77-80). Outside myth-ritual performances, God becomes a malleable object. In fact, we could easily trace stages in God's reification from sacred subject to 'dead' object as the speaker devoutly heeded becomes the one dispassionately described or storied. Further, as ritual erodes, God becomes privatized, known only in human depths and as a part of 'cheap family psychotherapy' (Berger's witty phrase [1969: 148]). Such a God does not easily find public portrayal.

Outside its ritual context, myth avoids the reduction of God to a mere character only if it is recognized as scripture. Thus, in the Western religious tradition, Zeus is a literary character, but YHWH is more than a mere character. Outside ritual, however, the scriptural status of myth increasingly depends on heroic interpretations, on liberal demythologizing or on fundamentalist harmonizing.

Beyond scripture, philosophy (and theology) objectifies God. The anonymous, objective narrative voice of the philosophical essay is not God, but a dispassionate scholar cataloguing God's attributes. Beyond scripture, story continues to render God as a character, but without myth's God-rendering (load-bearing) qualities of sacred context (ritual) and sacred genre (scripture, myth). As a result, God disappears as an ontological reality in story (Cossé adroitly avoids this problem; see n. 13).

The fictional portrayals of God by Miles, Morrow, and Ferrucci are such stories. While knowledgeable of and playful with the traditional Western depictions of God, Miles, Morrow, and Ferrucci re-symbolize God and transport him to new media, genres, and narrative styles for a new cultural era (see table below).[11]

Table 2

	Tradition	*Miles*	*Morrow*	*Ferrucci*
Symbol	sacred subject absent person	model human Hamlet	divine corpse Disney World	personal pan-theism Shirley MacLaine
Media	ritual	popular press	popular press	popular press
Genre	myth	historical criticism psychoanalysis	fantasy satire	confession romance
Narration	divine speech	objective, philo-sophical	3rd person omni-scient, non-divine	1st person limited
Culture	pre-modern	modern academy	modern entertain-ment	modern literature

11. Each of the authors maintains the traditional masculine imagery for God.

In terms of symbols, each of the authors conceives God personally and humanly. In two treatments, God has an interior, mental life replete with psychological problems ranging from internal tensions/conflicts to an anxiety bordering on neurosis. He desperately and humanly seeks self-awareness. In each treatment, God goes through 'life-stages'. Ultimately, he dies or simply fades away.

Each of the authors does symbol God somewhat differently. For Miles, God is Hamlet, the model of riven humanity seeking identity, integrity, and security. Miles's God desperately needs a Horatio, the biblical scholar turned analyst and narrator, to complete his psychic (mythic?) journey. For Morrow, God is Disneyland, a corpse at the whim of human aims—religious, political, and capitalist. Morrow's God desperately needs people of integrity—Van Horne, Ockham, Candle—to save his body and/or his reputation. For Ferrucci, God is Shirley MacLaine, a (not the) life-force evolving with the world and humans and intermittently interacting with humanity. Ferrucci's God needs humans to provide him with love and with self-understanding. Unfortunately, Ferrucci's humans fail God.

Despite their differences, then, in each of these divine portrayals, humans replace God. In each case, then, the ultimate source for each author's symbolism is common humanity, not the traditional Western sacred. Conscious artistic imagination has replaced myth.

Not surprisingly, the delivery systems for these modern symbolizations differ from those of the traditional depictions of the sacred. Where the medium of traditional gods is ritual, the medium for these modern gods is the popular press. As a result, the concern of these authors is sales, not worship or scholarship. An additional consequence is that these popular authors cannot assume a detailed familiarity with a myth-ritual tradition on the part of their readers. Thus, in contrast to the abrupt way that the God of Genesis 1, for example, appears on stage, fictional gods must be identified for their audience. The resulting treatment invariably appears superficial to readers steeped in a particular myth-ritual tradition.

Instead of myth, these authors' works are fiction. We could, of course, give each of them more precise genre designations. Thus, Morrow clearly writes fantasy. No one is expected seriously to believe that God died and fell into the sea. After one accepts that 'central impossibility' (Irwin 1976: 3-10), the story rolls along in a fairly 'realistic' fashion. The subsequent vagaries in reality are the result of that 'central impossibility' or of humor and/or satire. The heavy satire demonstrates, however, that Morrow has written more than an entertainment. While he is no prophet armed with a clear utopian vision, he does critique much in modernity, particularly institutional and capitalistic religion (on prophetic and poetic fantasy, see Walsh 1997a).

Ferrucci's novel is not a satirical fantasy although it often engages in flights of fancy. Ferrucci's novel is a 'tell-all' confession, the memoirs of an amnesiac, anxious deity. Not surprisingly, as befits modern memoirs, romantic exploits and self-justifications are the order of the work.

By contrast, Miles's work does not at first seem to merit the generic tag novel. Instead, it appears a more scholarly tome. In fact, Miles offers the work as a philosophical essay or, more specifically, as an exercise in historical criticism. Miles, however, so creatively transforms that style that his work is neither a history of Israel nor a traditional biography, but a highly imaginative fiction.

Not surprisingly, these popular novels also differ in narration from the word of God-style narration of ritualized myths. Not surprisingly, as Miles writes dispassionate academic prose, he comes closest to the authoritative, 'objective' style of the tradition. In fact, Miles's style resembles the classical philosophical descriptions of God.

While Morrow employs a third-person, omniscient narrator, his narrator is set apart from and unaware of the divine perspective. His stance is closer to the rebel of Nietzsche or Camus. Fittingly, then, in *Blameless in Abaddon*, Jonathan Sarkos (the devil) frequently interrupts the novel with first-person soliloquies. This narration stands in striking contrast to that of the Job narrative which it modernizes. There, the adversary's voice is carefully contained within another's narration and God has the impressive speeches. Here, Sarkos has substantially more stage presence than the divine corpse.[12] In fact, Sarkos gets the last word, although by then he has become the fading alter ego and archetype of a fading God.

Ferrucci's narration is the most distinct. He alone (leaving the end of *Blameless* aside) dares a first-person divine narration. Here, God

---

12. Job's adversary, clearly a divine underling, speaks only in the prose introduction which is narrated by an anonymous, omniscient third person. That narrative voice is typical of biblical prose and creates a 'divine word' narration: cf. Walsh 1997b: 77-80. In Job, if God does not get the last word in the poetry, the prose conclusion remedies the lack.

reveals his own mind, and its anxieties, directly. The striking feature of this narration, given its narrator, is, of course, the limited quality of the divine perspective. What this God does not know could fill volumes.

Of course, each of these narrators has an ideological perspective. Put simplistically, Miles writes from the perspective of and in favor of modern activism. Morrow and Ferrucci write against institutional religion. Ferrucci writes from and for a romantic individualism, a view of life which celebrates love, art, music, and a zest for life. In short, all of these Gods reflect the culture of modernity, a culture of humanism and/or individualism. Not surprisingly, then, the Gods are models of modern humans who are revolted at the lack of order in their worlds, who desperately seek self-awareness and meaning, and who lack a meaningful other with whom to dialogue. With the death of the traditional God and the end of meaningful transcendence, if meaning exists, it is in the world. Not surprisingly, then, these fictionalizations tout world-views and ethics which are modern versions of Stoicism (Miles, Morrow) or Epicureanism (Ferrucci) (cf. Toulmin 1985: 262).

More surprisingly, these human Gods are 'at home' in the late Western religious tradition. They juxtapose with the symbol God and with their very human depiction the trajectory of the Western religious tradition in which theism gives way to humanism. Not surprisingly, then, these Gods disappear (all the authors), are objectified (all except Ferrucci), and are privatized (particularly Ferrucci). Despite the fact, then, that these authors write for the popular press, their symbolizations do not depend upon popular religion. Instead, these irredeemably human Gods are parasitic on the Western intellectual and religious tradition. They fail to actualize that tradition only at one point. They see that God is 'person,' but, unlike their tradition, they do not 'x-out' his person. They make God accessible, but they do not mystify God.

Conclusion

When the half-gods go, the minimal gods arrive (Niebuhr 1970: 28).

It frolics—in myths, to be sure, but myths with no other depth than that of human suffering and, like it, inexhaustible. Not the divine fable that amuses and blinds, but the terrestrial face, gesture, and drama in which are summed up a difficult wisdom and an ephemeral passion (Camus 1991: 117-18).

We have, then, located these works in their intellectual and cultural context. They are not new myths arising from the people and resolving the tension between the death of God and the popular demand for religion. Instead, they belong completely to the Western intellectual, religious tradition. Their notions of the divine (location of the sacred) belong wholly to that trajectory (thus, some form of humanism). As a result, they do not resolve the dilemma of the death of God. They revel in it and market it. Their connection of the intellectual pole and the popular pole, then, is wholly economic and/or aesthetic (a reflection of purely personal philosophical choices).

Devoid of a myth–ritual context, it is difficult to see what else these fictionalizations could be. That genre-medium, along with its assumption of divine narration, carries most of the weight in traditional depictions of gods. Even when gods are absent from such performances, their presence is still 'felt'. Outside that genre-medium, gods become mere story-characters alongside other characters (or scenery or plot-device) as the books in which they occur are merely one among many. The questions of other media shifts—of academic or popular presentation, of essay or fiction, of third-person or first-person narration—are of lesser import.

Gods, then, live only in the myth-ritual genre-medium. Only there are they the sacred subject of religion. The gods of literature are not the *mysterium tremendum et fascinans* (Otto's famous phrase). No one fears or desires them. No one goes to them for power or meaning. In fact, if anything, they are pitiful objects, needing psychological help or burial.[13] As fictional creations, they have no 'reference', no ontological reality or connection thereto. As fictional creations, they have only a 'sense' or connotation which depends upon the cultural codes of their readers and the intertextual allusions that they construct (see Aichele 1997: 67-75, 87-116).

While readers may, indeed, read as they list, the texts considered here all 'fit' well within late modernity. Within that culture, they do not reflect Williams's 'popular religion', but intellectual and artistic reflection upon the West's traditional, institutional gods. Such literary creations can hardly be anything other than traditional. Even alien imports

---

13. The better part of wisdom in fictionalizing God would be to create an absent God. This is the *modus operandi* both of late biblical texts and of the recent novel by Cossé (1999). As a result, Cossé's still absent God is far closer to Otto's *mysterium tremendum et fascinans*.

would have their own tradition or would become 'westernized' in the process of communication.

These texts, then, are largely 'texts of pleasure', texts which cohere easily with the reader's ideology (Barthes's phrasing, see Aichele 1997: 124-27). They are not provocative or incoherent. Of course, this labeling is appropriate only if one reads the texts as popular fiction and locates them in Western intellectual history. If one introduced the texts into a myth-ritual setting (or to a fundamentalist), they would become 'writerly' indeed. Further, Miles might provide some moments of incoherence for a historical-critical academy and Ferrucci for the monotheistic Western tradition. Only Morrow, however, has truly fantastic, blissful possibilities, and he only with the crafty ending of *Blameless in Abaddon*. For the most part, the gods of these tales are entirely 'presentable'.[14] Notably, then, where the traditional depiction of God presented God as person 'xed-out', the modern fictions have only a person. They lack the mystery of the original. Not only are they not new myths resolving tensions in modernity, they also fail to expose the real tensions in modernity in any fantastic or postmodern fashion.

14. That is, the texts lack the major mark of postmodernism as depicted by Lyotard, 'the unpresentable in presentation' (cited in Aichele 1997: 15).

DISNEY'S POCAHONTAS AND JOSHUA'S RAHAB
IN POSTCOLONIAL PERSPECTIVE

Lori L. Rowlett

At first glance an ancient prostitute and a saccharine sweet cartoon character from Disney might seem poles apart.[1] However, upon closer examination, an analogy begins to emerge between the Bible's Rahab and Disney's 'Pocahontas' (Donaldson 1999). The story of Rahab (Josh. 2) fits a pattern of the way that female characters are used in accounts of conquest: she represents the 'good native' who acquiesces almost immediately to the conquerors, as though she recognizes from the start an innate superiority in them and in the colonizing culture. She is far too eager to turn her back on her own people, her indigenous religion and even her identity. The story of Pocahontas contains many of the same elements as the Rahab story. In both cases, the 'good native' who takes to the colonizers immediately is a woman who later marries into the community. In both cases, she serves as a savior, protecting the men from her own people, effectively allowing them to colonize her native land, and herself. A comparison of the Disney-fication of the colonized woman with her ancient prototype sheds light on our own cultural practices of self-representation and depiction of the 'other'.

Narratives of colonization, whether they are folk tales, official accounts, or literary representations, often evince a gender polarity in which the conquering culture (the one composing the story) gives itself characteristics which are considered masculine, while the colonized other is feminized. For example, in the early nineteenth century, Henry Rowe Schoolcraft wrote of the 'luxurious effeminacy' of the Native Americans (Pike 1992: 7). They were considered passive recipients

1. My 1996 paper for the AAR session on women and war in the Religion, Peace and War session focused on Smith's memoirs and several well-known visual representations of Pocahontas rather than the Disney cartoon (Rowlett 1996a).

(like ova) of 'civilization' brought in by the more 'active' (like sperm) imperialists (Pike 1992: 6). Native Americans were said to be stronger on feeling than reason and to be licentious, whereas the Europeans regarded themselves as rational and very much in control of natural impulses. As Frederick Pike pointed out in his book on the myths and stereotypes of civilization and nature:

> Wherever the imperialist process unfolds, daring colonists expect to be rewarded by readily available sex proffered by inferior creatures who ostensibly welcome seduction and subjection... Racist and sexist beliefs coincide to the point of being indistinguishable (1992: 8).

The accusation of excessive sensuality in indigenous people is closely related to the attribution of closeness to nature, as Pike also mentioned:

> The conflation of nature and woman has helped to perpetuate the widespread male conviction that woman is somehow outside the bounds of and antithetical to civilization. Men, as they tend to perceive the situation, are the creators of civilization and the architects of progress... (1992: 6).

Women, on the other hand, are viewed as the embodiment of the forces of nature which must be brought under the civilizing control of men. Similarly, the Europeans, who perceived themselves as the 'masculine' race, felt that they had a natural right to dominate those whom they stereotyped as effeminate (Pike 1992: 5-6). The fact that the Native Americans practiced (and still do practice) religions in which harmony with nature is highly valued adds to the perception that they were and are closer to nature and the body, both devalued as somehow 'base' and more feminine than those things European males attributed to themselves. Disdain for Native American beliefs and rituals was expressed in the missionary impulse to eradicate 'superstitions' (Pike 1992: 95) in favor of more supposedly rational forms of religion, and in the Christian tradition of labeling other religions as primitive, chaotic and even evil. The tendency to think of indigenous rituals as sensual rites, because of the emphasis on dance, drumming and singing, was intertwined with the general view of the indigenous people as more sexual.

Similarly, throughout most of the Bible, the beliefs and practices of the various ethnic groups lumped together as Canaanites are condemned as obscene. Prostitution is the prevailing image for neighboring peoples' religions in the Bible. Agricultural fertility and human sexuality are metaphorically linked in many ancient Near Eastern religions, as in the Sumerian myth of Inanna and Dumuzi, and the Egyptian myth of Isis and Osiris (Rosenberg 1994). Both connect the cycles of nature (the agricultural seasons) with the sexual relationship between a grain god and a fertile goddess,[2] whose reunion renews the earth. Therefore the deeply metaphorical sexual aspect of the polytheistic religions of the ancient Near East became a pretext for the condemnation of those participating in these religions as 'whoring after other gods'. As in the judgment of the Europeans concerning the Native Americans, who were said to be more given to temptation and less capable of marital fidelity (Pike 1992: 95), the accusation of heightened sexuality and infidelity prevails in characterizing Canaanite practices and beliefs. Added to the stereotype of the sensual Canaanite is the confusion of the Hebrew terms *zônâ* (prostitute) and *qᵉdēšâ* (holy woman, priestess, from *kodesh*, a root meaning holy) when talking about the so-called 'temple prostitutes' of Canaanite religion whose function evidently had to do with re-enacting the earth-renewal mythology mentioned above. Taking part in the associated ritual practices, which presumably involved a *qᵉdēšâ*, is referred to in the Bible as *zenut* (same root as *zônâ*). It is hardly surprising, then, that Rahab is a converted sex worker. She is a symbol of (among other things) the transformation of the land from sexually lascivious paganism (in Hebrew eyes) to colonized docility.

All four of the elements common to the Pocahontas and Rahab conquest stories are gender-related. First, the woman falls in love with, has sex with, and/or marries a conqueror. As Pike pointed out in connection with another (analogous) imperialistic situation:

> For a Yankee man to marry a Latin woman did not upset imperialist concepts about races meant to dominate and races destined for dependence. However, for an American woman to marry a Latin man did upset the natural balance. It meant that the woman of a race destined for dominance would be dependent (in line with sexist assumptions) on the man of a race naturally destined for submission (1992: 9).

Second, the indigenous woman saves conquerors from and helps them against her own people. Third, she wholeheartedly embraces the conquerors' culture, setting for them an example of converted and thereby 'improved' otherness. Fourth and most important, her body, and particularly her reproductive powers, are co-opted by the conquering culture.

---

2.   I prefer to refer to her as a fertile goddess rather than a fertility goddess, because she has attributes in addition to her fertility.

A comparison of the parallels between Rahab in the conquest of
Canaan and Pocahontas in the conquest of the Americas as represented
by Disney must include the rescue scenes. In the Disney cartoon, Pocahontas uses that occasion to proclaim publicly her romantic love for
John Smith. Rahab the prostitute uses the occasion to proclaim the
machismo of the Hebrews' god. Both cases are shaded by the gender
polarities so often found in narratives of conquest, but both also reflect
the values of their respective cultural contexts: military might in the
ancient Near East, and, in contemporary America, a valorization of the
male–female romantic coupling pushed so emphatically in popular
culture.

Easily the most famous scene in the Pocahontas legend is the one in
which she throws herself over the prostrate John Smith and begs for his
life. It probably never happened. The melodramatic salvation scene did
not appear in Smith's original travel accounts, but was added when he
wrote his memoirs in old age. Smith apparently fancied himself irresistible to women; his diaries contain several scenes in which women
go to extraordinary lengths to save his hide (Barbour 1986). An especially salacious story appears in his Turkish adventures. A married
woman who adored him (supposedly) helped him sneak out of her
country (again, shades of Rahab) so that he could escape through Eastern Europe and Russia. The description of Pocahontas throwing herself
upon him may tell us more about Smith's self-regard than it does about
the historical Pocahontas.

Likewise the biblical account of Rahab may be shaded by masculine
ego. Joshua's spies had gone into Jericho, enemy territory, to spy out
the land for conquest. Her 'inn' was a brothel in which she did business
(*zenut*). As frequently occurs in male fantasy, but not often in real life,
the sex worker seemingly was so overcome with the men's prowess that
she would do anything for them, although she had known them only a
short time, perhaps just long enough to service them.

Rahab too quickly abandons her identity and her roots to integrate
with the colonizing culture, as though she immediately recognizes the
superiority of the conqueror. Pocahontas too is presented as being
drawn right away toward Captain John Smith, and away from her own
culture. In both cases, the colonizing forces reflect their own self-con-
cept and inflated self-regard through the eyes of the colonized 'other'.
The woman in both cases risks her own safety to save the men's lives

from her own people, giving the impression that the woman prefers to ally herself to the conqueror.

One of the most disturbing aspects of the film is the Disney corporation's use of the rescue scene. Not only is the conquest of the Americas trivialized by having Pocahontas use the rescue as an occasion for announcing her romantic feelings for Smith, but additionally, the conflict is misrepresented. The English troops and the Native American warriors are shown as morally equivalent. Both are choosing warfare rather than peace, and both are scolded by Pocahontas, who argues for the peace and love 'path'. There is no mention of the real set of power relations underlying the entire situation: one of the parties was trying to conquer the other and take its land. Native Americans were not invading Europe; Europeans were invading the Americas. In the cartoon, men from both sides march toward each other, singing a song declaring the other side to be savage. Never mind the fact that the Native Americans were defending their homes from a brutal invasion, and the Europeans felt entitled to whatever they could take by force for colonization.[3]

Disney's film contains many errors of fact. Pocahontas would have been only about twelve years old when Smith was in Jamestown, not a well-developed woman as in the cartoon. The cartoon Pocahontas was made to look more Asian than Native American, which indicates that perhaps the Disney personnel thought that one 'other' was more or less the same as any 'other'. One wonders whether perhaps the (grossly unfair) stereotype of Asian women as submissive and dependent played into the decision. Whatever the reasons, Disney's artist used various models in creating the cartoon Pocahontas, including one from the Philippines (Edgerton and Jackson 1996: 95).

Pocahontas never was known to have had a romance with John Smith, although she later married another Englishman, John Rolfe. Furthermore, the religion of the Native Americans in the Disney cartoon is an absurd hodge-podge, representing no particular tribe. The talking tree is borrowed (probably unconsciously) from various European mythologies, and is therefore an example of the Euro-American filmmakers' projection of their own culture's dimly remembered and stereotypical idea of what indigenous closeness to nature might look like. In some European myths, trees can and do transform into deities or

---

3.   Conversation with Laura E. Donaldson at the annual SBL meeting, November 21, 1998; also mentioned by Edgerton and Jackson (1996).

people and back again.[4] Native American nations differ greatly from one another, and do consistently revere nature as alive, but the Powatans were never known to anthropomorphize in quite the way shown in the movie. Likewise, the concept of animal familiars is European, especially Celtic. Native Americans often have a totem animal, but, depending on the particular beliefs of a given tribe, it may be a clan totem or an individual one revealed in a vision. It would not be a pet. As one of Jamestown's historian-educators said to me, 'Pocahontas would not have thought of raccoons as cute. She probably would have thought of them as edible.'[5]

The Canaanites in the Bible are treated in analogous ways. They apparently exist in Joshua primarily to be exterminated in the battle scenes. Most of them are dehumanized (except Rahab herself) as though they were clones of one another. As with the Native Americans, who in reality belonged to distinctive nations, the individual cultures which made up the so-called Canaanites were treated as though most of them were interchangeable in the narrative.

The Disney cartoon and the biblical text both emphasize the voluntary aspect of Pocahontas's and Rahab's actions. When Rahab voluntarily places herself at the service of the conquerors, the episode is usually cited as an example of inclusiveness in the Bible.[6] Her 'profession of faith' is generally read by biblical scholars in a positive light, showing that all who place their faith in Yahweh can find a place among Yahweh's people. However, at the same time, she is used as an example of the 'good native'. Turning her back on her own people, she becomes a salvific figure for the Hebrew military men, helping Joshua's spies flee Canaanite guards. She converts to the conquering Hebrew religion, but she has had no time to learn about it. Instead, her reasons invoke a rhetoric of violence (Rowlett 1992: 19-22 and 1996b: 173-81):

---

4.   Examples which come to mind immediately include the story of Apollo and the laurel tree, Merlin's Oak in the Arthurian legends, and the figure of the Celtic 'Green King' or 'Green Man' (Rosenberg 1994, and Matthews 1998).

5.   Private communication with Irene Baros-Johnson, formerly an educator at Jamestown settlement in Virginia, 1995.

6.   For example, Elwell says that 'It was within God's purposes that those Canaanites who would give up their Canaanite identity in order to become Israelites, culturally and religiously, should be absorbed into the Hebrew nation and be allowed to survive' (1989: 138).

> I know that Yahweh has given you the land, and that the fear of you has
> fallen upon us, and all the inhabitants of the land melt away before you.
> For we have heard how Yahweh dried up the water of the Red Sea before
> you when you came out of Egypt, and what you did to the two kings of
> the Amorites that were beyond the Jordan, to Sihon and Og, whom you
> utterly destroyed (Josh. 2.9-10).

In other words, the god's chief virtue was his capacity to cause death.
She was subsequently absorbed into the Hebrew community, making a
complete break from her own ethnic group:

> The young men who were spies went in and brought out Rahab ... and
> all she had...and placed them outside the camp of Israel... Rahab the
> harlot and her father's household and all she had, Joshua spared. She has
> lived in the midst of Israel to this day, for she hid the messengers whom
> Joshua sent to spy out Jericho (Josh. 6.23-25).

Eventually she married (or at least had sex with) an Israelite. She relin-
quished her own identity, thereby becoming a part of the patriarchal
social order being asserted in the conquest narrative. She took a place in
the hierarchical system under Joshua's command. She functioned not as
an individual woman but as the embodiment of otherness being altered
and engulfed. The contrasting fate of the other inhabitants of Jericho is
graphically described:

> They utterly destroyed all in the city, man and woman, young and old,
> and ox, sheep, and donkey, with the edge of the sword (Josh. 6.21).

There are two ways to control living beings—eradication and domestication. Eradication means simply exterminating people; extermination
abolishes power by abolishing its object. Domestication, as in the
stories of Rahab and Pocahontas, represents an attempt to bring the
populace into line, so that the colonized support the dominating culture
without coercion (French 1985: 128-31). Therefore it is essential that
the colonizing culture represent the indigenous people as voluntarily
complicit in their own domination. We have no actual accounts of these
stories from the pens of Pocahontas or Rahab. Their willing, even
eager, compliance comes only from the words put into their mouths by
representatives of the colonizing culture.

Like Rahab, colonial Virginia's Pocahontas later married a conqueror, John Rolfe, with whom she had a son. Like Rahab, she converted to the conqueror's religion before her marriage into the colonizing culture. Conversion may be seen simply as one more manifestation

of domestication by the colonizer. One of the most famous portrayals of her (outside of the rescue scene) is the John Gadsby Chapman painting of her baptism. The painting depicts her wearing white English clothing, in the scene's center, in stark contrast to the other Native Americans lurking about the dark periphery in native garb. She became England's colonial 'good native', converting to England's Christianity from her native religion. The function of her baptism is analogous to that of Rahab's conversion in the biblical story. Instead of the old adage, 'the only good Indian is a dead Indian', one could say, 'the only good native (or Canaanite) is one who no longer is truly a native'. In other words, instead of exterminating the person bodily, the colonizer merely exterminated everything about her that made her who she was. Thus transformed, she was fine.

When Pocahontas was baptized, she was christened Rebecca. The biblical name is symbolic of her turn away from her 'savage' indigenous religion, but the name change is also indicative of her voluntary relinquishment of her identity. Colonized people have often found themselves addressed by names they do not recognize but which sound more familiar to those addressing them. Taking away one's familiar name, the primary means of personal definition, is domination through domestication at its deepest level. It leaves the person's self image completely vulnerable to any change a colonizer wants to impose on it. Likewise, a colonizer will usually change the name of conquered territory, symbolically altering an indigenous people's self-definition to suit their own purposes. Examples abound—New Spain, New England, Virginia (named for England's 'virgin' queen) and Louisiana (named for the king of France). Each place had its own Native American name supplanted.

Sexuality, marriage and reproduction are elements of both the stories. After her conversion, Pocahontas married John Rolfe. In one of his letters,[7] he gave as one of his reasons for the marriage the opportunity it would provide him to help assure her salvation. Actually her conversion seems to have been part of her acculturation: she was instructed in Christianity at the same time that she was taught English.

Before her conversion, Rahab was a prostitute, a very disreputable profession in ancient Israelite culture, although its meaning is ambigu-

---

7. Some of the letters of John Rolfe appear in Ralph Hamer's *A True Discourse of the Present Estate of Virginia* (1615) and are reprinted in part in Rasmussen and Tilton (1994: 28).

ous elsewhere in the ancient Near East, as discussed above. Her conversion, which included subsuming her into the conquering culture at the cost of her individuality and independence, elevated her to respectability and inclusion. She was transformed into the good native (good Canaanite) because she no longer had Canaanite characteristics.

An interesting point in the Pocahontas and Rahab stories is that the two women each gave their bodies willingly to the colonizer for reproduction. When children were born, they belonged to the conquering culture of the father. Therefore the woman not only lost much of her personal and ethnic identity, but she had to watch her children lose their ancestral heritage. In a sense the women's bodies, their wombs, were colonized.[8]

Nothing is said about Rahab's motivation for marriage, but she turns up in a New Testament text (Mt. 1) in the Davidic monarchy's genealogy, which is in keeping with the concerns of many of the biblical writers: the birth and lineage of certain very important males is often highlighted in stories concerning women.

On the other hand, Pocahontas married for love, especially in the Disney portrayal. In Disney's cartoon and in its recent sequel, Pocahontas appears as something of a love addict. She is madly in love with Smith in one episode, then he leaves and Rolfe comes along. She is wildly smitten again. Just as the biblical story of Rahab is a reflection of its time, the Disney version of Pocahontas reflects our own time. Young people are raised on the myth of the all-consuming romance. Girls and women are given a much stronger dose of the myth than are men and boys. Consequently, Disney, Hollywood and other producers of popular culture promulgate and reinforce over and over again the idea that a young woman's pathway to happiness lies in being swept away by a strong male who will marry her. The entire Disney movie was built on the patently false romance between Pocahontas and Smith, as though the only aspect of Pocahontas's life which could possibly be interesting was a whirlwind romance culminating in a passionate kiss.

There are political dimensions also to the romantic obsession. In addition to the dynamics of colonizer/colonized, strong male/acquiescent female, and civilized Christianity/'savage' paganism, the couple-

8.   I examined this topic more thoroughly in my 1996 paper (Rowlett 1996a: n. 1), in comparison with the 'rape camps' of Bosnia, in which Muslim women were raped to colonize their reproductive systems, making them bear the children of the conquerors.

dom-is-everything message is imperialistic. Our culture rules out of bounds the matrilineal and communal patterns of the Native American cultures located on the East coast (Hudson 1976) as somehow less legitimate than European patrilineal and patrilocal patterns. Probably it is because American culture's conservative agenda pushes the nuclear family as ideal, and denigrates alternative family structures. Even the traditional extended family is downplayed because of its association with communitarian values. Any communal or 'village' approaches to caring for children is usually written off as ridiculous. (Remember the ridicule directed at Hilary Clinton when she wrote her book called *It Takes a Village*?) In the Disney cartoon, then, when Pocahontas leaves her people in favor of seeking her fortune with a white man in a foreign culture, the stamp of approval is given to the 'couple' as the primary unit of society rather than the community, which would have centered on the mother's kin group. The romantic heterosexual couple and the resultant nuclear family are valorized at the expense of other options, such as a web of relationships.

Both Rahab and Pocahontas are, in a sense, cartoon figures. Neither is allowed to speak in a truly indigenous voice. The colonizing powers telling the story have given her words to speak in praise of themselves as conquering heroes. She is supposed to be grateful because she is allowed into their society. In both cases, the woman is regarded as worth saving and assimilating because she recognizes the specialness of the conquerors, making her the mirror which magnifies their own glory. She becomes the medium for transmitting the colonizing power's arrogance in its representation of itself to itself.

SOME DAY MY PRINCE WILL COME: IMAGES OF SALVATION
IN THE GOSPEL ACCORDING TO ST WALT

Susan Lochrie Graham

> Amen, I say to you, unless you turn around and become as little children,
> you will never enter the kingdom of Heaven (Mt. 18.3).

Children, as Frances Young points out, 'are selfish and aggressive little
beasts, easily jealous and ever demanding...' (1982: 5). In order for
them to become polite and agreeable adults like us, a good deal of education is necessary. That education is provided by their families and the
other institutions society has created for the purpose, especially schools,
churches and other religious bodies, and children's groups and clubs.
But the influence of the cultures in which we all live has arguably the
greatest effect, all the more so for being subtle and unrecognized. Those
of us who were born in the United States after the Second World War,
the 'Baby Boomers' who are now parents and, increasingly, grand-
parents, experienced childhood during a time of great cultural change.
The role of the United States, and by extension each and every American, as guardian of all that is good and true and beautiful in the world,
encouraged us as children to believe that the American Way was the
only right way to do anything, and that those who lived differently were
in some way deprived, in need of our help; or depraved, particularly if
they resisted our good will. In the time following the end of the War,
America thrived. How could anyone bear to be different? It is in this
time, roughly the period from 1945 to the early 1960s, that the perva-
sive consumer culture here developed, along with scientific and techno-
logical discoveries that resulted in the electronic shaping of education
and entertainment, neatly combined as 'edutainment'. As one of the
children of this era, one who remembers seeing some of the early animated features produced by the Walt Disney Studios when they were
first released, and who dreamt her own romantic dreams over a lavishly
illustrated spin-off book based on the film *Cinderella*, I want to take a
look now at the ways in which these films taught me and my brother

and our friends to be adult women and men in this culture. How did we learn, selfish and aggressive little beasts that we were, to be the people we are today? What did we learn?

In the years following the end of the Second World War, American society was transformed. In the late 1940s and 1950s, America was marked by complexity, diversity, and contradiction. It was, as historian James T. Patterson (1996: 13) characterizes it, 'a bewilderingly pluralist society'. Despite poverty and discrimination against racial minorities, Cold War jitters, and the restlessness of certain groups in society, including disaffected youth and some women, the mid-1950s were remarkably buoyant. Patterson comments: 'The whole world, many Americans seemed to think by 1957, was turning itself over to please the special, God-graced generation—and its children—that had triumphed over depression and fascism, that would sooner or later vanquish Communism, and that was destined to live happily ever after (well, almost) in a fairy tale of health, wealth, and happiness' (1996: 311). There was an optimistic spirit, a feeling that there was no end to progress, and a conviction that there was nothing American ingenuity could not accomplish (1996: 317).

The rapid demobilization of troops in 1945, with its sudden influx of young men anxious to 'get back to normal' and to make up for lost time, raised a number of issues. From the economic point of view, wanting to 'get ahead', the vets availed themselves of a number of government programs under the G.I. Bill which provided unemployment benefits, helped them to find work, provided opportunities to enter higher education, and enabled them to buy homes at favorable rates.

The ideal family in the 1950s was the nuclear family, with the father working outside the home and the mother primarily employed in childcare and housekeeping. When women worked, they overwhelmingly worked in 'pink collar' jobs. The desire for comfortable personal lives fuelled a consumer boom and created a time of prosperity for many Americans. Images of comfortable homes filled with 'labor-saving' devices inundated consumers, whether from magazines and billboards or from the increasingly widespread new medium of television, creating a market for the goods that were being produced. The children in these families were expected to flourish, and as they reached adolescence they were supposed increasingly to take on the role of consumers themselves. In this way, the American way of life, one of ever-increasing prosperity, would perpetuate itself.

In spite of increasing secularization, church and synagogue member-ship increased dramatically in the 1950s to a high of 69 percent in 1959. Of those who identified themselves, some 66 percent proclaimed themselves Protestant, 26 percent Catholic, and 3 percent Jewish. Part of this apparent religiosity, Patterson points out, was stimulated by the Cold War. Communism 'was evil in part because it was Godless', and the young Reverend Billy Graham 'explained that Communism, 'a great sinister anti-Christian movement masterminded by Satan', must be battled at every turn. America became 'one nation under God', and the words 'In God We Trust' were added to the currency. While such moves might seem to blur the separation of church and state enshrined in the Constitution, few people noticed. 'On the contrary, these actions reflected widely held and popular feelings that fused the ideals of Christianity and "Americanism" into a firmly anti-Communist "civil religion". God, many people believed, had endowed the United States with a mission to spread the sacred truths of the Declaration of Inde-pendence and the Constitution throughout the world and to destroy the diabolical dogmas of Communism' (Patterson 1996: 329-30).

Cultural life in America in the 1950s was not without its critics. They voiced a list of concerns: 'the mass media were debasing public taste, sexual license was threatening traditional morality, juvenile delin-quency was overrunning society, and generational change—a "youth culture"—was undermining the stability of family and community' (Patterson 1996: 343). It is within this context that the animated car-toons of Walt Disney were produced and viewed: *Cinderella*, *Sleeping Beauty*, *Alice in Wonderland*, *Peter Pan*, and *Lady and the Tramp*. Of the five, only *Lady and the Tramp* was written originally for the film; the others were adapted by the Studio from earlier oral and print sources. The Walt Disney Studios took the opportunities presented by television, combined with advances in animation techniques in film, and a visionary plan to create an integrated entertainment and leisure complex, with front-line advertising in the home on the daily 'Mickey Mouse Club' program, which attracted children and their families to the movie theaters to watch the new films, and ultimately provided a dream holiday destination for many in the new 'Magic Kingdom' of Disney-land in Anaheim, California.

Not surprisingly, the full-length animated features produced by the Disney Studios during the 1950s presented images of human relation-ships and work that idealized the new consumer family unit. Combined with postwar American triumphalism and economic growth, these images both created new desires and dreams and provided the means of fulfilling them, for a price. The pleasures of hard work and thrift that built the nation were increasingly relegated to a position of hallowed values, while leisure activities and consumption took their place as the birthright of those lucky enough to take advantage of them. 'A dream is a wish your heart makes', Cinderella sings, and sure enough, her dream of love, wealth, and power comes true. All you have to do is wish hard enough and keep on believing, no matter how faint the hope of fulfillment sometimes seems.

The religious values of faith, hope, and love are here associated with cultural meanings and means of fulfillment, at least for some. In Christian theology, the means have to do with belief in Jesus as the savior and redeemer of the world, a faith that will assure eternal life and bliss in God's kingdom. In popular imagery, God reaches out with open arms, the arms of Jesus the redeemer nailed to the cross, seeking to gather all into the loving parental embrace. Those who have allowed themselves to be thus gathered in seek to live their lives according to a moral code that emphasizes loving, self-sacrificial actions for the sake of others as appropriate to disciples of Jesus, who follow him as their Lord. Living as a Christian implies seeing one's experience through this lens. Believers are encouraged to create a sacred communal space, for which a key metaphor is the kingdom of God, where peace and justice prevail and where nonhierarchical social structures are possible. Satisfaction comes from belonging, living in unity and equality, rather than from achieving higher status than others. Dreams and desires are future-oriented, with the emphasis on life after death in ecstatic union with God. For children, especially the church-going children of the 1950s, the images of Walt Disney's fantasy films provided an important intertext for understanding these Christian concepts, but an intertext which functioned both to create the myth and to subvert it for other cultural purposes. In a *Time* magazine cover story in 1954, Walt Disney himself was described as 'the poet of the new American humanism'; Mickey Mouse was 'the symbol of common humanity in its struggle against the forces of evil'. Mark Pinsky, who writes for the *Orlando Sentinel*, notes, 'The Disney empire, by its own designation, is a kingdom of magic, almost totally without reference to any kingdom of heaven. There are no churches on Main Street at Disneyland or Walt Disney World', although the reasons for the omission are not clear. According to one biographer, Walt was raised in a fundamentalist home and attended a midwestern Congregational church, although he did not attend church regularly until he was in his forties; another biographer, Bob Thomas, admits that Walt 'considered himself religious yet he never went to church' (Pinsky 1995: A11). Although Disney's films seem consistently to reward the good and punish the wicked, according to Thomas he 'did not believe in mixing religion and entertainment' and Pinsky comments that 'Throughout his life Walt Disney steadfastly denied there was any great message in his work' (1995: A11).[1] The Reverend Clark Whitten, who comments that the films avoid any explicit Christian message, maintains that the Disney gospel is purely materialistic. 'They have a gospel: it's to make money,' he contends (Pinsky 1995: A11).

For a culture in which prosperity depends on creating markets for the goods which are increasingly being produced, the Christian theological vision is subversive and must be contained. Such containment entails a translation of religious dreams and desires into secular terms, where fulfillment is possible through the production and consumption of objects. Consumer objects of desire take the place of the desire for ecstatic union on the one hand, while controlling the sexual satisfaction of that desire on the other by displacing sexuality onto fetishistic objects. As the objects both create and satisfy desire temporarily, consumption provides immediate emotional gratification and the need for further consumption in the future.

With this in mind, it is worth taking a critical look at the intersection of the secular and religious intertexts in Disney's animated features of the 1950s. For church-going parents, Disney's 'new American humanism' provided an integrated way of inculcating in their children superficially Christian moral values and knowledge of culturally acceptable social roles. But because the films are not made with explicit religious material, the Christian intertext functions in the interests of creating and maintaining appropriate structures and roles in the newly emerging consumer economy. In these films, as we will see, the Christian myth

1.   Some commentators point out differences between the 'eras' of Walt Disney and his heirs, especially Michael Eisner; critic Michael Medved claims that Disney shared the values of his audience while Eisner and his team do not. He concedes, however, that some of the recent films 'teach wholesome and positive messages' (Pinsky 1995: A11). Whether or not that is the case, this article is focused solely on the films of the Disney era.

and the American dream come together powerfully to create what might be termed a Christian capitalist humanism with its own Christ figures and its own doctrine of salvation. Here, 'following Jesus' means acting according to his rules, being 'good', willing to sacrifice oneself for others, dutiful and obedient. From an economic perspective, those who are 'good' are supposed to prosper; social order is maintained by providing adequate wealth and encouraging consumption. In a political context, of course, duty includes duty to one's country and patriotism. Those who cannot be integrated into this vision are the evil Others: foreigners, particularly Asians and Eastern Europeans, blacks, and native Americans, who are seen as threats to the social order. Being 'saved' in this view means being integrated into the consumer culture where one can take advantage of the material rewards available. The biblical image of a liberating, redeeming Christ is here transformed into the means of this integration.

The transformation is clear in the images of the male heroes of three full-length animated features of the 1950s, *Cinderella*, *Lady and the Tramp*, and *Peter Pan*.[2] *Cinderella,* the earliest of the three films, opens with a lengthy sequence which moves from illustration to animation, so that the details included in Disney's version seem to be part of the original fairy tale come to life. But the long opening sequence in Cinderella's bedroom in the tower, the only part of the house where sunshine strikes, visually sets up the oppositions which govern one moral message of the film. Cinderella is associated with light, joy, peace, beauty and life, while the stepmother and stepsisters bear the weight of all the opposites of these. From the time of her father's death, Cinderella has lacked both paternal protection and the freedom due to her as a female member of her social class. The prince, a minor character in the plot, has two roles: he must recognize the young woman who is his appropriate mate, and he must provide heirs to the throne of his father. When he finds Cinderella, he is mesmerized by her, and falls immediately in love. She, magnificently dressed and groomed, is under a spell herself, and must escape before her identity is uncovered at midnight. She leaves one of her glass slippers, enabling the prince to find her.

---

2. The Disney Studios produced other films during this period, but I have limited my choice to one fairy tale, one classic children's story, and one modern fable. What I am arguing here might be said of the other films, particularly *Sleeping Beauty* and *Alice in Wonderland*, both produced during the 1950s, and perhaps also of another modern fable, *101 Dalmatians*, which appeared in the early 1960s.

Marriage follows immediately, and we are told that they live happily ever after.

There are numerous images of danger and bondage in this film. Cinderella herself, of course, is kept under control by her stepmother, who as a last resort, locks her in her tower room. It is from this place that Cinderella must be released, and the glass slipper, an object Cinderella loses and the prince finds, is the key to the resolution of the action. Because of it, he is able to rescue her, and she is united with him in his kingdom of peace and prosperity. The story avoids any hint of sin or guilt in Cinderella or in the prince. Those in need of the changes brought about by an act of redemption are forgotten, not forgiven, and as soon as Cinderella's foot slips into the glass slipper, they disappear. The rescue, easily undertaken, results in no transformation and no reintegration. Evil, in this view, is entirely external and can be removed. The desire to destroy the wicked stepmother and stepsisters is displaced in the (literal) fall of Lucifer the cat. Even in bondage, Cinderella seems not to suffer.

Thus while the film seems to suggest that the prince's action 'saves' Cinderella, she is in fact in no need of salvation. Those who are cannot be saved. The glass slipper, which functions as the metonymic index[3] of Cinderella's virtue, and so marks her as the chosen one, does not fit the others. The virtues of the feminine object are externalized: Cinderella's small feet enable her to be recognized as the chosen one, a sexual image which is further displaced in the glass slipper. But the slipper functions in other ways. Taken by the prince when Cinderella slipped out of his grasp, it represents both the object of desire and the means for satisfying it. It is, then, a fetishistic object of consumption.

This language of desire suggests an intertext other than the theological notion of salvation for reading these films, of course, and one which raises issues of gender as well as sexuality. When desire is represented by visual means, and particularly by objects of consumption, we can speak of the fetish, the visualization of desire. Consumer objects as fetish represent the coincidence of consumer culture and desire. In the politics of representation and gender, according to Laura Mulvey's early work (1975), the feminine appears as a response to masculine desire in two modes, the voyeuristic and the fetishistic.[4]

---

3.   For the terms related to the semiotic analysis of film images, see Metz 1974; a helpful discussion may also be found in Monaco (1981: 130-40).

4.   See Neale 1993.

The pleasure of the feminine as a voyeuristic object comes from asserting control, especially through punishment and forgiveness. Images of bondage associated with punishment function to make voyeuristic objects of the female characters in all three films, more markedly so in *Lady and the Tramp* and *Peter Pan*. In Mulvey's reading, the boy feels a guilty desire for his mother, and takes pleasure in images which enable him to control and punish the female. The pleasure of the feminine as a fetishistic object, on the other hand, enables the boy to displace his anxiety, created by the object of desire, his mother. By focusing his desire on some other object, and taking pleasure in its beauty, his fear is assuaged. While both modes provide pleasure for the male, in these films male recognition of the female as the chosen one, leading to mature sexuality of which the index is marriage, is the reward of the fetishistic object. Death is the reward of the voyeuristic object.

In *Cinderella*, this process is introduced in the tower which is Cinderella's domain. She cares for a number of animals whom she has domesticated, and for whom she functions as mother. Early in the film a new mouse is caught in a trap, and the film shows Cinderella rescuing him. She provides clothing for him, and most importantly, she gives him a name. The film depicts the ideal home, where boys are 'saved' by mothers and where girls find safety in the culturally prescribed roles of mother and wife. Girls in this scenario are not powerless, but their power comes from their goodness and innocence which serve to attract appropriate males. Cinderella is, in Mulvey's terms, a voyeuristic object at the beginning, but the action of the plot must release her to her proper role as wife and mother, where she becomes a fetishistic object for male viewers. In either case, she remains under control, and while after meeting the prince she becomes aware of the inappropriateness of her literal bondage at home, she never becomes aware that marriage might also limit her personal freedom. In this fairy tale world, 'good' female characters desire marriage and motherhood.

In *Peter Pan*, Wendy is the object of Peter's desire. She represents motherhood, a source of nurture and pleasure, to him and to the Lost Boys. Having just been banned from the nursery by her father, Wendy is no longer a child. She is growing up, becoming a woman, and the night when Peter comes looking for his shadow marks that transition. Peter, the boy from Neverland who comes to take her away with him, can be seen as a possible savior for her.

Wendy looks to escape her father's pronouncement, condemning her to maturity. Peter rescues her and takes her away, and in the course of the subsequent adventure, in the space of one evening, he rescues her several times, along with John and Michael, Tiger Lily and the Lost Boys. But in the end, when Wendy chooses to walk the plank, she has chosen to grow up. And although Peter rescues her once more, she no longer desires to remain in the childish fantasy world of Neverland. Salvation for girls is in acceptance of biological destiny. Wendy is ready for this transition, and it is her desire for Peter that causes problems in Neverland, 'women trouble'. Peter's desire for her as mother must be renounced, and he does not allow himself to desire her as a woman.

In the erotic economy of this film, his desire is displaced eventually onto Tinker Bell. The danger Wendy represents for Peter is represented in the gift Captain Hook sends to Peter, a time bomb which will explode, connoting Wendy's coming of age and mature sexuality. Tinker Bell snatches the bomb away from Peter at the last moment, and she nearly dies when it explodes. The crisis enables Peter to release Wendy and to recognize Tinker Bell as the most important person in the world for him, his chosen one. But since she is a pixie and not a real woman, she is a fetishized object which allows him to avoid taking on his proper paternal role. There are no appropriate objects for Peter's desire, since the film is careful to present Tiger Lily as a girl still under her father's control, unlike Wendy who is seen as a 'squaw'.

The images of a boy rescuer from the sky who leads an unruly group of male followers parodies the biblical image of Jesus and his disciples. Peter is an anti-establishment figure, like the other green men of the folk tradition, but the film suggests that the delinquency of young people is a phase that must be rejected; those who refuse to do so become Lost Boys. John's bowler hat and umbrella are symbols of appropriate male leadership and authority: it is not surprising that the Lost Boys immediately fall in line and follow him 'wherever he may go'. Peter cannot be integrated into the adult world to which John returns. He remains a dream figure, a childish memory for boys, whose salvation requires that they give up that vision and accept adult life, itself an illusion based on dependency on a mother-wife at home. The idea that salvation might be found in mutual interdependence, with both give and take, so that one's own salvation is intimately linked with the salvation of others is not a vision of this gospel. It requires, rather, that male heroes rescue female heroines and give them homes and protection, in return for integration into a nuclear family where the wife indulgently mothers the husband as well as the children. This is what Peter Pan wants for the Lost Boys, but is unable to give them, as he refuses to 'grow up' into the adult sexual role required. The proper result is shown in the Darling family, where George Darling has clearly given up the boyish fantasies of pirates and treasure, but has moved into a different fantasy of the wife who will mother him. If growing up means losing one's illusions, giving up the 'silly stories' of childhood, then he has not grown up. He simply tells himself other stories.

Other images suggesting the saving work of Christ shape the hero of *Lady and the Tramp*, but here again, the Christian imagery supports different values. Tramp, a stray from the wrong side of the tracks, protects several characters from danger and releases them from bondage. But as in the case of Peter Pan, he rescues rather than redeems them. He is seen early on opening the door to the dog catcher's van, and he fights off the hellish hounds that attack Lady. When she is muzzled and lost, it is Tramp who finds a way to free her, using the help of animals locked up in the zoo. And starry-eyed though she is, even daring to stay out all night with him, when he offers her the freedom of life in the wild, she places duty first. Lady's dedication to her duty of care for the baby, which keeps her from entering the promised land of adventure and freedom with Tramp, is represented by an index: the collar and shiny gold license tag. This object of consumption is presented as a fetishistic object, an object of desire which serves to identify Lady's virtue. She is properly registered, under appropriate social and legal control.

Caught and put in the pound on the way home, she is humiliated. In the pound, a dark place of voyeuristic control, the fetishized license tag saves her from the death that certainly awaits the stray dogs: 'What's a nice girl like you doing in a place like this?', the dog catcher says to her. Once more at home, chained to the dog house, she refuses Tramp's overtures. He is, as Jock says, 'a mongrel'. This rejection, losing Lady's affection, is the turning point for Tramp. He can no longer save her from danger or free her from bondage. Charm and wiles have their limits; when the rat attacks the baby, Tramp shows his true character by taking her protective role and risking himself. He kills the rat, but finds himself in the clutches of the dog catcher who has 'been after this one for a long time'. Unable to save himself, he appears doomed. But he is himself rescued by Trusty the bloodhound, who risks his life, chases the van and by frightening the horses gains enough time for Tramp to be released alive. Trusty, who had lost his sense of smell, and with it his identity, finds it again in this redemptive moment of heroism. Tramp, free from the dog catcher, is brought home, and the next scene shows him proudly wearing his own collar and license tag, with a basketful of puppies. His action has brought him into society, and he is able to play his proper role, no longer lusting after other females and dreaming of adventure on the open road.

Thus this story, with multiple examples of release from bondage, suggests that true heroism requires not only the desire to help others in trouble, but the willingness to risk one's own safety. But true freedom and love are not found out in the streets, or on the road in search of adventure; the best things in life are found in home, family, and order. 'Being good' and taking pleasure in submission are rewarded by the mark of one's virtue, a license of one's own. These pleasures, although they seem to have something in common with the virtues commended by the story of Jesus, in fact recontextualize the value of risky self-sacrifice by rewarding it. Tramp profits from his experience, and although Trusty breaks a leg, he too escapes harm. The strays, on the other hand, whose crime is not to be properly integrated into society, and in the case of Peg, not to be adequately chaste, receive a death sentence without reprieve.

Thus all three films image male and female desire. Freud's comment that 'every separate phantasy contains the fulfillment of a wish and improves upon unsatisfactory reality' (White 1993) is echoed in Cinderella's song 'a dream is a wish your heart makes', where faith is rewarded if one 'keeps on believing'. Peter Pan suggests the importance of faith, and the need to see the world with a child's eyes. But the dreams and desires of these films, while the images connote certain aspects of the Christ figure, are desires that commodify and fetishize the religious. The desire for unity with God through the saving figure of Christ in an eternal realm is one that must be controlled in a consumer culture where it is important to develop objects of desire that can be acquired, so that the pleasures of consumption can be available to more and more people. Religious desires lead to social relationships which are not defined by the pleasure of consuming objects for status and differentiation. So desire for union with God and the idea of the people of God as family are imaged here by the erotic desire which is displaced and fetishized in marriage, conjugal love, and children, where the family displaces both inappropriate sexuality and unattainable spiritual union. The hope for fulfillment in the future becomes an expectation of immediate fulfillment by consuming, making objects of desire one's own, to be used for pleasure.

As we have seen, the satisfaction derived from goods is related to socially structured access. Both satisfaction and status depend upon display and the ability to sustain differences within a culture of inflation, by creating both bonds and distinctions. In a society which values hard work and a certain inner asceticism, the controlled circulation of goods makes consumption an auxiliary to work: orderly, respectable, and conserving. The films provide the pleasure of inversion of cultural values. Peter Pan tempts us with Neverland; Lady strays onto the wrong side of the track. There is pleasure in the liminal journey, the view of what is forbidden, with a safe return home. The films offer a vision of transcendence in Neverland and the open road which the 'salvation' of the adult male figures in the films, George Darling and 'Jim Darling' as well as Jock and Trusty, has required them to give up. Their presentation as both objects of desire and of ridicule suggests that transcendence in moments of transgression is to be desired, but within the limits of a controlled consumer environment. Liminality, desire, sexuality and fetishism all combine in these films, providing us with the thrill of the possibility of disorder, which is resolved in a conservative fashion, leading to further desire which enables further consumption.[5]

If the Disney gospel is indeed to make money, it does so by imaging and offering forbidden thrills. As Mike Featherstone points out, within popular culture there remains a tradition of transgression, the carnivalesque, and liminal excess; we find these things displaced into the cinema and theme parks, favored sites of consumption. These places, where consumers experience excitement and excess, are liminal spaces for impossible dreams (Featherstone 1991: 79-81). The adults at the Walt Disney Studios who provide us with these images of adulthood and proper family life are, as it were, having it both ways: they are adult males who are paid to live a life of imagination so that others can temporarily experience the pleasures of both transgression and transcendence. The religious desire for transcendent community in unity with God finds immanent satisfaction in sites of consumption where shared experience and shared emotions create a sense of community,

5. For a detailed analysis of consumer culture, although not from a theological perspective, see Featherstone 1991.

however transient, in the effervescent pleasures available to all for the price of admission. Thus we find that in the very commodification of religious ideas found in the films, the excess leads back to the things lost in religion, a sense of community and union in the desire for the transcendent. So we come full circle in terms of desire, but desire fully commodified.

THEY'RE NOT JUST BAD, THEY'RE STUPID AND UGLY, TOO: THE DEPICTION OF BAAL WORSHIPERS IN NEST ENTERTAINMENT'S *ANIMATED STORIES FROM THE BIBLE*

R. Christopher Heard

The presentation of 'Bible stories' to children is nothing new. There is already precedent for such a practice within the Bible itself (e.g. Deut. 6.20-25). In recent years, animation has become a favorite medium in which to present such stories. Nest Entertainment was organized in 1992 by Richard Rich, formerly an animator and producer with Walt Disney Studios. Nest's first products were a series of *Animated Stories from the New Testament*, soon followed by its series of *Animated Stories from the Bible*[1] and *Animated Hero Classics* (featuring such widely varied figures as Judah Maccabee, Joan of Arc, Leonardo da Vinci, Christopher Columbus, Pocahontas, and Harriet Tubman). Nest's mission, according to its web site, is to 'help families share with children everywhere the Judeo-Christian morals so necessary to their development. We do this through storytelling, featuring famous biblical and historical figures as role models. They represent the positive qualities we want our children to emulate' (http://www.nest-ent.com/acm/info.htm). Since this mission causes Nest to see itself as 'the most important company in the world', it seems appropriate in this volume on 'culture, entertainment, and the Bible' to evaluate one of Nest's *Animated Stories from the Bible* and assess its fit with Nest's stated goals for the series.

Setting the Stage

Exterior. Temple—night
Ahab stands at the edge of a second-story balcony, gazing at a fountain bubbling in the palace courtyard. His clothing includes: an armored tunic, over which is draped

---

1. That is, the Hebrew Bible.

a purplish-red cloak or cape; a thin gold crown with two small triangular projections at the front; thin gold bracelets on his upper arms; gold braces on his wrists. His black hair is pulled back into a ponytail.

> *Baal priest*[2] (partially visible over Ahab's left shoulder): It's time for the dedication, my lord. We mustn't keep her waiting.

Ahab turns to walk inside. Baal priest now becomes fully visible. He wears a headdress that resembles white animal horns, and has three teardrop-shaped red marks (presumably cosmetics or tattoos) on his forehead. He is bald, but sports bushy eyebrows. Triangular gold earrings hang from his earlobes. He wears a thin gold necklace. Half a dozen gold bands encircle his upper arms, with similar jewelry on his lower arms. He wears a blue robe topped by a wide gold collar, from which hangs a small rodent-like skull. His fingernails are noticeably long.

Cut to: Interior. Temple, Upper Level
Jezebel lies on her stomach on a low couch behind a sheer curtain, wearing a white backless bodysuit, a wide gold belt, gold bracelets on her upper and lower arms, and a crown that resembles Ahab's except for the two red gemstones embedded in it (Ahab's has no such jewels). Her eyelids and lips are cosmetically colored.

> *Ahab*: Ah, Jezebel.

(Ahab kisses Jezebel's hand, which she has extended through the curtain)

> *Ahab*: Were it not for you, I never would have known how sweet life could be.
> *Jezebel*: Your people await your word, Ahab.

Cut to: Interior. Palace/Temple, Lower Level
Two dozen or more revelers celebrate on either side of a long blue carpet that descends from a short staircase.

Reverse Angle
Ahab walks to the head of the short staircase and raises his arms for silence.

> *Ahab*: Prophets of Baal, friends, noblemen; Jezebel, queen of all that is mine: the god of Israel is dead, and Baal has taken his place!
> *Crowd*: (cheers)
> *Ahab*: And tonight we dedicate this temple to the god of the sky, who alone has the power to bring rain and make Israel prosper! Long live Baal!
> *Crowd*: (cheers)
> *Ahab*: Long live Jezebel!

---

2.   This character is designated 'Baal priest' in the activity book, published by Nest, that accompanies the video. I will follow this designation in the 'screenplay' segments presented here.

Reverse Angle
The large, wooden double doors of the temple open, one by one, without any visible force being applied to them. Elijah stands there silently, fists clenched at his sides. He wears a red strap (perhaps cloth or leather) around his forehead, and a brown sleeveless tunic. A gray skirt, apparently made from an animal fur, covers most of his thighs and tapers to a point parallel with his knees between his legs. A knife with a foot-long blade rests in a sheath strapped to his chest; a horn (of the type for anointing oil) is strapped to his belt. Elijah walks to the base of the small staircase, where Ahab stands at the head.

> *Ahab*: Who…are…you?
> *Elijah*: Turn away from the worship of Baal, Ahab, or as the Lord lives, he will curse the land!
> *Ahab*: So. You're one of the prophets. I thought we put an end to your kind. No matter. We shall settle the issue here and now!

(Ahab draws his sword)

> *Elijah*: Listen and hear me well, Ahab. As the God of Israel liveth, there shall be no rain until I, Elijah, call on the Lord to deliver it.

(Ahab and Elijah trade harsh stares. Elijah turns and walks to the temple door)

> *Jezebel*: Kill him! Kill him!

(Elijah topples two large statues of Baal, one on each side of the temple door)

> *Jezebel*: Kill him! Kill him!

Cut to: Exterior. Temple steps

> *Ahab* (to soldier): Find Elijah!
> *God*: Elijah!
> *Elijah* (crouching behind large jars, brandishing his knife): I'm not afraid to die, Lord.
> *God*: Go eastward, Elijah, and hide thyself at the brook Cherith.[3]
> *Elijah*: Let me strike, Lord! Let me put an end to this wickedness!
> *God*: Go, Elijah. I shall provide for you there.

Thus begins the story of Elijah in Nest Entertainment's *Animated Stories from the Bible* series. It is immediately apparent that Nest found 1 Kgs 17.1 insufficiently interesting to stand on its own, for it has created a rather detailed narrative context for Elijah's simple pronouncement of drought.[4] The felt need for a narrative context to house and

---

3.   Nest's voiceover actor pronounces 'Cherith' as two syllables, placing the accent on the first and pronouncing it like the beginning of 'cheese'. Strange, this Yahweh who cannot speak Hebrew (*kᵉrît*) properly.

4.   Since I know very little about the individuals or groups of individuals

dramatize the biblical narrator's characteristically laconic report points at once to an important feature of adaptations of biblical narratives for film. The adaptation of any written work for the screen requires certain kinds of transformations that are semiotically meaningful.[5] Normally, written works adapted for film must be condensed, and in the process they tend to lose detail with regard to the events being portrayed.[6] Biblical narrators, however, tend to be much more reserved than narrators in British and American novels. Thus Nest—like the producers of almost all films based on biblical narratives—is constrained to transform its source material in a direction opposite that of the norm. Instead of condensing or abridging the details of incident in their source material, Nest's desire to have scenes of a reasonably interesting length drives it to create new dialogue, characters, and situations in order to fill up the allotted time or to fill in gaps in the source narrative.[7]

Inevitably, the move from a strictly verbal medium to a graphically rich medium requires a physical depiction of the characters involved. Film adaptations of biblical texts share this transformative feature with all film adaptations of written works. Such depictions can never be semiotically neutral, and the depictions themselves lie completely within the control of the filmmakers (although decisions about the meaningfulness of the image lie with the observer).[8]

> If we both read the words [*sic*] 'rose' you may perhaps think of a Peace rose you picked last summer, while I am thinking of the one Laura Westphal gave to me in December 1968. In cinema, however, we both see the

responsible for making the various creative decisions that inform the video, I have treated the video as a 'group work' and have cited 'Nest' as the source of such decisions.

5.   Indeed, George Bluestone (1957: ix, 5) sees these transformations as *so* semiotically meaningful that they constitute not so much 'adaptation' as creating an entirely new 'structure' out of the 'raw materials' of the literary work. See also Huss and Silverstein 1968: 105.

6.   On this and other aspects of the adaptation of novels for the screen, see Bluestone 1957: 5, and, more fully, Monaco 1981: 27-33.

7.   Alan F. Segal makes the same observation in his brief treatment of Cecil B. DeMille's *The Ten Commandments* (1995: 36).

8.   *The Ten Commandments* is again instructive here: DeMille cast Charlton Heston as Moses because of the latter's resemblance to Michelangelo's famous statue of Moses. Cf. Segal 1995: 36, and Fraser 1988: 9. For the importance of attending to how a film looks as well as what happens in it, see Sobchack 1983: 68-87.

same rose, while the filmmaker can choose from an infinite variety of roses and then photograph the one chosen in another infinite variety of ways. The artist's choice in cinema is without limit; the artist's choice in literature is circumscribed, while the reverse is true for the observer. Film does not suggest, in this context: it states (Monaco 1981: 128).

Nest's decisions about how to render Elijah and the leading figure among the prophets of Baal are particularly suggestive in this regard.

The leading figure among the prophets of Baal—for convenience, I will refer to him as 'Elibaal'—stands out noticeably against the other characters in the video.[9] To begin with, his skin tone is noticeably darker than that of all the other characters. To the extent that this artistic decision marks Elibaal as an 'outsider' *vis-à-vis* the Israelites, it is a convenient visual reminder of the biblical story's depiction of Ahab's Baal worship as an 'import' from Sidon. This association becomes explicit in the caption to one of the images on the back cover of the activity book distributed with the video: 'King Ahab, and his wicked priests, were almost successful in converting Israel to the worship of the phoenician [*sic*] idol Baal'. However, Elibaal's skin color may also send viewers the subtle message that a darker, or different, skin tone than the majority's, or one's own, is sinister and not to be trusted. Given that other Nest products present Pocahontas and Harriet Tubman as heroes, this particular element appears to be a vestige of old in-grained habits regarding the semiotic values of 'dark' and 'light' rather than a consciously racist choice. The ease with which this association of darker skin tones with evil slips into the *Elijah* video, however, demonstrates how powerfully that particular association has pervaded American culture even for a creative team that has explicitly sought to identify heroes from a variety of ethnic groups.

Elibaal also displays unique dress, wearing triangular earrings, a pattern of three teardrop-shaped cosmetic marks on his forehead, a gold necklace (with a clasp resembling the skull of a small rodent), and long fingernails. The only other character so accoutered is Jezebel. From one perspective, this ornamentation is a brilliant, if subtle, way of aligning the prophets of Baal with Jezebel, an association strongly implied, if

9. 'Elibaal' (*'ēlîba'al*), 'Baal is my god', is an obvious counterpart to 'Elijah' (*'ēlîyâ*), 'Yah[weh] is my god'. Compare also the name of Jezebel's father, Ethbaal. For another example of an interpreter assigning names to otherwise unnamed characters—an example in which it makes rather more difference than it does here—see Bal 1988: 41-68.

not quite stated outright, in 1 Kgs 16.31 and 18.3. On the other hand, one easily imagines that Nest's largely conservative Christian and Jewish constituency will associate these visual cues with conservative cultural codes.[10] In those codes, a variety of negative associations automatically attach to a male wearing long fingernails, cosmetics, and large earrings. Such associations may be encouraged by Nest's decision to give Elibaal a higher-pitched voice than either Ahab or Elijah, the other prominent male characters in the video. While no overt assertions of aberrant sexuality are made, the way Elibaal dresses and speaks may cause many members of Nest's audience to immediately categorize him not only as a pagan, but also as a transvestite and a homosexual— which, for such an audience, can only be to pile sin upon sin.

On top of all this, Elibaal wears an odd horned headdress. This head-dress may very well be a result of Nest's research into ancient Baalism. If Nest knew that the bull may have been associated with Baal in ancient Canaan, it may have modeled Elibaal's headgear after a bull's horns.[11] As a matter of reception, however, it is more likely that the video's viewers will associate the horns with popular western portrayals of devils than with bulls, thus adding another negatively charged image into the mix. The small skull that hangs from Elibaal's necklace might actually draw viewers away from bull associations to diabolical associations, since bulls, though sometimes violent, are hardly predators.

It seems clear at this stage that Nest has exploited (or, perhaps, has been 'taken in' by) selected cultural codes in a manner likely to increase viewers' perceptions of Elibaal as evil. But so what? Clearly, in the biblical story as well as in the video, the priests of Baal are the 'bad guys'. So what difference does it make if Nest makes Elibaal look *really* bad, if it piles cue upon cue to show that this character is one of the bad guys?

In terms of the success of Nest's own project (to 'help families share with children everywhere the Judeo-Christian morals so necessary to

10. On the general relationship between the cultural codes reflected in film and those held by the audience, see Monaco 1981: 131, and Rollins 1983a: 249 and 1983b: 32-48. The fact that Nest sees a significant part of its constituency as Jewish is clear from its decision to name its video series *Animated Stories from the Bible* instead of *Animated Stories from the Old Testament*. A companion series, *Animated Stories from the New Testament*, is clearly aimed at Christian viewers.

11. For the association of bull imagery with Baal, see Kapelrud 1952: 21; Toombs 1995: 38.

their development…through storytelling, featuring famous biblical and historical role models [that] represent the positive qualities we want our children to emulate'), it makes a difference because the visual 'otherizing' of Elibaal gives the contest between Yahweh and Baal a rather different flavor in the video than in the biblical text. Judging by the Yahwism that the former prophets and certain psalms promote against the backdrop of the picture of Baalism that emerges from the Baal myths known to us,[12] it seems that Baalism will have been attractive to ancient Yahwists precisely because it sounded so familiar, not because Baalism was strange and exotic. It was easy for Yahwists to adopt Baalism not because Baal was so different from Yahweh, but precisely because it was so hard to tell the difference. The powers predicated of the two and the manner of speaking of the two were so similar that they might prove rather difficult to distinguish.[13] By making Elibaal look so different from the rest of the characters in the video, the animators imply a starker conceptual difference between Baalism and Yahwism than is evident from their source material.

Elijah's visual appearance is also telling. He is drawn as a physically powerful individual. The strength implied by his muscular arms is confirmed by the video's depiction of Elijah toppling two statues of Baal. The video here reflects Nest's research into ancient Baalism, as these statues are modeled after statuettes generally identified as Baal (and/or Resheph), complete with conical hat and upraised club (presumably representing thunder).[14] No such event is narrated in 1 Kings 17. The biblical narrator leaves Elijah's physical appearance indeterminate, with the exception of his hairiness and leather belt mentioned in a later episode (2 Kgs 1.8). Nest's animators do not have that luxury. They are bound by their medium to give Elijah a physical appearance. They do, however, have a choice about what kind of physical appearance to give

12. This is by no means a self-evidently sound procedure, and care must be taken not to assume that either the biblical texts or the Baal myths constitute direct testimony to the everyday beliefs and practices of ancient Yahwists and Baalists. Nevertheless, there is a striking degree of correspondence between the literatures mentioned, as demonstrated repeatedly by Bronner 1968.

13. Bronner presents many examples of these similarities under the rubric of Yahwist anti-Baal polemic. Psalm 29 provides another classic example of the similarities; cf. Basevi 1990: 13; Craigie 1983: 70-71; Johnson 1955: 62; Weiser 1962: 261; and Margulis 1970: 346.

14. A photograph of such a statuette may be found in Pritchard 1958, illustration 134; cf. the 'Baal of Lightning' stele, illustration 136.

him, and they choose to give us a superhero: Conan the Tishbite. After announcing the impending drought and toppling the statues of Baal, Elijah flees the newly-dedicated temple. As in the biblical story, Elijah then goes to the Wadi Cherith (and then on to Zarephath) at Yahweh's command—but not before drawing his knife and begging Yahweh to let him slaughter the Baalists on the spot (another item not featured in the biblical narrative). Later, while at the Wadi Cherith, Nest's Elijah prays, 'But, how much longer must I wait here? Let me return and finish what I've begun!' Presumably, Elijah is wishing, as before, to physically overpower (and kill) the Baalists.

Praying for Rain

Before proceeding to the contest on Mount Carmel, the video offers Baal's prophets 'equal time' and gives viewers an imaginative look at what they might have been up to during the drought.

Exterior. Temple—day
Only the temple courtyard and the dried-up fountain are visible.

> *Baalist* (off-camera): Must we wear these silly outfits?

pan to: Baal priest, dressed as before.

> *Baal priest*: The object of our little play is to please Baal, not to quibble about costumes.

Follow Baal priest to: Four Baalists standing side-by-side. Each is bald-headed with bushy eyebrows. Each wears a simple, monochrome tunic (one is pink, one green, one blue, and one yellow) fastened at above the right shoulder. Each wears on his head a weather-oriented symbol—one sun, two clouds, one lightning bolt—with a hole cut in each symbol to accommodate each Baalist's head.

> *Baal priest*: Remember, by acting out the miracles of Baal, we show him that we have faith in his power. Places!

Cut to: Baal priest and the Baalists on a crude stage topped by a simple wooden frame. The Baalist wearing the sun cutout ('Sun Baalist') climbs to one of the top corners of the frame. Baal priest stands in the middle of the stage. To his right stand Cloud Baalists no. 1 and no. 2. Lightning Baalist stands behind the two Cloud Baalists on a barrel.

> *Baal priest*: Ready?
> *Sun Baalist*: Ready!
> *Baal priest* (clears his throat): Oh great Baal, we know that you and you alone can make it rain. Command the clouds to gather and pour out moisture on this barren land.

(Baal priest, annoyed, looks at Sun Baalist, who is daydreaming)

> *Baal priest*: Command the clouds to gather and…
>
> *Sun Baalist*: What's that I hear? Methinks a prayer for rain from yonder mortals below! Gather, all ye clouds! Send a mighty shower!

(Cloud Baalist no. 1 and Cloud Baalist no. 2 make blowing noises, then step away from one another to reveal Lightning Baalist behind them, who is sitting on the barrel, looking bored)

> *Baal priest* (to Lightning Baalist): You have to jump! First there's thunder, then the clouds separate, then lightning! Lightning strikes!

(Cloud Baalist no. 1 and Cloud Baalist no. 2 step back together, make blowing noises, then separate to reveal Lighting Baalist behind them, who is now standing on the barrel)

> *Lightning Baalist* (jumping off barrel): Hya!
>
> *Baal priest*: And now, oh Baal,

(Lightning Baalist climbs back onto barrel. Cloud Baalists no. 1 and no. 2 make blowing noises)

> *Lightning Baalist* (jumping off barrel): Ha!
>
> *Cloud Baalist* no. 2 (rubbing himself where he was struck by Lightning Baalist's costume): Ouch! Watch it with that thing!
>
> *Lightning Baalist*: I can't help it. This costume is too big.
>
> *Cloud Baalist* no. 1: Can I be the lightning? He's not very…
>
> *Baal priest*: Put that back on! We're almost at the part…
>
> *Lightning Baalist*: I refuse.

(Sun Baalist pours a bucket of water into the upper part of the frame. The water drips out through holes in the frame, simulating rain)

> *Baal priest*: No! We're not ready for that yet! Not until I say, 'Oh Baal, make it rain!'

(The Baalists on the stage, and the Baal priest, slip on the wet stage one at a time until all are lying prone with water pouring down on top of them from the frame)

The same 'myth and ritual' thinking that spent so much time early in the twentieth century trying to map out the precise contours of Israel's putative annual enthronement festival (or covenant renewal festival or royal Zion festival) has tried likewise to map out the uses of the Baal myths (as known chiefly from their Ugaritic exemplars) at an annual festival commemorating Baal's victory over Mot.[15] However, if Baal worshipers did in fact engage in ritual drama, such drama was surely

15. For a handy digest of such studies, see Smith 1994: 60-75.

richer and more reverent than the ridiculous skit depicted in the Nest video.

Besides the fact that the script of the Baalists' 'ritual drama' is banal if not downright silly, the Baalists themselves cannot remember their lines and, moreover, cannot keep from tripping over one another as they rehearse. The level of incompetence displayed by these Baalists is completely unprecedented. Nest has now added another negative element to its construction of Baal worshipers. Baal worshipers are, from the start, the bad guys, and Nest has encumbered their leader with visual elements they can assume will be negatively encoded among their audience. Now, in a completely fabricated scene, Nest charges Baal's prophets with gross professional incompetence. In Nest's video, Baal worshipers are not just bad, they're stupid and ugly, too.

The Baalists' Flintstones-style tunics and bald heads are also intriguing and semiotically ambiguous. Clearly, these elements of their appearance cause them to stand out starkly against the other Israelites, which is itself no doubt a distortion. Both the Bible and more contemporary accounts of Israelite popular religion suggest that the Israelites would not have seen Baal worshipers as strange and unusual, but rather as perfectly normal friends and neighbors. Why then does Nest depict Baal's prophets in this particular kind of dress and with this particular lack-of-hairstyle? This depiction may well be a reflex of Nest's awareness that shaven heads are sometimes associated within the biblical literature with non-Israelites, if not quite explicitly with non-Israelite worship (e.g. in Jer. 9.26; 25.23; 49.32). Similarly, biblical materials prohibit Israelite priests from shaving their heads on several occasions (e.g. in Lev. 21.5; Ezek. 44.20). On the other hand, biblical materials attest that Israelites did shave their heads for purposes of ritual purification (Lev. 14.8-9), discharging nazirite vows (Num. 16.18), and mourning (Isa. 22.12; Amos 8.10; Mic. 1.16). Since there are thoroughly respectable (from a biblical perspective) reasons for shaving one's head, and since baldness is not specifically associated with Baalism in the biblical literature, Nest may be guilty of hasty generalization if the choice to portray the Baalists as bald-headed is not simply arbitrary. In any case, one might wonder whether Nest's viewers will be so attuned to the various treatments of baldness in the biblical literature, which can hardly be said to form major themes. It is entirely possible that viewers of the *Elijah* video might notice bald heads and robes and consciously or unconsciously equate Baalists with Buddhists —with the possible concomitant result of a transfer of negative associations either direction, or both, between the two groups.

Testing the Gods

The story comes to a head, of course, with the contest between Elijah and Baal's prophets on Mount Carmel.

Exterior. Mount Carmel—day

> *Elijah*: We will place sacrifices on these altars, ready for burning. The prophets of Baal shall call on the name of their God, and I will call on the name of the Lord. The god who answers by fire, let him be God.

Three Baalists (the same as in the 'skit' scene, minus Sun Baalist) and the Baal priest shout an unintelligible shout, then begin dancing in a circle, bending at the waist and throwing their arms into the air. Amid their meaningless shouts ('ya!', 'heyoh!' and the like), some comprehensible phrases can be discerned:

> *Baalists*: Show these people that...
> Oh great god of the sky...
> Show us your power...
> *Baal priest* (tearing his robe): Oh great and mighty Baal, see how we wound ourselves for thee! Send down fire from your throne and reveal your power!

(Nothing happens)

> *Baal priest* (to the Baalists): Again!

(The dance continues. Elijah looks on, bemused)

Fade through to: The same scene, hours later. The passage of time is indicated by a circular trench, as much as eight inches deep, that the Baalists have worn into the ground by their continual dancing. The Baalists are now so exhausted they can barely walk.

> *Baal priest*: Hear us, oh Baal.
> *Elijah*: Come now! Louder! Louder! For surely Baal is a god! He's just not able to hear you! Maybe he's talking to one of your other gods? Or perhaps he's out hunting? Yes, that's it. I hope for your sake that he isn't away on a long journey. Continue! Continue!

The three Baalists have now fallen on the ground from exhaustion. Only the Baal priest remains.

> *Baal priest*: All-powerful Baal, send down your fire! Show them that you, and you are God!

(The Baal priest falls backward, exhausted)

To be sure, 1 Kings 18 itself is none too kind to the prophets of Baal, ascribing to them a 'limping dance' around the altar, self-mutilations (which Nest graciously declines to show in explicit detail), and loud shouts—all for naught. One might easily conclude that there is already a mocking tone in the narrative;[16] certainly Elijah's own speech is full of sarcasm. On the other hand, one might see the Baalists in 1 Kings 18 as almost tragic figures. Indeed, for the narrator of 1 Kings 18, the Baalists' lack of success is clearly not to be ascribed to defective performance of their rites, for they have conformed to their prescribed practices (v. 28). Rather, the Baalists' lack of success in 1 Kings 18 is due to the simple fact that Baal is not God. Similarly, Elijah's own sarcasm is not directed (in either the biblical story or the video) at the Baalists' performance of their rituals, but at Baal himself. The video depiction, however, somewhat shifts the focus from Baal's own failings (indeed, nonexistence) to the incompetence of the four dolts who prophesy in Baal's name. Perhaps Baal would have responded if he had been able to draft better prophets?

Where, by the way, are the other 446 prophets of Baal, not to mention the 400 prophets of Asherah? In 1 Kgs 18.19, Elijah's challenge goes out to 850 prophets, and he stresses in 18.22 that he is the only Yahwist prophet left to compete against the 450 Baalist prophets (though readers learn later in the biblical narrative that Elijah is not quite correct in his estimate of his own isolation). It is quite a gutsy thing to stand alone in front of 450 prophets armed with knives and spears (v. 28) and insult their god! Yet this is precisely what Elijah does in 1 Kings 18, so confident is he that Yahweh will be vindicated and Baal will be proven to be no god at all. In Nest's video, however, Elijah is facing four-to-one odds rather than 450-to-one (or 850-to-one should Asherah's prophets decide to side with the Baalists if a brawl breaks out).[17] Moreover, on Nest's Carmel, the Baalists' spears and knives are gone, and the one wearing a weapon is Elijah—who has already performed feats of strength and daring-do to rival Samson's. 1 Kings' Elijah stakes his very life on the outcome of the Carmel contest. Nest's Elijah, however, risks very little.

16. Bronner's study (1968) seems to suggest this.
17. Asherah's prophets cannot be presumed to side automatically with the Baalists, as shown by Freedman 1987: 241-49.

Do We Want Our Children to Watch This Video?

In the final analysis, however, do the various transformations discussed above materially affect Nest's goal? Does this video 'help families share with children everywhere the Judeo-Christian morals so necessary to their development…through storytelling, featuring famous biblical and historical role models [that] represent the positive qualities we want our children to emulate'? Do we want our children to watch this video?[18]

Nest has taken one key element within the story told in 1 Kgs 17–19—Elijah's sarcasm toward the prophets of Baal during the contest on Mount Carmel—and has woven that into the very fabric of its own narrative. Moreover, it has shifted that sarcasm from an unflattering depiction of Baal to an unflattering depiction of Baal's prophets. To some degree, this no doubt misrepresents Baal worshipers as a class. More importantly for Nest's own project, however, is the fact that this transformation at once cheapens and exaggerates Elijah's accomplishments. It exaggerates Elijah's accomplishments by inadvertently shifting the focus from a contest between Yahweh and Baal to a contest between Elijah and the prophets of Baal. It cheapens Elijah's accomplishments by portraying the prophets of Baal as inept morons, which leaves little doubt or suspense about who is going to win this contest (if there were any doubt to begin with). There is simply no way the powerful, competent Elijah can possibly lose out to these bozos, and the numeric reduction of the opposition from 450 prophets of Baal to one Baalist prophet with three or four cronies so evens the odds that Elijah's eventual victory is never in doubt, even for viewers who are unfamiliar with the biblical story. 1 Kings' Elijah is a gutsy prophet who stands up for his God at significant personal risk and is wholly dependent upon his God for a successful outcome to his greatest challenge. Nest Entertainment's Elijah is little more than a bully who probably could (and indeed wants to) just beat up his opponents should his God fail to come through.

In the end, of course, Elijah *does* kill his opponents in 1 Kings 18. Nest's video implies as much, though it does not depict the actual slaughter in the Wadi Kishon. To that extent, the eagerness of Nest's Elijah to strike down the Baalists at the beginning of the video is con-

18. Cf. Fewell and Gunn 1993: 20, and Landy 1997: 157-76.

sistent with the biblical characterization of Elijah (if perhaps in too proleptic a fashion). Murder (or, more generously, execution) of those with whom we disagree on religious matters is, one hopes, *not* a quality we want our children to emulate. Nevertheless, this moral problem arises from the biblical source material itself and not from Nest's transformation of it.

The depiction of the Baal worshipers in the video is, however, another matter. Nest exercises considerably more freedom here, since the biblical narrator says so little about the Baalists themselves beyond mentioning their existence. It is entirely clear that the biblical narrator regards the Baalists as *wrong*, both epistemically (Baal is not God and does not have the powers ascribed to him) and morally (one ought not worship Baal). Should anyone wish to dispute this, the matter will have to be taken up with the source material itself rather than with Nest's transformations of it.

What Nest adds, without warrant from the source material, is the characterization of Baalists as not just bad, but stupid. Some might object that the Baalists' incorrectness about Baal's divinity and/or power is proof of their stupidity. In this regard the narrative sequence must be honored. The final 'evidence' for whether Yahweh or Baal is God has not been gathered until 1 Kgs 18.38. The three-year drought itself might be cited as 'data' that should have caused the Baalists to conclude that Yahweh, not Baal, was truly God. However, it is unlikely that anyone making that particular claim would support the corresponding notion had the tables been reversed. That is to say, if a Yahwist (rather than a Baalist) were to cling to the belief that Yahweh could cause rain even after a three-year drought, Nest and its constituents would probably applaud that Yahwist's faithful endurance. This point seems not to be lost on Nest itself, as halfway through the video Elibaal attributes the lack of rain to Baal's *unwillingness*, not Baal's *inability*, to bring rain.

It is with this element in its characterization of Baalists that Nest threatens to undermine its own project. As already discussed above, Nest's Elijah is somewhat less of a positive role model than the biblical Elijah, precisely because the biblical Elijah comes off like an underdog and Nest's Elijah comes off like a bully. Beyond even this, though, one of the video's implicit messages is that those who worship any god other than the Judaeo-Christian God—or, by extension, those who adhere to any religion other than Judaeo-Christian monotheism—are not just incorrect or even sinful, but just plain *stupid*. It will not do to argue that the comedic presentation of the Baal worshipers in *Elijah* simply has entertainment value, not educational (or ideological) value. Nest itself 'believes that education is not always entertaining, but that entertainment is always educational, especially with these young minds; when a child is being entertained, he is being educated'. Thus the burden of modeling positive qualities for children to emulate must be borne not only by the characters in the video, but also by the video itself.[19]

This mocking attitude toward adherents to other religious outlooks hardly seems to be the sort of positive quality that children should be encouraged to emulate. To think that those who do not share one's own religious commitments are stupid hardly seems an auspicious starting point for any encounter with those others—whether the ultimate goal of such an encounter is evangelism, dialogue, or mere civil coexistence. In the final analysis, then, Nest's Elijah (the character) provides a somewhat less positive role model than 1 Kings' Elijah. More strikingly, however, Nest's *Elijah* (the video) itself serves as a somewhat negative role model in its characterization of Baal worshipers as stupid. And it is precisely Nest's departures from, and imaginative embellishments of, its biblical source material that draw it away from its stated goal.

19. So the Nest web site (http://www.nest-ent.com/acm/intro.htm).

Part II
ART, LITERATURE, MUSIC

THE CUT THAT CONFUSES, OR: IN THE PENILE COLONY

Tina Pippin and George Aichele

[W]e already believe unconsciously, because it is from this external
character of the symbolic machine that we can explain the status of the
unconscious as radically external—that of a dead letter (Žižek 1994:
321).

Slavoj Žižek writes about the Freudian interpretation of dreams (1994:
297-300), or perhaps we should say, about his reinterpretation of the
Freudian interpretation, by way of Marx and Lacan, among others.
According to Žižek, the dream as a mental phenomenon is a translation
formed by a 'short circuit' between the 'latent thought' of the dream
and unconscious desire. The dream is thus composed of three 'elements': the manifest dream itself (the text), the latent thought expressed
in it (its content), and unconscious desire which fuses the other two
together (Žižek 1994: 298).

Although Žižek makes no mention of Charles S. Peirce, the dream
structure that he describes here is remarkably similar to Peirce's triadic
description of the sign. According to Peirce, the sign is composed of a
'representamen' (the physical signifier), an 'object' (the signified referent), and an 'interpretant' (the signified sense).[1] What Žižek calls the
manifest dream or 'text of the dream' (1994: 297) is analogous to the
representamen. The dream as a text is a 'rebus', a signifying product,
that must be deciphered. The latent content of the dream consists of
'entirely "normal" thought which can be articulated in the syntax of
everyday, common language.' This latent thought is the apparent referent of the dream—Peirce's object. Žižek notes that this thought is *not*
generally unconscious. Finally, and most important, the unconscious,
otherwise repressed desire, *'which has nothing whatsoever to do with
the "latent dream-thought"'* (1994: 298; [Žižek's emphasis]) serves as

---

1. In this we follow Frege 1952 in the use of 'sense' and 'referent'.

the mechanism that translates the latent content into the manifest dream. This desire is analogous to Peirce's interpretant, which meaningfully connects the object to the representamen. It is the sense of the dream, which psychoanalysis seeks to bring to light:

> This desire attaches itself to the dream, it intercalates itself in the interspace between the latent thought and the manifest text; it is therefore not 'more concealed, deeper' in relation to the latent thought, it is decidedly more 'on the surface', consisting entirely of the signifier's mechanisms, of the treatment to which the latent thought is submitted (Žižek 1994: 298).

Peirce argued that the three components of the sign are interchangeable—that is, that every interpretant may be the representamen of another object, and so on. It is on this basis that Umberto Eco and others have argued that semiosis is unlimited. Every signifier may also be a signified, and vice versa. In other words, there is no stopping point for signification, no Final Signified, no Absolute Signifier. Is it likewise true that there is no limit to the significance of the dream? The dream is a sign. We do not want to press our comparison of Žižek to Peirce too far, but this line of thought does suggest the approach to intertextuality that we pursue in the following. We will look at three texts, and each of the three texts will become the representamen, the interpretant, or the object, of one of the others.

First Text: the Dream Text: Embellished to Death

> [W]riting is only a transcription of the divine word, or even writing from the finger of God, but in any case it is a copy, a double of a spoken word that already exists without the writing, itself doubled on the two tables and their two faces as if to indicate its character as carbon copy, as repetition. Its function is to make God's word stable, durable, and obligatory, to be his Law (Kristeva 1989: 100).

Jacques Derrida (1979) speaks of writing as though it were an act of cutting into a surface or plowing the ground. Derrida presents the image of the spur or the point: the point of the pen spearing the page, which bisociates into the 'point' of the utterance and the present as a 'point' in space-time. Meaning and presence both emerge from and conceal the violence of inscription. The meaningful reading both contains and overlooks the meaningless writing.

In Franz Kafka's story 'In the Penal Colony' (1948) an officer of the penal colony explains the design and the operation of a peculiar machine to an explorer who happens to be visiting the colony. The machine, designed by the colony's former Commandant himself—whom we are told was a man of 'perfect organization' (Kafka 1948: 193)—consists of three parts: the Bed, the Designer, and the Harrow. The condemned man is initially laid face down on the Bed. The Designer is a mechanism of cogs that operates the Harrow according to a pre-set pattern or program, not unlike a player piano or mechanical loom. The Harrow is a glass plate that slides back and forth on a steel ribbon. It operates like the print head of an electric typewriter or dot matrix computer printer. The Harrow supports movable needles that are made to vibrate in such a way, once the machine is turned on, that they inscribe the sentence of the condemned man on to the page of his naked flesh, etching it with 'acid fluid' (Kafka 1948: 209) and rinsing away the blood.

The sentence is always a death sentence. The condemned man is letter by letter and word by word 'sentenced' to death. This writing of the Law is writing gone mad, writing pushed to the nth degree. The machine in the penal colony is a writing machine; it is a word processor. Žižek says that 'the dependence of the Law on its process of enunciation…must be repressed into the unconscious, through the ideological, imaginary experience of the "meaning" of the Law, of its foundation in Justice' (1994: 319). In Kafka's story, the words of the sentence refer in two distinct ways. They are not only symbols, in the Peircean sense, of the abstract judgment of the Law. The words are also potent indices of the concrete suffering of the man. Writing is violent and cruel and ultimately lethal. The man's skin becomes a 'carbon copy' (Kristeva 1989: 100) of the written sentence that has been programmed into the Designer. The body of the condemned man is slowly rotated on the Bed so that his skin is eventually entirely covered by the inscription of the sentence. 'Of course the script can't be a simple one', the officer calmly explains, 'it's not supposed to kill a man straight off, but only after an interval of, on an average, twelve hours; the turning point is reckoned to come at the sixth hour' (Kafka 1948: 202). The embellishments and flourishes of the alphabetic script provide for most of the actual writing. However, writing is never anything but embellishment, the meaningless little marks that distinguish one letter from another. If you take away the embellishment, then only a meaningless line is left. Embellishment is the semiotic difference that enables writing to signify.

Kafka's story is about writing, but it is also about reading, about understanding and misunderstanding. The Derridean spur is also the trace, or residue (Derrida 1979: 39-41). It is the text. Like all of Kafka's stories, 'In the Penal Colony' is a dream text. It is possessed by a dreamlike quality that cries out for interpretation, whether allegorical or psychoanalytic. It also resists the reader's attempts at understanding. Just as, at the end of the story, the explorer refuses to allow the soldier and the condemned man to accompany him as he flees the island of the penal colony, so this story never lets its reader get 'on board'. This non-understanding appears in the story as well. Neither the condemned man nor the soldier who guards him ever understand what the officer and the explorer are talking about. They are silly slapstick figures—'like a submissive dog' (Kafka 1948: 191)[2]—nightmarish comic relief in Kafka's fantastic world. When the explorer tries to read the text of the machine's plans, all he sees is 'a labyrinth of lines crossing and re-crossing each other, which covered the paper so thickly that it was difficult to discern the blank spaces between them' (Kafka 1948: 202). Once again, semiotic difference disappears as the blank spaces that are essential to this difference disappear. The explorer finds that the judicial procedures of the officer, like the script in which the sentence is written and the working of the machine itself, are incomprehensible. Much as in Kafka's novel *The Trial*, the accused is never told his sentence, or allowed to contest it. As Walter Benjamin (1968: 115) says, 'In Kafka the written law is contained in books, but these are secret; by basing itself on them the prehistoric world exerts its rule all the more ruthlessly.'

With each rotation of the condemned man's body the machine's needles cut deeper and deeper, and the man eventually bleeds to death. Only by *becoming* the text is the condemned man enabled to read his own sentence. The violence of reading necessarily corresponds to the violence of writing:

> Enlightenment comes to the most dull-witted [the officer says]. It begins around the eyes... Nothing more happens than that the man begins to *understand* the inscription, he purses his mouth as if he were listening. You have seen how hard it is to decipher the script with one's eyes; but our man deciphers it with his wounds (Kafka 1948: 204, *emphasis added*).

---

2. This is also reminiscent of the final words of K., the hero of *The Trial* (Kafka 1956: 286).

Like its central object, Kafka's story is also a semiotic machine. By reading this story we 'become' the explorer, and we learn that the officer and his writing machine have fallen on hard times. The new Commandant is not as wise as was the former one, the one who invented the machine. He does not understand the importance of the machine and refuses to encourage its use. Consequently the performance of the machine is no longer up to its former levels of perfection—it now makes disturbing noises—and the officer fears that his executions will soon be shut down altogether. The next death sentence may be for the machine itself. The officer begs the explorer to lend his support to the machine, but the explorer refuses, revolted by the entire gruesome process. In desperation, the officer releases the condemned man, readjusts the settings on the Designer, climbs into the Bed himself, and inscribes on his own body his own sentence: 'BE JUST' (Kafka 1948: 219).

In response to the officer's commands, the machine obeys perfectly, in absolute, uncanny silence. It is as though it 'knows' its master's desires and welcomes him to its embrace. Nevertheless, as the process continues, the machine begins to fall apart. The cogs pop out of the Designer, and the needles of the Harrow begin to jab randomly at the body of the officer. The officer dies quickly and without his 'sentence'. He also does not achieve understanding. The writing machine jams, and it leaves the page of the dead man's body smeared and illegible. His body is left hanging, impaled on the motionless Harrow, dangling over the pit into which the machine had previously discarded the dead bodies, a grotesque crucifix:

> [The officer's face] was as it had been in life; no sign was visible of the promised redemption; what the others had found in the machine the officer had not found; the lips were firmly pressed together, the eyes were open, with the same expression as in life, the look was calm and convinced, through the forehead went the point of the great iron spike (Kafka 1948: 225).

'In the Penal Colony' is a story about the incarnation of justice, and about its failure. As a story about death and judgment, it is also an eschatological story. Eventually the explorer flees the island of the penal colony, but only after he has visited the grave of the former Commandant and seen the inscription on it (written 'in very small letters'): 'the Commandant will rise again and lead his adherents from this house to recover the colony. Have faith and wait!' (Kafka 1948: 226). The messianic Commandant will restore his machine to its former excellence, and all will be well. Nevertheless, this epitaph is described as 'ridiculous'. The former Commandant's few remaining followers appear to be 'poor, humble creatures'. Benjamin's comment again seems pertinent:

> Kafka's world, frequently of such playfulness and interlaced with angels, is the exact complement of his era which is preparing to do away with the inhabitants of this planet on a considerable scale. The experience which corresponds to that of Kafka, the private individual, will probably not become accessible to the masses until such time as they are being done away with (1968: 143).

Second Text: the Latent Thought: a Full Monty

> This word to be circumcised, this word of someone's to be circumcised, this word to be circumcised for someone, this word is an *open* word. Like a wound, you will say. No, first of all like a door: open to the stranger, to the other, to the guest, to whomever (Derrida 1986: 342).

The written diagram of the machine, the sentence written on the skin, the writing on the Commandant's tombstone—in Kafka's story, writing is the circumcision of the body, the sentence of law that we must understand in our flesh although not necessarily in our minds. The indexical *circumscription* of the officer's body is also its symbolic *circumcision*, demanded by the colony's law, the revelation of radiant justice (Kafka 1948: 209). It is also futile, and doomed. As Jorge Luis Borges (1964) says, Kafka creates his precursors, and one of them (although not so noted by Borges) is St Paul, writing in the New Testament.

Paul seems to agree with Jesus' words in the gospel of Thomas, saying 53: 'If [circumcision] were beneficial, their father would beget them already circumcised from their mother. Rather, the true circumcision in spirit has become completely profitable'. Paul says that those who are already circumcised should not reverse the process—whatever that might mean!—and those who are not yet circumcised should not become circumcised (1 Cor. 7.18). Because it belongs to the 'flesh', circumcision is indifferent to salvation. In the letter to the Galatians, Paul uses even stronger language:

> Now I, Paul, say to you that if you receive circumcision (*peritemnēsthe*), Christ will be of no advantage to you. I testify again to every man who receives circumcision that he is bound to keep the whole law. You are severed from Christ, you who would be justified by the law; you have fallen away from grace (Gal. 5.2-4).

If you cut off your foreskin, then you cut off Christ. The foreskin is an index of the flesh; it *is* the flesh (Boyarin 1994: 77). But once again, the foreskin is also a Peircean symbol, and like all symbols it requires interpretation.

Paul frequently conjoins circumcision and the law. Circumcision 'binds' one to the law, just as the prisoner is bound to the Bed of Kafka's machine. One must be bound in order to be cut, and vice versa. The flesh is not mentioned in Gal. 5.2-4, but the spirit appears in the very next verse:

> For through the Spirit, by faith, we wait for the hope of righteousness. For in Christ Jesus neither circumcision nor uncircumcision is of any avail, but faith working through love (Gal. 5.5-6).

Thus the writing on the flesh prescribed by the law is superseded for Paul by the spirit, by faith, and by love.

Kafka resists this hermeneutics of the spirit. As Benjamin says of Kafka's writings, 'modern man lives in his body; the body slips away from him, is hostile toward him. It may happen that a man wakes up one day and finds himself transformed into vermin. Exile—his exile— has gained control over him' (Benjamin 1968: 126). Paul's world is dia-metrically opposed to Kafka's. Yet Paul still has some use for cutting, for after a few verses of exhortation to his readers to remain loyal to him, he concludes this passage in Galatians, 'I wish those who unsettle you would mutilate (*apokopsontai*, castrate) themselves!' (5.12)

We find a similar conjunction or rather opposition between mutila-tion and circumcision (as well as spirit and flesh) in Phil. 3.2-3:

> Look out for the dogs, look out for the evil-workers, look out for those who mutilate the flesh (*tēn katatomēn*). For we are the true circumcision (*peritomē*), who worship God in spirit, and glory in Christ Jesus, and put no confidence in the flesh.

These two Greek words, *apokoptō* and *katatomē*, both translated as 'mutilate', denote different types of cutting (chopping off vs carving), but from let us say a 'phallocentric' point of view there is very little difference in connotation. Furthermore, the line between *peritomē* and *katatomē* may be a fine one indeed! Has not the officer in the penal colony, that servant of the law, mutilated himself by carving if not by chopping off? The mutilation of circumcision/castration is fitting for those who stand on the side of flesh and the law, and in opposition to Paul and the Holy Spirit. For those who follow Paul's teaching, no circumcision is necessary. For those who do not, circumcision does not cut deeply enough.

But there is no talk of *writing* in these Pauline passages. For that we must search elsewhere in the Pauline corpus, and we find it in Paul's opposition between the letter of the 'written code' and the Holy Spirit, in a passage in 2 Corinthians:

> Are we beginning to commend ourselves again? Or do we need, as some do, letters (*epistolōn*) of recommendation to you, or from you? You yourselves are our letter of recommendation, written on your hearts, to be known and read by all men; and you show that you are a letter from Christ delivered by us, written not with ink but with the Spirit of the living God, not on tablets of stone but on tablets of human hearts…not in a written code (*grammatos*) but in the Spirit; for the written code (*gramma*) kills, but the Spirit gives life (3.1-3, 6).

Paul even sounds a little bit like one of Kafka's characters in this passage! The physical writing, on 'tablets of stone' or 'with ink', is opposed to the spirit who writes on human hearts. [3] This is not the writing on the flesh, the writing of the law, but rather the 'true circumcision' which is associated with Paul's gospel for the Gentiles. An even more explicit juxtaposition of circumcision and writing appears in Rom. 2.26-27:

> So, if a man who is uncircumcised keeps the precepts of the law, will not his uncircumcision be regarded as circumcision? Then those who are physically uncircumcised but keep the law will condemn you who have the written code (*grammatos*) and circumcision (*peritomēs*) but break the law.

Just as the Holy Spirit and the grace of God, in Pauline theology, stand opposed to both 1) circumcision and faith in the flesh, and 2) the physical forms of writing, so reciprocally, these two are aligned with one another and perhaps even at some deep level they are identical. Although it does not explicitly figure in any of these passages, Elizabeth Castelli's assessment of Paul's language of *mimēsis* seems appropriate here as well:

---

3. This language is also strikingly similar to that of Socrates in the *Phaedrus*. We should also recall that the parchment on which manuscripts such as Torah scrolls are written is indeed flesh.

> [T]his language identifies the fundamental values of wholeness and unity
> with Paul's own privileged position vis-à-vis the gospel, the early Chris-
> tian communities he founded and supervises, and Christ himself... To
> stand for anything other than what the apostle stands for is to articulate
> for oneself a place of difference...to stand in opposition, therefore, to the
> gospel, the community, and Christ (1991: 87).

Both Paul's rejection of the necessity of circumcision, or even its desir-
ability for the uncircumcised, and his rejection of the 'written code' are
aspects of Paul's larger project of 'spiritualizing' the body as it appears
in the Jewish scriptures (Boyarin 1992, 1994). Daniel Boyarin argues
that, '[s]ince for [Paul], these physical entities and connections have
been fulfilled/annulled by their spiritual referents, 'according to the
flesh' becomes a hermeneutical term referring to the literal, the flesh of
language as well' (1994: 77).[4] Boyarin stresses that the question here
concerns *reading*—that is, whether the physical text of the scriptures is
to be read 'according to the flesh' (that is, the local truths of the penis,
the body) or 'according to the Spirit' (in a universalizing way).

Third Text: the Hidden Desire: a Close Shave

> Progress in reading is preceded by an act that traverses the material
> solidity of the book to allow you access to its incorporeal substance...
> The margin of the pages is jagged, revealing its fibrous texture; a fine
> shaving—also known as 'curl'—is detached from it, as pretty to see as a
> wave's foam on the beach (Calvino 1979: 42).

Paul's letters do not make the connection between writing and circumcision or mutilation explicit and central in the way that Kafka's
story does. However, when we take Paul as Kafka's precursor, albeit a
precursor by way of opposition, that connection becomes clearer. Then
the scriptures themselves entice us to read circumcision not only
according to the flesh but also according to the spirit. We find this invitation both in the metaphoric rewriting of circumcision (of the lips or of
the heart) within the Hebrew scriptures themselves and also (and much
more so) in the colonizing reappropriations of Jewish circumcision in
the New Testament. Paul does not mention Moses in the letter to the
Galatians, but he does mention Abraham (Gal. 3.6–4.31) and Abraham's 'offspring' (Greek *sperma*, 3.16). One of Abraham's sons is even

---

4.   See also Boyarin's continuing discussion of this relation (1994: 77-81).

described as 'according to the flesh' (4.22-23) and the other, Paul suggests, is 'according to the Spirit' (4.29). But if Paul may be read as a precursor of Kafka's story, then the Jewish scriptures may also be read as precursors of both Paul and Kafka. Thus we establish a sort of reverse trajectory in which later texts explain earlier ones.[5] Isn't this how we always do in fact read?

The story of Zipporah circumcising her son in Exodus 4 interrupts what looks like an otherwise continuous story. God tries to get Moses ready to go back to the people of Israel in Egypt, but Moses resists God at every turn. There is talk of Israel as the first-born son of God and also of the first-born sons of the Egyptians (4.22-23). Finally, however, Moses takes leave of his father-in-law Jethro and goes on his way, returning to Egypt with his wife, Zipporah, and his son.[6] He is to go to Pharaoh and threaten him with the death of the Egyptians' sons. In the wilderness Moses encounters Aaron, who has come out to meet him on the holy mountain. Moses and Aaron return together to Egypt, where they preach and perform miracles, and are believed by the Israelites.

Zipporah's story appears as a dream-like intrusion that interrupts this sequence. Dare we call it 'Kafkaesque'? Apparently this story reverberates in some way with God's threat to kill the Egyptians' first-born sons, because it appears immediately after that threat, and before the reunion of Moses with Aaron. The verbal ambiguities of this 'intractable narrative' (Burns 1992) and of its relation to its larger context—the birth of the son of Moses, Israel as the son of God, the sons of the Egyptians—remind us of Roland Barthes's well-known discussion of the ambiguities in a similarly mysterious and violent story, the wrestling match between Jacob and the angel in Genesis 32 (1988: 246-60). We cannot keep track of all these sons, and the pronouns outrace their antecedents.

Zipporah's story appears in the Revised Standard Version as follows:

> At a lodging place on the way the LORD met him and sought to kill him. Then Zipporah took a flint and cut off (*perietemen*, LXX) her son's foreskin, and touched Moses' feet with it, and said, 'Surely you are a bridegroom of blood to me!' So he let him alone. Then it was that she said,

---

5. Borges (1964) also does not list Genesis and Exodus among Kafka's precursors. Nor do we claim to have touched every point on this trajectory. There are doubtless many other texts that belong just as well along this curve.

6. Or sons. The LXX text of Exod. 4.20 is 'sons'. Only one son is mentioned in the preceding (Exod. 2.22) and following (4.25) stories.

Culture, Entertainment and the Bible

> 'You are a bridegroom of blood', because of the circumcision (*peri-tomēs*, LXX) (Exod. 4.24-26).

A strikingly different translation of this same passage is offered by Michael Fishbane (1979: 70):

> And on the way, at a resting spot, YHWH encountered him and sought to kill him. Then Zipporah took a flint and cut off the foreskin of her son and touched his penis, saying: 'You are now a bridegroom of blood with YHWH'. So he released him, and she said: 'You are a bridegroom of blood through the circumcision'.

Whose life is threatened by God? Has God mistaken Moses for an Egyptian, and is he trying to kill his son? Or is it Moses himself that God wants to kill? The fantastic ambiguities of the text of Exodus will never settle these questions, but clearly Zipporah has understood what the reader cannot. Zipporah is a good reader. But how is it that Zipporah knows just what to do?

Who really is saved by Zipporah's quick flint? Zipporah carves the body of her son, releasing the curl of his foreskin to touch it to the genitals of her husband (according to the RSV). Or does she touch Moses with her *knife*? Eissfeldt (1965: 192) suggests this latter reading. Are there two separate cuts here—two circumcisions? Or yet again, do these ambiguous words merely mean (as Fishbane's translation suggests) that she touched Gershom's penis while circumcising him? In any case, Zipporah must be not only a good reader but a good writer as well—that is, handy with the knife—for whatever it is that she does, it works!

Enigmatically, the text says, 'He let him go'. Are we still talking about God here, or might this phrase refer instead to a father-son confrontation? The strangely erotic (and possibly incestuous) suggestion of the bloody foreskin (or knife!) touched to Moses's (or maybe the son's) 'feet' and the sleazy horror-movie overtones of the 'bridegroom of blood' suggest a monstrous, albeit salvific, crime. Boyarin notes that 'erotic implications were to be most fully developed in the midrashic and (later) mystical readings of the rite of circumcision. In those readings, the performance of that rite was understood as a necessary condition for divine-human erotic encounter—for seeing God' (1992: 485).

Just who is this monstrous 'bridegroom of blood', anyway—is it Moses, Gershom, or God himself? The two translations cited above reveal remarkably different readings of Zipporah's words in Exod. 4.25: are 'you' a bridegroom of blood to *me* (that is, Zipporah) or to *YHWH*? Fishbane bases his translation on the cryptic signifier *LY* in the

Hebrew text (1979: 70, note). What is explained in the final sentence ('Then it was that she said, "You are a bridegroom of blood", because of the circumcision', 4: 26, RSV), and what need is there to explain anything? In the RSV, this statement looks like a later commentary, attempting to explain an otherwise intrusive and apparently irrelevant story. Fishbane (1979: 70-76), however, makes a strong case that the story belongs with Exodus 1–4. Fishbane's translation renders this sentence more coherently, and the NRSV similarly moves the text in this direction ('It was then she said, "A bridegroom of blood by circumcision" '). The LXX offers no help here, for instead of Zipporah's intriguing 'bridegroom of blood' language, the much tamer statement, 'I stop the blood of the circumcision of my child!', appears twice.

Love Bites

Circumcision, after all, is another name for deconstruction (Caputo 1997: 262).

It is that resistance, the nightmare which attends the loss or dissolution of the male essence, that constitutes the most persistent turn of the patriarchal imagination (Rutledge 1998: 17).

Fate or some mysterious force can put the finger on you or me for no good reason at all (character in Edgar G. Ulmer's *Detour*, quoted in Žižek 1997: 3).

In a dramatic scene in James Morrow's fantasy novel, *Towing Jehovah*, a Catholic priest is driving a Jeep down the two mile long dead body of God that has fallen into the ocean and is being towed by an oil tanker to an ice cave for preserving. A particular body part caught the priest's attention:

the great veiny cylinder floating between the legs (a truly unnerving sight, the scrotal sac undulating like the gasbag of some unimaginable blimp)... It wasn't just that the sharks had wrought such terrible destruction, stripping off the foreskin like a gang of sadistic *mohels*... A God without a penis would be a *limited* God, a God to whom some possibility had been closed, hence not God at all (Morrow 1994: 115-16).

We hear Mary Daly complaining, 'God doesn't have a penis'. Morrow's idea that the deity is uncircumcised but requires the bloody, sacrificial covenant of his male followers raises interesting aspects of this ritual event.

In the late twentieth century there was a plethora of anti-circumcision groups, all arguing in a rather Greco-Roman way that circumcision of the foreskin is a barbaric, unnecessary (for health reasons, at least) act. These groups' basic argument is that 'Every circumcision…is an assault on a child's sexuality and a violation of his right to an intact body' (Infant Male Circumcision Fact Sheet). Groups such as NOHARMM, National Organization to Halt the Abuse and Routine Mutilation of Males, call for 'genital integrity' and children's rights. The Jewish Alternate Bris Support Group suggests naming ceremonies as a sub-stitute to circumcision. Many internet sites point to the ethical principle, first, do no harm, and to the right to an intact body. The Declaration of the First International Symposium on Circumcision refers to Article V of the United Nations Declaration of Human Rights: 'No one shall be subjected to torture or to cruel, inhuman or degrading treatment.' So is circumcision in various cultures a viable sacred marking? Or is it abuse of children and adolescents? In Judaism and Christianity, is the cir-cumcision ritual another way to keep women out any direct member-ship in the covenant, entering only through their circumcised husbands?

Exodus 4.24-26 does not blink at any of these more modern question-ings of the ritual. In this weird story Zipporah takes care of business, offering the deity what he is apparently after. Imagine—the deity attacking Moses and being appeased by the flesh of a child! The rabbis have multiple readings of this text: God or an angel attacks Moses, the first or the second son is circumcised, Zipporah acts to clear Moses of murder charges in the Egyptian incident, Moses or one of the sons is attacked, Zipporah holds the foreskin up to Moses or God's genitals. Or as in Tobit, circumcision is a necessary rite to hold back the demons on the wedding night. 'It is also possible to think that a protective efficacy is ascribed to circumcision' (Houtman 1983: 99).

This circumcision is a cut, a bodily scarification mark, a sign of the covenant with the deity. James Nohrnberg describes this scene: 'One is not born circumcised, but, once circumcised, or symbolically scarified for life, one dies this way' (Nohrnberg 1995: 163). Nohrnberg believes that 'His [Moses's] vicarious circumcision is not a fragment, but a frac-tion: not a stray trace, but a carefully placed sign' (1995: 163). This carefully placed sign is centered on the male's genitals; God is out for murder but in this case settles for a part of the male body. A few chapters later the (most likely circumcised) Egyptians lose their first-born sons to God's wrath. Moses is saved as an infant, but God always stalks him.

This passage in Exodus 4 is as dark as its desert night setting. It's unclear who's who or why God wants to kill Moses, but there is the nagging sense that any relationship is located in or on the bodies of his believers. On the body as the scene of conversion, Elaine Scarry relates, 'The human child, the human womb, the human hand, the human face, the stomach, the mouth, the genitals (themselves circumcised, marked)—it is in the body that God's presence is recorded' (1985: 204). Moses is a man of 'uncircumcised lips' (Exodus 6.12, 30), and so God marks Aaron for the speech act task. In the circumcision ritual in Orthodox Judaism 'blood must be drawn from the wound either by mouth or, today, through a suction pump' (Beidelman 1986: 512). The continuation of the covenant in both testaments demands a blood sacrifice—foreskins of males, Christ as the foreskin, etc.

This fantastic story in Exodus 4 blurs the lines between gods and demons. Is the deity mad? Stalking around in the desert in search of male children, like some cohort of the 'demon' Lilith whom he cursed to roam the night, giving birth to sons that die? Or is God like 'Aluqah the vampire demon who fed on flesh and blood' (Houtman 1983: 83)? Is God doing a practicing run for the genocide of the first-born sons of the Egyptians? Are Moses and God now 'blood brothers'?

Is this deity a morphing deity—preferring to act in demonic ways: unleashing floods, tearing down towers, thwarting journeys, sending plagues, and killing first born sons? Do we desire to encounter God this way? Late at night in a dark desert? The monster in the Bible's closet? Do we have here something like the 'death wish' that accompanied Victorian fantasies, according to fantasy theorist Rosemary Jackson:

> Whereas more subversive texts activate a dialogue with this death drive, directing their energy towards a dissolution of repressive structures, these more conservative fantasies simply go along with a desire to cease 'to be', a longing to transcend or escape the human (Jackson 1981: 156).

Exodus 4 is a more radical fantasy, a conversation 'between the imaginary and the symbolic' (Jackson 1981: 156) that leaves a cut in the text.

Žižek relates that for Schelling, '*the inertia of external material reality is a proof of the divine madness, of the fact that God himself was 'out of his mind'*' (Žižek 1997: 11). God can put the finger on you or me for no good reason at all. Job can certainly testify to this divine action. But as monster God always escapes, because the monster always 'turns immaterial and vanishes, to reappear someplace else'

(Cohen 1996: 4). Jeffrey Cohen notes that '[t]he monster's body quite literally incorporates fear, desire, anxiety, and fantasy (ataractic or incendiary), giving them life and an uncanny independence. The monster's body is pure culture' (Cohen 1996: 4). We are not so sure that we agree with Louis Ginzberg that the space of demons is 'morally neutral' (1955: 98-99). The murdering deity as wilderness demon is odd, excessive, and untrustworthy.

A recent poem by Shirley Kaufman on Zipporah further raises issues of vampirism; Kaufman makes reference to 'this blood on [Zipporah's] fingers' and 'this cut flesh red as a love bite' (1990: 69). Is this circumcision as a way to remove the child from his 'foreign mother' and her 'idolatrous' indigenous religious practices? Or is Zipporah enacting a salvific sorcery to save her family? Does the deity need blood to live forever? Does God cannibalistic of God's own creation hunger and thirst for blood sacrifice, never to be satisfied? Does God need more than animal blood and meat, extending the desire for human blood and flesh? Foreskins piled upon foreskins? Is this insatiable thirst finally quenched at the crucifixion? (In the Christian tradition) is God's need for blood ultimately only satisfied (once and for all as in the Book of Hebrews) by God's own blood drawn on the cross? Is the crucifixion a love bite, the marks of a bloodthirsty God turned in a final act on himself in order to live forever? One structuralist analysis of Exodus 4 reads for 'the transformation of Moses from a product of human birth into one of divine rebirth' (Kunin 1996: 16). So through (symbolic) circumcision is Moses made 'divine'?

God in (the circumcised) Jesus comes to earth and is murdered by humans, thereafter stalking the earth as an undead, the bite marks of crucifixion still fresh on his flesh. God is left for dead, a corpse in a tomb, but disappears before the light on the third day, before the tomb is opened. The priest in *Towing Jehovah* tells of the problem a corpse can cause:

> 'The corpse is taking hold', is how Ockham explains our situation. 'Not the corpse per se, the *idea* of the corpse—that's our great enemy, that's the source of this disorder. In the old days', says the padre, 'whether you were a believer, a nonbeliever, or a confused agnostic, at some level, conscious or unconscious, you felt God was watching you, and the intuition kept you in check. Now a whole new era is upon us' (Morrow 1994: 135).

An interpretive check is needed here. The discourse of theology and vampire theory can tread into dangerous territory—already laid by the Nazi's imaging of Jews as Nosferatu—dangerous and in need of being destroyed (Dijkstra 1996: 425-34). Dijkstra summarizes: 'It is the old story: the Jew's hypersensual erotic degeneracy creates the effeminacy that causes him to hunt for blood' (1996: 431). This anti-Jewishness was echoed centuries earlier by Herodotus (*The Histories*, II.37): 'They practice circumcision, while men of other nations—except those who have learnt from Egypt—leave their private parts as nature made them… They are religious to excess…' In the Tanakh there is a prohibition for humans against drinking the blood of animals (Deut. 12.23), but God does not follow these rules. God demands foreskins, Egyptian sons, and then blood on the doorposts at Passover.

In Exodus 4 it is the deity who is prone to vampirism; God is out for blood and flesh. As in vampire stories, death and erotic desire are linked. Howard Eilberg-Schwartz comments that in this Exodus 4 scene 'Israelite masculinity has been sacrificed to God', for 'circumcision was for the ancient Israelites a symbol of male submission' (1994: 161). God takes on the role of Lestat in the Anne Rice vampire novels; it is as if God echoes Lestat, 'My fangs are too small to be noticed unless I want them to be; but they're sharp, and I cannot go for more than a few hours without wanting human blood' (Rice 1995: 3). Nina Auerbach adds, 'Vampires are neither inhuman nor nonhuman nor all-too-human; they are simply more alive than they should be…they are also hideous invaders of the normal' (1995: 6). Auerbach continues, 'it is impossible either to exorcise or to trust a species whose immortality has given them supreme adaptability' (1995: 8). Vampires cross centuries, retaining many archaic ideas from their original times. In traditional vampire stories, Satan is a vampire, not God. But the biblical story mixes the roles of demons and gods.

The symbols of blood and flesh take a strange turn in Christianity in the eucharistic feast. According to Dijkstra:

> The symbolic bond of blood, this gift of God's blood-sacrifice, the essence of God ingested by the faithful, holds the promise of eternal life. Among those given to blasphemy, this holy ritual (which undoubtedly can be traced to an origin in analogue pre-Christian ceremonies) could easily be mistaken for a form of 'energy vampirism' through which the communicants would gain immortality by ingesting the 'blood' of the Son of God. (1996: 89)

January 1 is the Feast of the Circumcision in the Christian calendar. Christian martyrdom is seen as a baptism of blood. 'There is a fountain filled with blood, that is filled with Immanuel's veins' goes a popular hymn. In the eucharistic tradition Christians renew the covenant every time they drink Christ's blood—blood on the lips so they can live forever, members of the revenant.

Conclusion

Derrida (1986 *passim*) notes that to circumcise is also to inscribe. The biblical text invokes not only the circumcision of the body, but also an inevitably ideological circumscription of narrative and of language. Once again, the spirit replaces the flesh. The foreskin is a fetish; it is uncanny. The bloody foreskin is a metaphor for the written page of scripture, a curl or 'scroll' of the text that saves. The son's body is inscribed with the law; he is 'sentenced', not unlike the officer in Kafka's story 'In the Penal Colony', although perhaps more like the original condemned man of that story, the 'submissive dog', rather than the officer who eventually 'sentences' himself. But the foreskin is also Christ, whose blood redeems, but only if (contrary to Paul's larger claims) he is 'cut off' from you, circumcised, circumscribed. As the foreskin, Christ is the residue, the 'leftover', the curl of the page:

> [T]here is always a residue, a leftover, a stain of traumatic irrationality and senselessness... [and] this leftover, far from hindering the full submission of the subject to the ideological command, is the very condition of it: it is precisely this non-integrated surplus of senseless traumatism which confers on the Law its unconditional authority (Žižek 1994: 321-22).

The foreskin is the 'paradoxical object-cause of desire' through which the subject is ideologically trapped by the Other (Žižek 1994: 322). The foreskin is the leftover, the fleshy page of scripture, the material aspect of the signifier. In this sense, perhaps, Paul is the great ideological critic, and the great psychoanalyst to boot, seeking to liberate us from our bondage to this desire.

But this sense is not enough. As Régis Debray (1996: 56) notes, 'having too fully deciphered the world as a sign, we forget there is a world underneath, and that the letter itself has a body'. In the story in Exodus 4, the foreskin is both more and less than a metaphor; it is narrative incarnate. It is simply the simple flesh of story, which we discard once we have understood its meaning, and Zipporah is its scribe. As Freud might have said, sometimes a penis is just a penis. As in Kafka's story (but not in Paul's), we have here both symbol and index. Zipporah's knife divides as it unites—the flesh of the son, the son and the father, Israelites and Egyptians, and eventually Jews and Christians. Like the anonymous narrator, Zipporah has no need of these oppositions—there is no circumcision for *her* in this story—even as she creates them. Zipporah blurs the oppositions in the very act of establishing them. She is the Nietzschean immoralist, the Lyotardian *differend*, who rescues the moral order and the possibility of meaning from 'outside' of the system of meaning.

In a similar fashion this story affirms the law even though it is itself beyond the law, or better, 'before the law' (see Kafka 1958: 60-79). Boyarin (1992: 496) argues that, in Jewish tradition, circumcision enables the male Israelite 'to take the position of the female' in the faith-relation to God—that is, to become a 'Daughter of Zion'. Instead of the female becoming male, as in the gospel of Thomas 114, the male must become female. Or as Boyarin puts it, the foreskin is an ugly blemish that must be removed. In this context, Paul's association of the foreskin with Christ, and the connections that Paul makes between circumcision and castration, are particularly remarkable.

We are still, of course, reading along a reverse trajectory. Circumcision, however, is not simply 'in' these texts. Rather, it emerges from the tension *between* the texts, a tension that is made clearer by our retrospective reading, our dream text analysis, because it is *created* by that retrospective reading. Circumcision carves out and around the texts just as the texts themselves carve in or circumscribe a relation between father and son, or between the LORD and 'him', whoever he is. Zipporah's story both invites and staves off the threat of chaos. How, and of what, might this text function as an ideological symptom—that is, a kind of circumcising? Ideology here masks itself as not-so-subtle fantasy—mythic fantasy—even as the fantastic narrative provokes the unraveling of ideology:

> The fundamental level of ideology...is not of an illusion masking the real state of things but that of an (unconscious) fantasy structuring our social reality itself... [I]n the opposition between dream and reality, fantasy is on the side of reality: it is, as Lacan once said, the support that gives consistency to 'reality' (Žižek 1994: 316, 322).

APOCALYPSE, ART AND ABJECTION:
IMAGES OF THE GREAT WHORE

Caroline Vander Stichele

Time and again the book of Revelation has been a source of inspiration
for art. That is not so surprising. Its visionary character appeals to the
imagination and, moreover, is essential to the message of the book,
which claims to show what must soon take place (Rev. 1.1). At the turn
of this century and millenium a renewed interest in Revelation can be
noted, as images and themes from this book are revived and revamped.
In what follows, I want to focus on one of the few female but popular
characters of this book, namely the Great Whore, who features in Rev.
17.1–19.3. First I discuss a number of visual representations in which
this character appears and then I explore the underlying cultural codes
operating in both the text and its representations. I concentrate here on
material which originated in Europe in the course of the twentieth century. Before turning to this material, however, I will introduce the
underlying source text and say a few words about the representation of
this character in earlier centuries.

   The Great Whore only makes her appearance at the end of the book
of Revelation. The previous chapters of this book (Rev. 15–16) describe
how seven plagues, representing the wrath of God (16.1), were poured
out over the earth by seven angels. Then, at the beginning of ch. 17, one
of these angels appears to John and tells him: 'Come, I will show you
the judgement of the great whore who is seated on many waters, with
whom the kings of the earth have committed fornication, and with the
wine of whose fornication the inhabitants of the earth have become
drunk' (17.1-2).[1] Then follows the description of what John sees:

---

1.   The Bible is quoted here according to the NRSV.

> I saw a woman sitting on a scarlet beast that was full of blasphemous names, and it had seven heads and ten horns. The woman was clothed in purple and scarlet, and adorned with gold and jewels and pearls, holding in her hand a golden cup full of abominations and the impurities of her fornication; and on her forehead was written a name, a mystery: 'Babylon the great, mother of whores and of earth's abominations'. And I saw that the woman was drunk with the blood of the saints and the blood of the witnesses of Jesus (17.3-6).

In the following verses, the angel explains this vision to John and tells him that the woman 'is the great city that rules over the kings of the earth' (17.18). Now another angel appears who announces the fall of Babylon (18.1-3) and John hears a voice from heaven exhorting 'my people' and describing the fate and reactions of those who gained from the city (18.4-20):

> Then a mighty angel took up a stone like a great millstone and threw it into the sea, saying, 'With such violence Babylon the great city will be thrown down, and will be found no more' (18.21).

Next, the angel describes the desolation of the city (vv. 22-24) and his words are welcomed by a great multitude in heaven, glorifying God for his judgment of the Great Whore (19.1-3). It is the last time that she is mentioned in the book of Revelation.

As far as the reception history of the Great Whore in art is concerned,[2] I have to limit myself here to some observations which are relevant to the material from the twentieth century under discussion in this article. First of all, it should be noted that no representations of the Great Whore have come to us from antiquity. Not that Revelation played no role at that time, but preference seemed to be given to its more peaceful and triumphal motives, such as the lamb on mount Zion, rather than to the cataclysmic scenes from this book. The earliest pictures of the Great Whore appear in illustrated manuscripts of the book of Revelation. This material forms a major source of information to document her presence in art, especially from the Middle Ages onwards, although some illustrations may have their origins in late antiquity.[3] Very often the Great Whore is represented as described in

---

2. A major source of information from the viewpoint of art history is Van der Meer 1978. References in this article are to the Dutch edition.

3. This may for instance be the case with the Apocalypse from Trier, dated in the first half of the ninth century. See Van der Meer 1978: 40, 93-101.

Rev. 17.1-6, sitting on the beast with the cup as her distinctive feature. For instance, the colorful illustrations in manuscripts of Beatus's commentary on Revelation, dating from the ninth to the thirteenth century, are famous. An illustration from one of these manuscripts, the so-called Facundus manuscript, dated 1047, shows the woman on the beast, holding a cup and wearing a large crown on her head. The animal on which she is seated looks like a horse. She rides it astride, wearing the same type of outfit as the other (male) horse riders depicted in the manuscript do. Her horse, however, is a hybrid creature. Apart from its seven heads, its feet are claws and upon closer inspection its tail appears to be a snake. The miniature also contains a textual element in Latin, namely: *ubi mulier sedet super bestia*.[4]

Outside the manuscript tradition of that time depictions of the Great Whore are hard to find. She is only seldom depicted in churches, although a few cases can be noted. Very early (1080–1120) but also unusual is for instance her representation on the capital of a column in the choir of a Romanesque church, Saint Pierre of Chauvigny in the Poitou region of France. This case seems to be the only one in its kind in Roman sculpture.[5] It shows the Great Whore in an ornamented dress, with two attributes: a cup and a small bottle. Her smile makes her look innocent, but one can see that, although veiled by her dress, she takes an obscene posture. It is her identity as a whore which is accentuated here. The small bottle which she holds in her left hand may well be a perfume bottle, symbol of her seductive luxury as described in Revelation 18. The woman is identified by the words on the capital as *Babilonia magna metrix*. Another case is her representation on one of the frescoes devoted to the Apocalypse in the apse of the baptistery of the cathedral of Padua (Italy). The frescoes date from 1376–78 and were painted by Giusto De Menabuoi. One of them shows the more traditional picture of the whore on the beast holding her cup and another one, referring to Rev. 18.21, shows an angel throwing a millstone in the sea.

Later on, with the printed bibles, also wood-carved versions of these scenes appear. This is for instance the case in the *Kölner Bibel*, dating from 1478, where both the woman on the beast and the angel throwing a millstone in the water appear together on one picture. Behind the woman one can also see a demolished tower, representing the fallen

4.   See Zink 1988: 49, Bild 22.
5.   See Oursel 1975: 225.

city.[6] A well-known woodcarving is the one made by Albrecht Dürer in 1498. The angel with the millstone reappears here as well as the destroyed, now burning, city. Here, the beast on which the whore is seated has seven different heads and the body of a bird with four feet. The woman, looking drunk, shows a luxurious chalice to the bystanders, who are gazing at her.[7]

In later times, we also find more secular appropriations of the Great Whore. She appears for instance on a tapestry, one out of a series of eight devoted to the Apocalypse, which were manufactured in Brussels during the sixteenth century.[8] On the left side of this tapestry she appears sitting on a throne, on the right side sitting on the beast and in the middle lying in a pool of fire. In all three cases she is dressed like a queen and holding her cup. A more curious item is a sixteenth-century jar from Siegburg, Germany, on which she is depicted as a naked woman wearing jewelry, holding a cup in one hand and a snake in the other. The subscript on the jar identifies her as *de Hor von Bapel, genant Dempas und allen Goten wol bekant* (the whore from Babylon, named Dempas and well known to all Goths). In this case her attribute, the cup, has itself become the object of decoration with her image (Caron 1988: 99).

Although it is hard to draw any general conclusions from this short and selective overview, we can at least note here that most depictions of the Great Whore occur in illustrated manuscripts of the book of Revelation or other works devoted to Revelation, such as the frescoes in Padua or the tapestries from Brussels. It is in this larger context that the Great Whore most often appears. With this observation in mind we can now turn to the material dating from the twentieth century.

The Great Whore in the Twentieth Century

The first picture I want to mention here dates from 1916 and may well reflect the apocalyptic atmosphere of 'the great war'. It is a lithograph by the German painter Lovis Corinth, which shows the whore lying naked but still laughing, with the beast standing at her head (Pippin

6. See *Apocalypse*. Keulse bijbel. H. Quentel, ca. 1478. Utrecht (the Netherlands): Rijksmuseum Het Catharijneconvent, Inv.nr. AMB i1.

7. See Van der Meer 1978: 303.

8. See Van der Meer 1978: 325, 327.

1992: 139). She holds a cup in her right hand, spilling its content. With her left arm she embraces one of three figures who are wearing a crown and are literally devouring her flesh as predicted by the angel in Rev. 17.16. Another picture of that time worth mentioning here as well is an etching by Erich Erler, showing a disturbing blending of woman and beast wading through a pool of blood and corpses, called 'The Beast of the Apocalypse'.[9] The head of the leopard showing its teeth merges with the pubic hair of the naked woman. What these two drawings have in common is that they are unusual, compared with those of earlier times. Erler's etching is unusual because it blurs the separation between woman and beast. The unusual character of Corinth's lithograph lies in the choice of the theme, because, although sometimes the punishment of the whore as described in 17.16 is depicted, in most cases the focus is on her being burned.[10]

With the twentieth century we also enter the era of a new medium: the movie. Here too Babylon makes her entry, more specifically in the silent movie *Metropolis* directed by Fritz Lang in 1926. It tells the story of a mammoth city around the year 2000, which is ruled by industrialist John Frederson. The workers of the city are led by a woman called Maria. Frederson, fearing a revolt, orders a scientist to kidnap Maria and make a robot replica to replace her. To test if the workers believe the replica to be a woman of flesh and blood, a show is set up starring the robot. At one point in the show, she makes her appearance on stage, scarcely dressed in a futuristic oriental outfit, holding a cup in her right hand, and standing on a beast which looks like a giant turtle or snail with seven heads.[11] The workers in the forefront stretch their hands out to her. In the end, however, the robot undergoes the same fate as the Great Whore, because the same workers burn her as a witch. In this case an interesting dialectics takes place between the robot 'playing' the Great Whore and the Great Whore, reincarnated as robot. Thus the distinction between woman and machine is blurred.

9. See Dijkstra 1986: 364.

10. See for instance Van der Meer 1978: 39, the burning whore according to the *Hortus deliciarum* (seventeenth-century copy; original: twelfth century), and 230, naked whore in pool of fire (from a manuscript with Revelation in Flemish, dated around 1400).

11. Serres 1995: 214-15. The outfit of the whore may well be inspired by the Western representation of oriental dance popular in the first decades of this century. See, for instance, Buonaventura 1998: 117-46.

Another German artist, who like Lang fled from the Nazis, is Max Beckmann. He made a series of 27 lithographs illustrating the Apocalypse during his stay in Amsterdam in 1941–42. The 21st picture in that series shows a pale, red-haired, naked woman with a lovely face, holding a cup and sitting on a black animal which looks like a wolf. The animal has prominent teeth, yellow eyes and horns in the shape of guns. On the right, an angel with a dark face descends from heaven, holding two swords, possibly a reference to the angel in Rev. 18.1 who announces Babylon's fall. The angel is surrounded by the heavenly light of a rainbow, contrasting sharply with the night blue background.[12] The woman holds the cup close to her mouth as if she will drink or has already been drinking. Neither she nor the beast seem to notice the angel, who faces the woman. Particularly striking in Beckmann's version of this scene is the appearance of the beast with its horns in the shape of weapons as well as the swords of the angel, suggesting aggression and violence. Rather than the beast, however, it is the unarmed, naked woman on its back, who is about to be slaughtered.

Forty years later and closer to our time Charles Sahuguet, a French artist, devoted a series of paintings (dated 1980–82) to the book of Revelation. Other than the lithographs of Beckmann these pictures literally illustrate the word rather than interpreting or actualizing it. One of these pictures represents the famous prostitute, seated as an amazon side-saddle on a horse-like beast (see Figure 1).

She is dressed in red, wearing a cape, long skirt and oriental-style bra decorated with gold, jewels and pearls, as mentioned in Rev. 17.4. With a smile on her face, she looks seductively at the viewer, holding her cup invitingly in her right hand. The words *Babylone la grande* (Babylon the Great) appear around her head like a halo or crown. She is surrounded by the many waters mentioned in Rev. 17.1. The picture resembles most the one in the Facundus manuscript of the Beatus commentary already mentioned before, but some interesting differences can be noted as well. An important difference is that the woman wears a crown in the Facundus manuscript. She also looks more triumphant there, holding her cup high. Another difference concerns her outfit and the way she sits on the beast. In the Facundus manuscript the woman's body is completely covered, she is wearing pants and rides the horse astride. In the painting of Sahuguet, however, the upper part of her

12. See Zink 1988: 68, Bild 37.

body is partly naked, she is wearing a skirt and sits side-saddle. In my view, this difference is relevant because it reveals the orientalistic elements in Sahuguet's representation of the Great Whore.[13]

Figure 1. 'Apocalypse XVII, 1–6: La prostituée fameuse'; illustration from *L'Apocalypse de Jean* vue par Charles Sahuguet (Saint-Maurice [CH]: Editions Saint Augustin, 1998).

13. With the term 'orientalism' I mean the European representation of the Orient, especially the Middle East, dominant in the nineteenth and first half of the twentieth century. See Said 1991: 1-4. Also here the outfit of the whore may be inspired by oriental dance in the beginning of this century.

Another series of paintings featuring scenes from Revelation was made by the Dutch artist Anneke Kaai in 1989 (Kaai 1997). These paintings were executed on silk. Interesting here is that, apart from the familiar elements already discussed, her picture of the Great Whore also contains elements which we have not yet encountered. The beast on which the woman sits has names written on its heads, composed of the four letters of the name of God in Hebrew, but put in a different order, thus representing the 'blasphemous names' mentioned in Rev. 17.3. Corresponding with 17.5, the woman herself wears a mark on her forehead. Blood is spilling from the cup which she holds. Similar, but smaller female figures appear on the left. They represent the other whores, implied in the description of Babylon as 'mother of whores' (17.5). In the background a skeleton arises from the burning city, symbolizing the burning woman, with kings, merchants and the ship's crew mourning at her feet. On the right, an angel appears carrying a millstone. In comparison with Sahuguet, this painting from Kaai has more in common with the later manuscript tradition and the lithographs from the *Kölner Bibel*, in that it is composed of different scenes. The woman's long black hair and dark complexion, however, make her look even more oriental than Sahuguet's version of the whore. Her outfit has equally orientalistic overtones, but instead of a cape she wears a short jacket, revealing her naked breasts.

The painting representing the Great Whore by Phil Vermeer, another Dutch artist, and dated 1993, is quite unlike the ones we have seen so far (see Figure 2).

Here the woman appears stretched out naked on the beast, while she pours the content of the cup in her mouth spilling it over her own body, its color merging with the red skin of the beast. Its seven heads are turned towards the woman, but the face of the woman herself is turned away, towards the four naked backs depicted in the background, symbolizing fornication. The attention of the viewer is drawn towards the woman's sex, which forms the middle point of the whole picture and thus, the viewer finds her/himself in the same voyeuristic position as one head of the beast, which is peeping in the same direction. This picture has some resemblance with the one from Beckmann, in that he too depicts the woman naked, but the major difference is that her sex is hidden there, as she sits upright on the beast with her legs high and closed. Moreover, she holds the cup, but doesn't drink it as is the case here. As we have seen, the whore on the jar from Siegburg was also depicted naked, although her sex is covered there with a burning heart, symbol of desire and passion.

Figure 2. 'The Great Whore' (1993) by Phil Vermeer, from a series of 87 drawings about Revelation, with oilstick.

A different interpretation of the Great Whore, both with respect to content and genre, could be seen in the evocation of the Apocalypse, as played by the Dutch group called *Monsterverbond* (Monsteralliance) in

September 1998 in Utrecht (the Netherlands). On stage John was reading aloud his version of Revelation 17 and 18, in which Babylon is identified with Amsterdam. The Great Whore appeared on scene first as a scarcely dressed woman in furs, symbol of luxury and all that is left from the apocalyptic beast. She took out an apple and bit it. Then another version of the Great Whore arose (see Figure 3).

Figure 3. Evocation of the Apocalypse by the Dutch group *Monster-verbond* in Utrecht, The Netherlands, September 1998 (photograph Jan Jans).

An interesting feature of this evocation is that a number of traditional elements, such as the cup and the beast are absent. The identity of the woman is largely established through the words of the prophet. This is also the case with the woman depicted on the capital of the Romanesque church in France and on the jar of Siegburg. There too it is the textual element which discloses the identity of the woman in question. A unique feature of the evocation, however, compared with other representations of the Great Whore, is the conflation with Eve suggested in biting the apple. Thus both the element of seduction and of transgression are being transferred from one story to the other.

By way of conclusion I want to make the following observations with respect to the material from the twentieth century. When looking at the representation of the Great Whore in this century, both elements of continuity and discontinuity with the past can be seen. A remarkable element of continuity with the past is that not so much isolated motives but series of pictures are created which serve as illustration or visual commentary on the book of Revelation. Text and image often complement each other. This is clearly the case with the paintings of Sahuguet and Kaai, which have been published in book form with the image on one page and texts from Revelation on the other. But also in the evocation of the *Monsterverbond*, the spoken word complements what is being shown. The most striking difference compared with earlier representations of the whore is that in all cases under discussion she is depicted partly or completely naked. In order to get a fuller grasp of this shift in focus, we will further analyse the relation between text and image, more specifically the underlying codes operating in both the text and its representations.

Evil and Abject

In what follows, I will first concentrate on the negative image of the Great Whore Babylon, as portrayed in Revelation 17–18, in order to determine what textual elements contribute to this negative image. Then I will analyse which elements recur in the artistic representations. Finally, I will use Julia Kristeva's notion of the abject to explore the underlying cultural codes. Because I want to create a distance between myself and the negative image in the text, I will use the designation woman/Babylon instead of the term 'whore'.

In focusing on Rev. 17.1–19.3, one should of course not overlook the rhetorical context and genre of the book in which this section occurs. An important and relevant feature of Revelation as a whole, for instance, is its dualistic worldview. Good and Evil are forces seen at work in this world and the reader is urged to side with the Good. The woman/ Babylon presented in Rev. 17.1–19.3 is clearly on the wrong side. As woman/city she is quite literally caught in the middle between the positive images of the woman giving birth in ch. 12 and the new Jerusalem in ch. 21.[14]

14. By 'positive', I mean from the viewpoint of and presented as such by the author. For a feminist-critical evaluation of these images, see further Pippin 1992: 68-86, Selvidge 1992: 157-67, and Keller 1996: 64-73, 80-83.

Why does she appear as evil? In my opinion, there are three semantic fields which give rise to this negative image. The first semantic field is related to sexuality and consists of all the words related to fornication.[15] From the very first time Babylon is mentioned, she is portrayed that way: 'Fallen, fallen is Babylon the great! She has made all the nations drink of the wrath of her fornication' (14.8). This theme also recurs in Rev. 17.1–19.3.[16] A second semantic field has to do with food and especially with drinking. The woman/Babylon is said to hold a cup and to be drunk with the blood of the saints and the blood of the witnesses to Jesus (17.6). Moreover, she has also made others drink the wine of her fornication, namely 'all the nations' (14.8) and 'the inhabitants of the earth' (17.2). Another image, which is more specifically related to food, can be found in 17.16, where it is said that her flesh will be devoured. Here, however, the woman is no longer the subject but the object of such action, as part of her destruction. A third semantic field covers value judgments made in the text, which are related to 'sin'. The word for 'sin' (*hamartia*) explicitly occurs in Rev. 18.4-5, where the sins of Babylon are said to be heaped high as heaven. Other value judgments present in the text are blasphemy, impurity, abomination, iniquity, deceit, and corruption.[17] As far as they also contain a value judgment, the words for fornication fit into this category as well.

Looking at the artistic representations with these observations in mind, the question now is which elements reappear in the depiction of the woman/Babylon. In most cases, the cup serves as her distinctive attribute, sometimes revealing its abhorrent content of wine and/or blood. The beast is another recurring element. Its monstrous appearance often stands in sharp contrast with the attractive woman seated on it. Where the beast is absent, the woman's identity is made explicit through textual elements. Especially in the older material, the woman is depicted as a queen or an otherwise wealthy woman. She is often wearing a crown, jewels, and royal dresses. In the context of Revelation, this

15. *Pornē* (whore) occurs in 17.1-5; 15-16; 19.2; *porneia* (fornication) in 14.8, 17.2-4, 18.3 and 19.2; the related verb *porneuō* (commit fornication) in 17.2 and 18.3-9.

16. Moreover, the same terminology is also used with respect to the woman prophet called Jezebel in Rev. 2.20-21.

17. The corresponding Greek words in the source text are: *blasphēmia* (17.3), *akatharton* (17.4, 18.2), *bdelugma* (17.4-5), *adikēma* (18.5), *planaō* (18.23), and *phtheirō* (19.2).

is not a distinctively negative element in the portrayal of the woman, but it can be meant that way in later appropriations. This element becomes less prominent in the twentieth century where she is more often depicted (partly or completely) naked, thus focusing on her female sexuality and stressing her identity as a whore.

In reproducing the negative depiction present in the text the artistic representations of the woman/Babylon recreate and promote a perception of this woman as evil. In order to explore how this effect is reached, I will use Julia Kristeva's notion of the abject as developed in her essay *Powers of Horror*. In my view, her observations make it possible to analyse the mechanism of abjection at work on a more subconscious level of perception. According to Kristeva (1982: 4), the abject is 'what disturbs identity, system, order. What does not respect borders, positions, rules. The in-between, the ambiguous, the composite'. She sees the phenomenon of abjection as coextensive with social and symbolic orders, on the individual as well as on the collective level, although it assumes specific shapes and different codings according to the various symbolic systems. As some of its variants Kristeva mentions defilement, food taboo, and sin.

Especially the two last ones are relevant to our subject.[18] With respect to food taboos, Kristeva discusses the distinction between pure and impure as developed for instance in the Torah, where certain categories of food are excluded from consumption and, therefore, considered abject. An explicitly forbidden practice is the consumption of blood: 'If anyone of the house of Israel or of the aliens who reside among them eats any blood, I will set my face against that person who eats blood, and will cut that person off from the people' (Lev. 17.10). The reason given for this prohibition is that the life of the flesh is in the blood (Lev. 17.10-14; Gen. 9.1-7). Against this cultural background the woman described in Rev. 17.6 as being drunk with the blood of the saints and the witnesses to Jesus appears as particularly repulsive. Not only is she 'drunk' with blood, but, moreover, it is human blood. The distinction between pure and impure at stake here is also mentioned explicitly in our text, as the content of the cup is said to be 'full of abominations and the impurities of her fornication' (17.4). Moreover, Babylon is further described in 18.2 as becoming the dwelling place of

18. The notion of defilement is not completely absent, but plays a more marginal role in this text. It is present more specifically in Rev. 18.4 where the people are exhorted not to take part in her sins or to share in her plagues.

impure spirits and animals. The notion of impurity as related to the species may also explain why the hybrid beast with its seven heads is perceived as a particularly abject creature.

Besides these elements related to the issue of food taboo, also elements related to the notion of sin appear in the text, especially in the form of moral judgments about the woman's behaviour. In fact, food taboo and sin are related to each other in so far as the logic of separation between pure and impure is now interiorized and a movement 'from abomination to morals' (Kristeva 1982: 103) takes place. Most prominent in Rev. 17.1–19.3 is Babylon's depiction as a whore, a woman whose behaviour implies the sexual transgression of borders, especially the ones set for and by the institution of marriage. Particularly relevant in this respect are prophetic texts playing in the background, which serve as paradigms for the imagery developed in these chapters. Parallels can, for instance, be found in Ezekiel 16 and 23, and, though less elaborate, also in Nah. 3.4 and Isa. 23.17. In Ezekiel 16 Jerusalem is addressed directly by God through the prophet as a woman (vv. 3-14). In vv. 15-41 the woman is more specifically depicted as a whore. In Ezekiel 23, two women are introduced who are first specified as Oholah and Oholibah and then identified with Samaria and Jerusalem (23.4). They too are criticized for playing the whore and judged accordingly. We find the reversed situation in Nah. 3.1-7, where Nineveh is first addressed as city and later compared with a whore. In Isa. 23.15 it is the fate of Tyre which is compared with that of a whore. The comparison is repeated in v. 17, where it is said that Tyre 'will prostitute herself with all the kingdoms of the world on the face of the earth'. In these texts the behaviour of a city is described in terms of fornication and explicitly condemned on theological grounds as unfaithfulness to the one God/husband. The image is by no means gender neutral, since the type of sinful behaviour is directly informed by the gender of the subject. The transgressive female is pictured as abject and therefore the violence, including sexual violence, done to her is presented as justified. Ultimately, she gets what she deserves.

The elements related to food taboo and sin, prominent in Rev. 17.1–19.3, are also prominent in its artistic visualizations. Although they too are informed by partly the same culturally determined codes, the power of these images of the abject seem to go deeper than that. According to Kristeva, they reach beyond the unconscious. She points more specifically to the source of the subject as the ultimate source of abjection.

Rooted in the struggle of the infant to separate from the mother and to differentiate between subject and object, the experience of want is the foundation of its very being. For Kristeva, purifying the abject, through catharsis, is something religion and art have in common: 'The various means of *purifying* the abject—the various catharses—make up the history of religions, and end up with that catharsis par excellence called art, both on the far and near side of religion. Seen from that standpoint, the artistic experience, which is rooted in the abject it utters and by the same token purifies, appears as the essential component of religiosity' (1982: 17, Kristeva's emphasis). This may well explain the power which archetypal images such as the one we encounter in Revelation 17–18 still have after two millenia. Babylon may change clothes and attributes, but she still plays the harlot.

PORTRAYALS OF POWER IN THE STORIES OF DELILAH AND BATHSHEBA: SEDUCTION IN SONG

Helen Leneman

This chapter will explore commonalities and differences between the stories of Delilah and Bathsheba, and will discuss the gaps in plot that have led to a wide variety of interpretations of these stories. After a review of these interpretations, there will be an overview of Talmudic and other post-biblical interpretations, including current biblical scholarship. Following this will be a discussion of literature and music from the sixteenth century up to the present inspired by the stories of Delilah and Bathsheba.

Although the songs referred to in the title of this paper depict seduction, the thesis of this paper is that these were not true seductions but only misrepresented as such by the popular media; this was due largely to post-biblical interpretations of the stories beginning in Talmudic times and continuing through twentieth-century literature.

In addition to character and plot similarities, there is also a theme common to both stories. A sexual act between the most powerful man of his time and a 'seductive' woman is at the center of both stories, and this brings up the theme of rape and seduction as acts of power. Temptation and the male response to it are part of this theme. *Who has the real power in these stories?* is the question posed to the reader.

Though both Delilah and Bathsheba have been commonly portrayed and perceived as seductresses, a review of the literature does not show discussion of parallels between their stories. Yet parallels do exist: both are assumed to be beautiful, virtually irresistible women; though in a sense both could be seen as victors, this essay will attempt to show they were both victims and pawns of men. As elsewhere in the Bible, motives and responses in both stories are ambiguous, leaving the reader unclear even as to who the hero is. This ambiguity has led to a great deal of interpretation and midrashic emendation, most at the expense of Delilah's and Bathsheba's reputations. Ultimately both these women are denigrated in order to elevate the men with whom they are involved, so the men can remain the focal point and hero of their respective sagas.

There are obvious differences between the stories as well. Bathsheba's story is part of the Davidic chronicles, believed to be fairly historical; the story of Samson and Delilah has a folk-tale tone and is likely to be more myth than history. Yet in both cases the writer's agenda was to elevate the male hero, so ultimately it may not matter to which genre of biblical literature the stories belong.

Taken simply as two stories, the most obvious difference is in the type of woman involved: one reputable (Bathsheba), the other disreputable (Delilah). This distinction was crucial to the biblical writers, who took any opportunity to warn men of the dangers of disreputable women. And clearly Delilah posed a greater danger to Samson than did Bathsheba to David. The other major distinction between the stories is in the conclusion: Bathsheba resurfaces to become a much more well-rounded and important character in the ongoing story of David's reign, while Delilah simply vanishes. The fact that he was tempted by a reputable woman rather than by a Delilah was an advantage not only to David but also to Bathsheba herself.

The story of Samson and Delilah (Judg. 16.4-30) is too well known to warrant a lengthy introduction: Samson falls in love with Delilah, who is paid by the Philistines to find out the source of his great strength; she nags him until he tells her the secret, which is his hair. She has it cut off, Samson is captured, blinded and imprisoned. When his hair grows back and he is put on display in the Philistines' temple, in a final show of superhuman strength Samson brings down the whole temple.

Prior to the episode with Delilah, Samson had been involved with other women, none of them Israelites. Most significant are the opening three verses of this chapter, wherein Samson meets and has sex with a prostitute in Gaza. He escapes a planned ambush, then grasps the posts of the town gate and carries them off on his shoulders. Then the story continues:

> After that, he fell in love with a woman in the Wadi Sorek, named Delilah. The lords of the Philistines went up to her and said, 'Coax him and find out what makes him so strong...'[1]

---

1.   All Bible translations are from the JPS *Torah* (Philadelphia: Jewish Publication Society 1962).

The placement of the meeting with Delilah immediately after the episode with the prostitute is significant. Is it not possible, as some scholars have suggested, that some of the attitude towards the prostitute could wash over Delilah? Possibly because of this association with the previous verses, Delilah has often been considered a prostitute herself, butnowhere is she thus identified. Contrary to common misconceptions, and unlike Bathsheba, there is actually no description of Delilah at all.

The story of Bathsheba to be treated here is from 2 Samuel 11 and 12.1-25, in which David spots Bathsheba bathing, has her brought to him, sleeps with her and makes her pregnant. David then orders her husband Uriah, a soldier in his army, home from the front and strongly encourages him to visit his wife. Uriah refuses, several times, leaving David with only one option, namely, to arrange to have Uriah killed in battle. After this deed has been accomplished, he marries Bathsheba. The prophet Nathan then comes to David and, by use of a parable, makes it clear that God is displeased with David's actions and that David will be punished. The punishment is the death of their firstborn child. The fact that this is at least as much punishment for the mother, Bathsheba, as for David, is never mentioned by the writer. David mourns and then another child, Solomon, is subsequently born to them, destined to be king following his father. (According to 1 Chron. 3.5, Bathsheba had four sons: Shimea, Shebab, Nathan and Solomon). It is quite possible that the account of David and Bathsheba is a case of layering a story on top of an historical reality, whereas that of Samson and Delilah is the opposite, an attempt to historicize a folk tale.

Unlike Delilah, who is never described, Bathsheba is described as 'very beautiful'. In addition, she is identified by her relationship to males: 'She is Bathsheba daughter of Eliam, wife of Uriah the Hittite.' (2 Sam. 11.4) However, her reactions and point of view are not revealed by the writer any more than are Delilah's.

Delilah is arguably the most famous woman in the book of Judges, her name a synonym for the mature seductive woman. Though not identified as a prostitute, she was obviously a woman available outside marriage, overtly using sexual attraction to entice Samson. Delilah, the only woman named in Samson's story, is identified not by the name of any male relatives (as was common when introducing an Israelite woman such as Bathsheba), nor even by her home town, but rather by a whole region, the *nahal soreq. Nahal* means wadi, a gulley which becomes a virtual torrent after a rain; and *soreq* alludes to a choice wine grape.

Thus the place name itself, Lillian Klein suggests, could imply passion and loss of control. Even more importantly, Delilah is identified as an unattached woman, whom biblical writers often depicted as seductively leading men astray (Klein 1993: 62).

The great importance of names in biblical tradition has led some to stretch for meaning in explicating both Delilah's and Bathsheba's names. The name Delilah itself may derive from *dalal*, which as a Hebrew root means to be weak, or, to hang, to let low. The Arabic root *dalla* means to behave amorously. So the name could mean 'falling curls' or 'flirtatious'. It might also mean 'one of the night', since her name in Hebrew, *de-layla*, could be based on the Hebrew root *layla*, meaning 'night' (although in Hebrew her name is pronounced *de-lîla*). Interpreted this way, Delilah would be the night who extinguishes 'one of the sun' (*Šimšon,* the Hebrew for Samson, from the Hebrew word *šemeš*, sun) (Klein 1993: 62).

The name Bathsheba *(bat* = daughter, *šeba* = oath, or a name) might refer to uncertain parentage (though her father's name is known) or an oath. Yet she is rarely even called by her name after her initial identification in 2 Sam. 11.3. Her name is uttered only after her infant dies (12.24), and only here is she called 'David's wife'; otherwise she is always called 'Uriah's wife' or simply 'the woman'.

Bathsheba's feelings are not relayed to the reader. In fact, the delineation of her character is so sketchy that it leaves virtually everything open to the imagination. In these early scenes, Bathsheba is a nonperson, merely part of the plot. Adele Berlin points out that she is not even a 'type', but rather an 'agent', an Aristotelian term which describes the performer of an action necessary to the plot. Where the plot called for adultery, Bathsheba became the agent. Berlin claims that Bathsheba is not considered guilty of adultery because she was only the means whereby it was achieved (Berlin 1994: 26).

Similarly one could claim that Delilah is also an 'agent', since the Philistine leaders are acting through her. Partly because these Philistines come to her, it has commonly been assumed that Delilah is herself a Philistine, although it is not stated in the biblical account. But why would an Israelite woman betray her people's hero? Lillian Klein admits, though, that there is only the 'suggestion' that she is Philistine (Klein 1993: 62 n. 1). Tikva Frymer-Kensky, on the other hand, sees no compelling reason to assume this. The text, she points out, 'never tells us that Delilah was a foreigner. The valley of Soreq is only thirteen miles west-southwest of Jerusalem...Danite territory, still occupied by Israelites. It was a border area that may not even have been under Philistine control... Since the text does not mention that Delilah was a Philistine, there is no reason to assume it' (Frymer-Kensky 1992: 260).

Delilah was often assumed to have been a Philistine in order to make the lesson of the story one of a warning against foreign women. For example, Cheryl Exum writes: 'The lesson of this text is to teach the Israelite male a lesson about the dangers of foreign women; nationalism reinforces gender ideology' (Exum 1993: 87). Lillian Klein writes: 'Delilah may not be a prostitute; the text is ambiguous, showing that the Israelite male cannot comprehend foreign women's words, values, or allegiances' (Klein 1993: 63). But the warning could just as well be against any independent, unattached woman, regardless of nationality. Part of the androcentric agenda of biblical writers was to portray women as powerful and dangerous, yet still subject to control by men. The narrator of this story seems to attach the blame for Samson's downfall to women, who are themselves victims of exploitation, since the Philistine men act through Delilah (rather than the usual reverse).

Cheryl Exum has called this story a 'variation of a traditional folktale whose latent meaning discloses male fear of women' (Exum 1993: 82). In a more recent interpretation, Exum coins the phrase 'Samson complex', by which she means 'the man's desire to surrender to the woman and his fear that he will be destroyed by her...Samson yielded, and look what happened to him, says our story. If even an apparently invincible man like Samson can be undone by a woman, how much more so should the ordinary man be on his guard. Such is the fear the woman inspires' (Exum 1996: 221). The point is that Delilah does not betray Samson so much as he betrays himself, by revealing his secrets to her.

In a similar interpretation, Betsy Merideth points out that this story 'is at least as much about Samson's pride and pretensions to immortality as it is about Delilah's harm to him'. Merideth's thesis is that 'betrayal' is not the appropriate term for Delilah's actions, since Samson is depicted as knowing what is going on. As an active participant in the events, he is not merely a victim (Merideth 1989: 72).

Whoever was the guiltier party in the story of Samson and Delilah, both paid a price in the end. Samson dies as a hero, destroying himself along with the Temple of Dagon. Delilah dies a textual death, vanishing from the story with her fate unknown to the reader.

Bathsheba, on the other hand, is notable as the only woman in

David's life who participates in the ongoing story of his reign, for she vanishes from the text only to resurface later (in the Book of Kings) as a much stronger person, the Queen Mother. As Alice Bach points out, the length of a female's textual life seems connected to the extent of sexual pleasure she provides her male creators (or the males in the story)! (Bach 1990: 36)—or, of course, how many sons she provides.

There are many disturbing aspects to the account of Bathsheba and David's initial encounter, as well as gaps in the narrative. The ambiguity has led to a wide range of interpretations around the simple issue of Bathsheba's role: was the act of bathing innocent or intentionally provocative? If innocent, then surely she is blameless. The text, and later commentaries, never blame Bathsheba for adultery, implying she was coerced, if not actually raped. Yet virtually all painters of later eras depicted Bathsheba as a seductress, fully in control of the situation. And these paintings had their impact on the public imagination, leading to popular songs and stories that have continued to perpetuate this idea. Most people today cannot separate the artistic renditions of the story from the biblical account.

The reason so many have felt the need to fill in the blanks in this story is because it is one of the briefest and most abrupt passages to relate such events. One and a half cold, stark verses (11.26-27a) sum up the condition of a woman who has had an adulterous affair, become pregnant, lost her husband, married her lover, the King of Israel, and borne his child. Only five actions—three on David's part, two on Bathsheba's—are minimally described. David sent, he took, he lay—verbs signifying control and acquisition, as Cheryl Exum points out. By contrast, Bathsheba 'came' and 'returned' (Exum 1996: 21). Meir Sternberg notes that the suppression of essentials, the narrator's pseudo-objectivity, and the tone rendering horror like an everyday matter, all create an extreme ironic discordance between the mode of presentation and the action itself (Sternberg 1987: 191). Stylistically this differs from the story of Samson and Delilah, probably because of the difference in genre.

The sexual act itself is reported very rapidly, with minimal dialogue; as Robert Alter points out, the elaborate scheme involving Uriah is much longer and has much more dialogue. Alter thinks this implies that the writer is directing our attention to the murder, not the sex act, as the major crime (Alter 1981: 182). The male writer (or reader, for that matter) would probably not have found fault with the sexual encounter.

The sex act between Samson and Delilah is not reported at all. It is assumed to be the means by which Delilah enticed Samson's secret from him. But the reader does not know if, how or when the act takes place. The text only says 'She lulled him to sleep on her lap', and this presumably would follow sexual intercourse.

Delilah's motives are never stated. Her primary motive could have been patriotism. The fact is, she betrays Samson for a price. If she loved him, this would show a lack of ethics and morality; yet nowhere in the text does she ever claim to love him. As Mieke Bal rightly points out, the fact that Delilah is given a name of her own, that she possesses her own house and associates with high-placed people, places her in the category of a successful and independent woman (Bal 1987: 50). So Delilah is not in dire need of money; she simply engages in a business transaction, either out of patriotism or simple practicality. To call it greed would be an unwarranted value judgment.

Delilah's goal might be to aid her people by eliminating an outside threat, while at the same time taking care of her own financial security. It is the *men* who direct Delilah in how to learn Samson's secret. She is not paid for sexual services, only for information.

Just how much money was she offered? This is of some importance in determining motive. In the text, the 'rulers' or 'princes' (Hebrew *seren)* of the Philistines tell Delilah 'we'll each give you eleven hundred shekels of silver' (Judg. 16.5). Robert Boling points out that 'tyrants' (or 'rulers') is a technical political title connecting the five great Philistine cities on the southern coastal plain with an Aegean homeland. Assuming there were five men involved, this amounts to a bribe of 5,500 shekels, an incredible figure (even accounting for inflation) when it is recalled that Abraham had paid only 400 shekels for a family burial place (Gen. 24.15, 19), Jeremiah paid seventeen shekels for a piece of property (Jer. 32.9) and thirty shekels is the value of a slave according to the covenant code (Exod. 21.32). Boling suggests that the source for the figure of eleven hundred could be the story that opens the following chapter, where Micah's mother budgets 'eleven hundred of silver' for the manufacture of a metal sculpture (Judg. 17.2) (Boling 1975: 249, n.). David Noel Freedman suggests that the term 'elef', translated here as a thousand, can also be understood as a term for the military district of which each tyrant was leader (Boling 1975: 249 n.). George Foot Moore points out that the number 1100 is unusual and is meant to seem enormous (Moore 1949: 352). So the financial motivation to follow the Philistines' order would have been high. In addition, coercion could have played a part: how much choice did Delilah really have? When all five leaders of the surrounding territory approached her, what would the consequences of refusing them have been? She was as much the victim or pawn of these men as Bathsheba was of King David.

Once she has agreed to do the job, Delilah is not devious; she says exactly what she wants. She never says she loves Samson; she uses his emotions without compromising her own. In Lillian Klein's words, 'she uses a man's love to bring him down—an age-old ruse' (Klein 1993: 63). Delilah's point of view is never given.

Determining Bathsheba's motives is still more difficult, since the author consistently withholds her point of view, creating an ambiguous portrayal. In the crucial scene, the initial sex encounter with David, neither she nor David has a voice. The question of Bathsheba's guilt or innocence in this encounter has occupied many commentators. Rabbis writing in the Talmud were much more concerned with the question of *David's* guilt, yet closer to modern times Bathsheba became the focus. Some male commentators believe the text hints that 'she asked for it'. Two commentators, H.W. Hertzberg and Randall Bailey, argue for Bathsheba's complicity. Hertzberg feels Bathsheba knew the place she was exposing herself was overlooked by the palace, implying a possible element of 'feminine flirtation' (Hertzberg 1964: 309). Randall Bailey argues for Bathsheba as a 'prime mover, a willing and equal partner to the events which transpire', and he turns the whole David–Bathsheba narrative into a 'tale of political deal-making and intrigue' (Bailey 1990: 85). These are both prime examples of 'blaming the victim'.

Cheryl Exum's response to such male commentators is that they are too quick to blame Bathsheba. She points instead to the responsibility of the *narrator*, who after all was the one who decided to portray Bathsheba in the act of bathing. The narrator, using David as his agent, 'makes Bathsheba the object of the male gaze'. Since the narrator chose to portray her bathing naked, how can we blame her or assume she might have known she would be seen? Readers of this text are watching a man watching a woman touch herself (purifying herself after her period, implying where she was touching). Looking at the female body is a cultural preoccupation and an accepted expression of male sexuality (Exum 1993: 187-89). By contrast, when David had exposed himself publicly (2 Sam. 6.14) he aroused *anger*, not desire, in his wife Michal.

Trevor Dennis points to Bathsheba's *vulnerability*. The narrator chooses to show Bathsheba bathing naked, which the reader could view as provocative behavior. But if she did not know David was watching, then she is vulnerable and actually humiliated (Dennis 1994: 145). As J.P. Fokkelman points out, the story puts David 'in the position of a despot who is able to survey and choose as he pleases' (Fokkelman 1981: 51)—which was probably the case. The unresolved question is whether or not Bathsheba was aware of being watched, and this depends on the actual physical layout of her house vis-à-vis the palace rooftop. Several chapters later, in 2 Sam. 16.22, Absalom, in a bid to take control of the monarchy, is described as publicly taking his father's concubines in a tent on the palace roof, 'in the eyes of all Israel'. The expression in Hebrew, *le-ênê,* can be interpreted as 'with the knowledge of' but it literally means 'before the eyes of'. Therefore, the reader understands the palace rooftop to be low enough for the people to view Absalom's activities. How much lower than that might Bathsheba's roof have been? Was she even bathing on the roof? If she was bathing indoors, with a door open, this would make David a true voyeur, not an innocent bystander.

Tikva Frymer-Kensky points out that Bathsheba was not out to get anything by using her beauty. The Bible in general, she notes, 'does not consider beauty a power or strategy of women'. In fact, Bathsheba's beauty is her vulnerability, not her power. Beauty only begins to be seen as a *power* of women in the postbibilical period (Frymer-Kensky 1992: 140, 262 n. 132).

The issue of love between these two people is never raised. Whereas Delilah is introduced as the woman with whom Samson fell in love, the question of whether David ever loves Bathsheba (or vice versa) is left unanswered. The minute she announces her pregnancy, his interest is in the paternity of the child, conceding her to Uriah from the start, which does not suggest great love. Once pregnant, Bathsheba is de-sexualized: this is how patriarchy severs the relationship between eroticism and procreation, to render a mother's sexuality non-threatening (Exum 1993: 191). Delilah, of course, is not destined to become a mother because that is not her purpose. Therefore she remains a threat to the very end and must disappear from the story. A close reading of the story of Samson and Delilah still leaves obvious gaps. Mieke Bal highlights three unanswered questions: Why doesn't Samson reproach Delilah for her betrayal? Why does he accept her reproaches without giving his own view? And most vital of all, why does he finally give her the crucial information? (Bal 1987: 40)

Two opposing viewpoints have been offered to explain most of these gaps. Samson was either incredibly stupid, in which case the story could be read as an indictment against the institution of both Judges and Nazirites (since he was considered a Judge and a Nazirite); or he was too smart for his own good, and thought he could play games with Delilah and still come out ahead.

Both of these stories were interpreted by post-biblical commentators, including rabbis in the Talmud. Later interpreters generally chose to keep Samson as a hero by in some way denigrating Delilah, a pattern that can also be seen in interpretations of the David–Bathsheba story. Pseudo-Philo was one of the first to retell the Samson and Delilah story. He combines the first four verses of ch. 16 with the subsequent verses:

> Then Samson went down to Gerar, a city of the Philistines, and he saw there a harlot whose name was Delilah, and he was led astray after her and took her to himself for a wife. And God said, 'Behold now Samson has been led astray through his eyes…and he has mingled with the daughters of the Philistines… Samson's lust will be a stumbling block for him, and his mingling a ruin… And his wife was pressuring him and kept saying to him, 'Show me your power and in what your strength lies, and so I will know that you love me.' …the fourth time he revealed to her his heart. And she got him drunk, and while he slept, she called a barber and he cut the seven locks of his head.[2]

The notion of making Delilah a respectable woman by marrying her off to Samson actually probably was motivated more by a need to make *Samson* more respectable and settled. This idea, plus that of getting Samson drunk, was picked up by much later writers who might have been familiar with this text.

Similarly with David and Bathsheba's story, the rabbis' preoccupation was with exonerating David. Thus in *Ket.* 9b, they explain that:

> Everyone who goes into the war of the House of David writes for his wife a deed of divorce (so if he falls in battle his wife can be free to marry without 'halitza').[3]

2.   *Ps.-Philo* 43.5-7, in Charlesworth 1983: 357.
3.   All Talmud quotes are from the Soncino Talmud. Another example can be found in tractate *Šab.* 56a: 'R. Samuel b. Nahmani said in R. Jonathan's name: Everyone who went out in the wars of the house of David wrote a bill of divorcement for his wife.'

The divorce was conditional, in the sense that it became retrospectively valid if the husband died. Thus, since Uriah died, Bathsheba was a free woman from the time he went out, and was not married when David took her. This typically ingenious rabbinic exegesis essentially absolves David (and Bathsheba) of adultery.

Other passages go even further. *Sanh.* 107a contains this elaborate midrashic retelling:[4]

> R. Johanan said...David forgot there is a small organ in man which satisfies him in his hunger but makes him hunger when satisfied... Now Bathsheba was cleansing her hair behind a screen, when Satan came to him, appearing in the shape of a bird. He shot an arrow at him, which broke the screen, thus she stood revealed, and he saw her.

This interesting retelling exonerates both Bathsheba (of immodesty) and David (of lust—'the Devil made me do it!' excuse).[5] Other attempts to exonerate David utilize extensive quotes from Psalms (supposedly composed by David) to prove he could not be guilty.[6] The rabbis used numerous means to exonerate David of guilt; never do they deal with the issue of Bathsheba's guilt or innocence.

Commentaries on both these stories continued through the centuries. In a much later period and different place, Baroque Europe, Delilah was seen as a heroine. Milton wrote *Samson Agonistes* (the original Greek term meant, in antiquity, one who contended for a prize in public games) in 1671. Delilah acts out of patriotism, and even tries to be

---

4. This lengthy passage opens with: 'One should never intentionally bring himself to the test, since David king of Israel did so, and fell... (David said) "Sovereign of the Universe, examine and try me"—as it is written, "Examine me, O Lord, and try me" (Psalms). (God) answered "I will test thee, and yet grant thee a special privilege, for I inform thee that I will try thee in a matter of adultery." ' (Round brackets indicate my additions.)

5. The passage goes still further: Bath Sheba, the daughter of Eliam, was predestined for David from the six days of Creation...the school of R. Ishmael taught likewise: She was worthy (i.e. predestined) for David from the six days of Creation, but he enjoyed her before she was ripe [before she was his legitimate wife]. (Round brackets indicate my additions; square brackets, the Soncino editor's.)

6. For example, ' *Abod. Zar.* 5a contains the following: David was not the kind of man to do that act, as it is written, 'My heart is slain within me' (meaning, David's inclinations had been completely conquered by himself). Similarly in tractate *Šab.* 56a, R. Samuel b. Nahmani said in R. Jonathan's name: Whoever says that David sinned is merely erring, for it is said, 'And David behaved himself wisely in all his ways, and the Lord was with him' (Ps. 18.14).

reconciled with Samson. Seeing her as simply motivated by greed was unconvincing. Like most other later writers, Milton saw Delilah's love for Samson as conflicting with her patriotic duty.

Samson Agonistes opens in the prison, that is, near the end of the biblical story. Some 700 verses into the epic poem, Delilah enters, announced thus:

> Some rich Philistian matron she may seem;
> And now, at nearer view, no other certain
> Than Dalila thy wife (ll. 722-24).

To which Samson replies:

> My wife! my traitress! let her not come near me (l. 725).

A dialogue ensues in which Delilah entreats Samson's forgiveness:

> With doubtful feet and wavering resolution
> I came, still dreading thy displeasure, Samson;
> Which to have merited, without excuse,
> I cannot but acknowledge... (ll. 732-35).

Delilah continues:

> If aught in my ability may serve
> To lighten what thou suffer'st, and appease
> Thy mind with what amends is in my power—
> Though late, yet in some part to recompense
> My rash but more unfortunate misdeed' (ll. 743-47).

To which Samson replies:

> Out, out hyena! These are thy wonted arts,
> And arts of every woman false like thee—
> To break all faith, all vows, deceive, betray;
> Then, as repentant, to submit, beseech,
> And reconcilement move with feigned remorse... (ll. 75-54).

Milton offers a new motive for Delilah's actions, namely, to gain power over him in order not to lose him. Delilah's words are:

> I saw thee mutable of fancy;
> Feared lest one day thou would'st leave me
> As her at Timna; sought by all means, therefore,
> How to endear, and hold thee to me firmest;
> No better way I saw than by importuning
> To learn thy secrets, get into my power
> Thy key of strength and safety' (ll. 793-99).

Samson asks her why she revealed his secret to the Philistines, and Delilah replies that they had reassured her no harm would come to him. Further on she also implies that great pressure was applied to force her to betray him.

William Blake (1757–1827) wrote a short Poetical Sketch called *Samson* which opens:

> Samson, the strongest of the children of men, I sing: how he was
> foiled by woman's arts, by a false wife brought to the gates of death!
> For Delila's fair arts have long been tried in vain; in vain she wept in
> many a treacherous tear... (Blake 1979: 179).

Altogether this is not a very flattering portrait of Delilah, but one which has influenced modern views of Delilah more than the biblical story itself, by its use of prejudicial adjectives such as 'false' and 'treacherous'. The biblical account, like the Bible in general, has virtually no descriptive adjectives.

Attempts at humanizing the characters and filling in the gaps were copied by several later writers. Eugene Moore wrote *Delilah, A Tale of Olden Times* in 1888. Delilah, in this version, is not only in love with Samson, but also is impressed with his God. Her Priest tries to convince her to betray Samson but she never agrees. Delilah's words to the Priest are:

> Priest! Fool! A pliant tool thou thought'st to have
> Wherewith to work thy will; but there's one page
> Which thou with all thy craft hast failed to read—
> That page whereon is writ in letters large—
> 'The love that woman giveth unto man
> Is stronger than the fear she hath of gods' (Moore 1888: 27).

Samson rebels against the Nazirite vows made for him by his mother, gets drunk deliberately, and when drunk reveals his secret. Delilah never means to betray him at all, but she cuts his hair in a sort of trance, wondering if he spoke the truth in his stupor. She says:

> Yes, I this hair will shear away, and thus
> My will may have and hold him at my side.
> If truth to me he told, if he grows weak,
> He'll here abide...
> While he's weak, upon my arms he'll lean,
> And for a space dependent be on me... (Moore 1888: 65).

Moore suggests the same motive for Delilah as did Milton: by weakening Samson, she can hold him to herself by making him dependent.

Woman here is depicted as manipulator rather than betrayer. It now becomes a struggle for power. Delilah tries to save Samson from the Philistines, follows him to prison and ultimately to the Temple of Dagon, to die by his side.

These modern retellings must have been well known to contemporary writers, such as Austrian writer Felix Salten (of *Bambi* fame), who in 1931 wrote his novel, *Samson and Delilah: A Novel*, based on the biblical tale. He makes numerous interesting changes, qualifying the novel as true modern midrash. Delilah was a virgin who had never as yet known a man's kiss, until meeting Samson. She lives with her parents and comes to believe in Samson's God. Her unsavory mother makes a deal and acts as go-between to bribe Delilah. In a subplot, her sister is lusted after by the Philistine leader, giving her a motive to side with their mother and persuade Delilah to betray her lover. She cleverly asks Delilah how she would find out if someone loved her. When Delilah starts asking Samson questions about his strength, he first tells her his secret is too 'holy' to reveal. But when he does finally reveal it, the sister is eavesdropping and it is she who cuts his hair! Delilah remains by Samson's side to the very end. The novel is vividly written, particularly the blinding sequence, in which the red hot points coming toward Samson's eyes are described as the last things he would ever see. In a particularly poignant and humanizing touch, Salten invents a pet dog who comes to visit Samson and Delilah in prison every night and who ultimately dies, trustfully, by their side. (Well, what can you expect from the writer of *Bambi*?)

The story of David has also been retold in many ways through the centuries, but the encounter with Bathsheba is more often than not simply excluded. Not having Talmudic means of discourse at their disposal, later writers utilized a simpler technique: whitewash. The goal was to make David into a hero, albeit a complex one, and it was too difficult to integrate the incident with Bathsheba into this picture.

One interesting exception is a 1923 play by David Pinski, originally in Yiddish, *David and His Wives*. The final chapter deals with Bathsheba. It opens with Nathan confronting David, telling him the parable as a *warning*. When Bathsheba is then brought to David, she refuses his advances, even reciting some of his own psalms as part of her argument! Nathan sends Uriah into the room. Bathsheba tries to convince Uriah to take her away from the palace, but he insists he must follow his king's orders. Exasperated, Bathsheba rips open the message delivered to Uriah, which he was to take back to the front. Even after she has proved David's evil intentions, Uriah still will not disobey his king's orders. Finally Bathsheba sends him away with the words, 'I have loved a slave! Now I shall love a king!' (Pinski 1923: 126). Just as in the modern retellings of Delilah's story, this modern midrash makes Bathsheba into much more of a real person, and turns many pre-conceptions on their head.

Composers, too, have found inspiration from these stories in every era. The two most famous musical renditions of the story of Samson and Delilah are by Handel and Saint Saëns. The libretto for the Handel opera of 1735 is by Hamilton Newburgh, based on his play, which is based more on Milton than the Bible. Most of the opera takes place in the prison, and Delilah, 'Samson's wife', appears only briefly in Act II to sing two successive arias (one is traditionally cut) in which she pretends to be penitent and submissive. The music itself does not convince the listener of Delilah's duplicitous nature, however, and in this sense may not have achieved the librettist's goal.

The libretto for the Saint Saëns opera of 1877 is by Ferdinand Lemaire, who makes Delilah a cold, calculating seductress. This is an important point, because this portrayal has probably molded modern views of Delilah's character far more than the biblical account ever did. The story has been altered somewhat. In her first appearance, Delilah, in the company of other Philistine women, greets Samson in a public place. In the first of her three arias, 'Printemps qui commence', she reminds Samson of their earlier liaison as her compatriots dance sinuously. Praising spring, she sings to Samson of how eagerly she awaits the renewal of their relationship. The listener is hard pressed not to feel some empathy for her. The music paints a softer portrait of Delilah than the librettist probably intended! However, in her second aria, 'Amour, viens aider ma faiblesse', the only one *not* sung for Samson's benefit, Delilah 'shows her true colors'. Such is the power of music to move the listener that even in Delilah's famous seduction aria, 'Mon coeur s'ouvre à ta voix', the music is so lush and seductive that the listener simply has to empathize with poor Samson. Who could resist such music? The fact that the biblical Delilah nags and cajoles rather than seducing is immaterial to composers: seduction music is far more appealing than nagging music, so Delilah became imprinted in all opera lovers' minds as the temptress par excellence. And no amount of scholarship or commentary can undo the power of music. The arts have done a great deal to popularize biblical stories, but this popularization has not resolved the ambiguities of the original stories in a favorable way for the female characters.

This is even more true in more popular renditions of the Samson story. In all of these, Samson is the poor sap and Delilah the temptress. Three such versions are 'Delilah Done Me Wrong', or 'The No Haircut Song', written by Gerard Calvi with words by Harold Rome for the 1963 musical *La grosse valise*; the 1957 song 'Samson, Mighty Samson', by Hamilton Henry (Terry) Gilkyson, popular singer, songwriter and guitarist of the 1940s and 50s; and the 1974 mini-epic oratorio *Samson and Delilah* by Sam Pottle, composer of the 'Muppet Theme Song'.

Musically, Bathsheba has fared no better than in most artists' representations, generally being depicted in popular songs as the temptress who brought David down. Numerous operas and oratorios entitled *David* completely ignore Bathsheba. Several examples are operas by Alessandro Scarlatti, Arthur Honegger, and many lesser known composers. One notable exception is Darius Milhaud's *David*, with text by Armand Lunel in French and Hebrew. This work was commissioned by the Koussevitzky Foundation of the Library of Congress. Milhaud dedicated the work to 'the people of Israel, on the occasion of the 3000 year anniversary of the founding of Jerusalem'. It was written in 1952 and received its world premiere at La Scala in 1955. The initial encounter between David and Bathsheba is not depicted but is referred to in a duet which takes place after their firstborn has died. Both express sadness and regret at what happened between them.

There is also a popular rendition of this story in which the lyrics show total ignorance of the story but use it as a vehicle to warn men of the dangers of women's charms, much as the popular Delilah songs do. This song, 'David and Bathsheba', is a true product of the 1950s, written in 1951 with words and music by Gordon Jenkins, Robert Allen, and Allan Roberts, who have their roots in vaudeville. This song is both a wonderful and horrible example of how biblical women have fared in popular interpretations that unfortunately have always been more accessible to the general public than scholarly books such as this one.

The fascination of these modern retellings, whether through drama, poetry, novels or music, is the way they illustrate the prismatic quality of the original story. The biblical writer left so many ambiguities and unanswered questions that the story may be understood any number of different ways without contradicting the actual text. Artists, writers and composers all felt the need not only to fill in the gaps, but to make their version the most emotionally compelling one. Each viewed the light through a different angle of the original prism. And each has opened new windows which illuminate the texts for readers of every generation.

RAHAB: FROM PESHAT TO PEDAGOGY, OR:
THE MANY FACES OF A HEROINE

Phyllis Silverman Kramer

Introduction

This paper examines a range of interpretations about Rahab. A review
of textbooks used for Bible study in elementary Jewish day schools has
been conducted to see how these educational materials present Rahab
and whether or not they mirror the Bible, and/or reflect a vast rabbinic
literature, and/or create some other perhaps more contemporary image
of her. This paper is intended as a pilot study in the area of Bible *vis-à-
vis* elementary school education to ascertain whether there is stereo-
typing and the manipulation of female role models in Jewish Bible
textbooks. The choice of Rahab as a touchstone biblical female stems
from her narrative being exciting and exhilarating, suspenseful and fast
paced, and highlighting a female's bravery and heroism.

Rahab in the Bible

The Character of Rahab

Appearing early in the book of Joshua is Rahab, the first post-Penta-
teuchal female. Although not an Israelite, she was unique in deeds of
bravery, aiding two Hebrew spies in need of help. In nineteen verses,
the reader learns of her heroic, benevolent deeds and her reward. Rahab
participated in extensive dialogue by giving instructions to the spies
and beseeching them to save her family, and by speaking with the king
who had summoned her.

Rahab's Heroism

Two spies, sent by Joshua to scout out Jericho, found lodging in the
house of Rahab, an innkeeper and/or a harlot. When the king of Jericho
demanded Rahab bring the spies to him, she hid them, lied to the king

saying they had left at night when the city gates were being locked, and suggested they be pursued quickly (Josh. 2.1-7).

Surely Rahab is to be classified as a heroine who acted independently, endangering her life three times for the spies: she first hid them among the flax on her roof (2.4), then deceived the king of Jericho by having him think he was pursuing the spies when actually they were still in her home (2.5-7), and finally helped them escape over the city wall (2.15). Rahab's deception followed a motif seen in the books of Genesis and Exodus, where women lied in order to save someone. An example from each book was Sarah pretending to be Abraham's sister, and Shiphrah and Puah telling Pharaoh the Hebrew women delivered their babies before their arrival.

In choosing to be civilly disobedient, Rahab demonstrated strength and judgment, betraying her people in order to abet another nation. Perhaps her recognition of the spies' powerful God, and the miracles wrought for them (Josh. 2.9-11) mitigated against a response from her that would have cost them their lives. Therefore, she not only aided them, but spent the rest of her life among the Israelites. As she had protected the spies earlier, she later resided peacefully among them. Rahab's residence, having been located inside the city wall, could symbolically have been construed as her having been poised or caught between her own people and outsiders.

Rahab's acts of kindness to the spies were two in number and had a paired or balanced aspect to them. First, she hid the men (2.6) and then facilitated their escape to safety (2.15). Thus, two acts of kindness and two acts of rescue were evident. So, too, when the spies returned to conquer her town, the Israelites performed two acts of benevolence. First, they saved Rahab's family from danger (6.23), and then she was able to reside with the Israelites (6.25). Another example of symmetry in Rahab's story involved the rope. Rahab expedited the spies' flight by having them climb down a rope from her window (2.15). Subsequently, a rope was placed back in the window to facilitate keeping the spies' promise to rescue Rahab and her family (2.21). The balancing of Rahab's heroism and humanity with her being able to have her family rescued augured well to confirm the magnanimity of her deeds, and garnered respect for the significance of what she had done.

Rahab's Request to Save her Family
For her part in having saved the spies, Rahab asked that her entire family be rescued and kept safe when the Children of Israel would capture

her city. She did not request that any material wealth be saved. Setting forth rescue conditions with Rahab before being let down on a rope from her window, leading outside the wall, the spies escaped. Subsequently a red rope was hung from her window indicating where her family would be when the victorious enemy arrived. When Joshua conquered Jericho, the spies' promise was kept: Rahab and her entire family were saved whereupon she lived out the remainder of her life among the Children of Israel.

A discrepancy was noted in the Bible text. In three different verses, there was mention of who was to be saved in Rahab's family. The first verse stated Rahab asked that her father, mother, brothers, sisters, and all belonging to them be saved (2.13). The spies then told her of a plan to rescue her father, mother, brothers, and all of her father's household gathered together in the designated place (2.18). Finally, at the time of the conquest, her father, mother, brothers, Rahab herself, and all of her families (*kol mišp^{e}hôtehā*) were rescued (6.23). The question being raised is why Rahab's sisters were accounted for only in the first verse cited, whereas the other immediate relatives were listed individually in all three verses. Rahab acted alone and was not portrayed as part of a family that included a husband or children; only her extended family was mentioned. Given the emphasis on the domestic role of biblical females, this omission is unusual.

Rahab in Jewish Interpretation

The Character of Rahab

Rahab was introduced as a *zônâ* (2.1). Commentators translated this word as harlot or innkeeper, or a combination of the two definitions. While 'harlot' had negative connotations, the innkeeper explanation depicted Rahab as a moral person to whom the spies went for succor. Targum Jonathan used the euphemistic translation of *zônâ*, an innkeeper, and Radak later opined that *zônâ*, which meant harlot, was also an innkeeper, one who dispensed food as well as provided other services, sexual in nature. Abravanel said both the literal and euphemistic denotations of the word were correct. The Babylonian Talmud referred to her as a harlot (*Zeb.* 116b). Midrashim were more expansive than the targumic and talmudic sources, calling her a harlot and implying immorality (*Num. R.* 3.2 and 8.9; *Ruth R.* 2.1; *T.d. Eliyy.* 32 [Braude and Kapstein 1981: 509]; *Pes. R.* 40.3/4 [Braude 1968: II, 706]; *Pes. K.* 13.5 [Braude and Kapstein 1975: 256]; *Mek. Amalek* 3 [Lauterbach

1933: II, 163, 176; and *Mek. Shirata* 3 [Lauterbach 1933: II, 28]). Rashi and Altschuler agreed with the Targum, i.e. Rahab was an innkeeper providing all types of food. *Zônâ* (harlot) and *mazôn* (food) were connected midrashically to make such a translation feasible.

Rahab was noted as one of the world's exceptionally beautiful women, along with Sarah, Abigail, and Esther. When Rahab's name was mentioned lust was enkindled in men (*Meg.* 15a). R. Yitzchak said by saying 'Rahab, Rahab' a seminal discharge would immediately ensue. R. Naḥman responded that such an incident did not happen to him. R. Yitzchak countered, saying the sexual response would come from one who knew her. Another condemnation of her sexual puissance was the assertion that she had been possessed by every prince and ruler (*Meg.* 15a).

After being a harlot for 40 years, at age 50 Rahab became a proselyte (*Zeb.* 116b and *Mek.* 3 [Lauterbach 1933: II, 164]). Her seeking forgiveness was a result of her having saved the spies by lowering them through her window (*Zeb.* 116b). Her praises were sung when she was called a proselyte (*Exod. R.* 27.4; *Cant. R.* 1.63 and 4.2; *Eccl. R.* 8.13), and a righteous person (*Num. R.* 8.9; and *Eccl. R.* 5.14). The reasons for her having become a believer were because she saw God's miracles (*Exod. R.* 27.4) and because of Joshua. The latter argument meant she was not chosen by God to become a proselyte; rather another person influenced her (*Eccl. R.* 8.13). Rahab had strong faith in God (*Mek. Shirata* 9 [Lauterbach 1933: II, 74] and *Mek. Amalek* 3 [Lauterbach 1933: II, 163, 176]) whom she placed in the heaven and on earth (*Deut. R.* 2.28). Rahab also received praise for turning from prostitute to believer so God favored her with descendants who included prophets and righteous men (*Pes. R.* 40.3/4 [Braude 1968: II, 706). Eight prophets, who were also priests, descended from Rahab. The prophetess Huldah was descended from Joshua and Rahab, who married following Rahab's conversion to Judaism (*Meg.* 14b). Jeremiah was also of her lineage (*Pes. K.* 13.5 [Braude and Kapstein 1975: 3]).

A number of commentators addressed the issue of her becoming a convert, the key factor being whether or not she converted on her own recognizance: she heard about the Israelites and their God, came, and cleaved as a proselyte (*Exod. R.* 27.4). She drew near but was not chosen (*Num. R.* 3.2). R. Isaac stated Rahab was an example of vanity because she did not become a proselyte on her own; rather Joshua caused her to become converted, and R. Aḥa said it was not vanity

(*Eccl. R.* 8.13). Finally, Rahab repented, as a result of which her descendants included seven kings and eight prophets. 'She was called Rahab...because her merit in repentance was so substantial (*reḥôva*)' (*T.d. Eliyy.* 37 [Braude and Kapstein 1981: 509]).

An early comment, citing proof texts from the Book of Joshua about Rahab's actions and contrasting them with Israel's actions, offered a unique interpretation about Rahab and concluded: 'You find that all those words of Scripture which are used in tribute to Rahab contain a reproach to Israel' (*Pes. K.* 13.4 [Braude and Kapstein 1975: 255]). God's favor was bestowed upon her because she had the foreknowledge the spies would have to hide for three days; she knew the time because she saw the Divine Spirit (*Ruth R.* 2.1 and *Sifre Devarim* 24).

Rahab's Heroism
Rahab's heroism was twofold, saving both the spies and her family. For having allowed the spies to enter her home and rescuing them, God rewarded her, blessing her with special descendants, daughters who married into the priesthood and whose sons served in the Temple and blessed Israel (*Num. R.* 8.9).

Rahab saved not just her own immediate family, but those related in an extended familial pattern (*Ruth R.* 2.1; *Eccl. R.* 5.4). She exhibited an act of loving-kindness in having saved the spies and her family, and saved the spies without thought of recompense. However, when she realized that, by saving the spies she had saved their fathers' house, she asked for her father's house to be safeguarded likewise. This reciprocal arrangement assured the lineage of her father's house (Radak).

Post-Talmudic commentators gave insight into Rahab's actions in a verse by verse pattern, some verses eliciting varying opinions (Hoenig 1969). Rahab hid the spies two times. Initially, she hid them (*watisp^{e}nô*) (2.4) in a place where they would be safe from searchers, and later, she hid them (*watiṭm^{e}nēm*) (2.6) by covering them (Malbim). Altschuler had a different interpretation showing how careful Rahab was in protecting the spies. In the first instance (2.4), she hid each man in a special place because it was easier to hide them singly. The second time (2.6), she hid them in a better location.

Rahab's Request to Save her Family
In asking that her family be rescued, Rahab asked for a sign of truth from the spies to enable her to trust their word. The sign agreed upon would indicate her life would be spared (Rashi 2.12). She asked for a

sign so as not to be deceived (Radak). Radak, Ralbag, Altschuler, and Malbim (Hoenig 1969) also wrote about Rahab's deed of exceptional kindness to the spies who would later recompense her by saving her father's house. Abravanel commented she asked for her family to be saved, meaning her father, mother, and siblings (Josh. 2.13) because, being a harlot, she had no spouse or children. In interpreting the same verse, it was averred that, when Rahab asked for their lives to be saved, she was implying a spiritual salvation and the thought of becoming a proselyte (Malbim).

Commentaries on v. 2.21 explained Rahab's thought processes as she worked out her plans with the spies. One opinion was that she placed the scarlet thread in the window right after the spies left. In order for her not to call attention to herself when the victors would return, and neighbors think she was signaling to the enemy, she put the thread in her window immediately and left it there (Abravanel and Malbim). The second view was that she put the scarlet thread in the window at a later time when Israel came to conquer (Radak and Altschuler).

General Observations about Rahab in Rabbinic Literature
Rahab was seen as a woman of extraordinary beauty, exuding lust. Her profession (*zônâ*) was explained as a duality in an attempt by exegetes to present a more pristine image. They tempered her role as immoral harlot with her being an innkeeper. The combination of the two aspects would thereby lessen or soften the negative 'harlot' interpretation.

Biblical interpreters seem to have held Rahab in esteem for the part she played in connection with the Israelite spies. Not only was she protected by the exegetes in connection with her 'profession', but she was credited with a revered lineage. For her part in saving the two spies, and for her faith in God, she was rewarded with marriage to Joshua and illustrious descendants. She had shown protectiveness and loving-kindness in having safeguarded the spies with no initial thought of recompense, and for saving her family as well. She was extolled as a proselyte and may even have had communication with God, enabling her to know how long it would take before the spies would return with their nation to conquer her people.

Rahab in Jewish Educational Materials
Rahab's story is exciting for young girls and boys to learn. The tale is action packed, suspenseful, and fast paced; the hiding of two spies, the

deception of the king's soldiers, the promise, escape, and eventual rescue mission are told tersely and exhilaratingly, and have great appeal to children who are captivated by her bravery and heroism.

The Character of Rahab

Introducing the character of Rahab to young children presents a problem to educators who must translate the word *zônâ*. Bible commentators interpreted the word to mean either prostitute or innkeeper; the educational books seem to skirt the issue and concentrate on what they perceive were Rahab's personality traits. She was called 'a kindly woman who ran an inn' (Skulsky 1961: 39). The spies 'stopped at an inn, owned by a kind woman named Rahab' (Samuels 1973: 4). The students learned about 'Rahab, a woman of Jericho, and Rahab gave them a place to sleep' (Newman 1985: 12). The trait of kindness was further amplified by her being referred to as 'a very kind and friendly woman' (Daniel 1971: 11-12). She was also spoken of as a woman who 'can be trusted' (Benagh 1986: 22). Another book of tales said: 'A woman by the name of Rahab owned the inn. She gave them food and drink' (Cohen 1936: 13). Their gratefulness for her kindness was also recognized (Samuels 1989: 5). Another textbook containing the Bible text, included commentaries by Rashi and Altschuler. Students learned Rahab was an innkeeper (Rashi) and sold food (Rashi and Altschuler).

In examining the educational materials, effort was not directed specifically to what types of Jewish day schools used different texts. The books themselves were examined for content and fealty to the *peshat*. However, a glaring surprise surfaced. In a book of midrashim (stories based on the *peshat*), published by an Orthodox firm, the issue of who Rahab was, was confronted in a wonderfully and tastefully candid manner. The text describes a conflict between the beliefs of the spies and who Rahab is: upon entering Jericho, the spies went to a hotel owned by 'a well-known, beautiful woman named Rachav. She was friendly with all the kings of Eretz Canaan as well as many other important people. They used to discuss their war plans with her' (Weissman 1995: 8). In the hopes that they can glean information for Joshua, they decide to lodge in her hotel. 'In reality it was not appropriate for two *tzaddikim* [righteous men]…to stay at such a hotel. The owner was a non-Jewish woman who was known to be friendly with many men. But they had no choice. They did it *leshaim shamayim* [in the name of God], for they felt it would help them accomplish their mission' (Weissman 1995: 9).

The midrash goes on to call Rachav 'a special woman' (1995: 9) who realized her guests were holy, righteous men whom she treated 'respect-fully' (1995: 10). The midrash expresses praise for Rachav: having recognized the power of the Israelites, she could now effectuate a way to serve this Being although she knew she could 'be burned alive' (1995: 10) for doing so.

Rahab's Heroism
The primary focus both in text explanations and workbook exercises was the elucidation of Rahab's relationship with the spies. In one exer-cise, a question was posed: why did the spies go to gather news at Rahab's house rather than in the center of the town, the gate of the town, or on the streets? (Zielberman and Korach-Seger 1987: 21) I believe the answer to this question could involve discussion of the sociology of the town and society in which Rahab lived and also the position of a woman innkeeper. Were only women innkeepers? What power might Rahab have possessed, considering the king's soldiers came quickly to the inn searching for the spies? What role did the inn, in fact, play in the life of the town? One other biblical reference to *bêt zônâ*, found in Jer. 5.7, might be referred to as clearly alluding to a harlot's house where prostitution is committed. (Teacher discretion would come into play as to whether or not this verse would be appropriate.)

A most suspenseful part of this narrative was her hiding the spies and subsequently aiding them in their escape. In one workbook, thirteen pages were devoted to an examination of Rahab's story, including many questions about her abetting the spies: her words to the king's messengers and why she deceived them, how she hid them, and what the danger was she encountered in her home. Thought exercises included writing a paragraph about a punishment the king would give to Rahab for having disobeyed him and drawing a picture of Rahab and the spies (Yonay and Yonay 1989: 22-34). Pollack asked two salient questions: (1) 'What did Rahab do to save the spies from death?', and (2) 'Why did Rahab save the spies from death?' (Pollack 1934: 14).

Insight into Rahab's character was seen in an introduction to a com-position students were to write where it said she was prepared to sacrifice her own life in order to save the spies. The children of Israel recognized her goodness, and saved her and her family when they became the conquering nation (Shevell 1953: 8). Other questions in this same book related to how Rahab helped the spies escape, that is, her request to them, and her need to be given a sign they would be truthful with her. Attention was focused on Rahab's belief in the God of Israel, and a question was raised about how the spies felt when they heard Rahab's words (Yonay and Yonay 1989: 28). Often in the pages of Scripture, it is not evident that females have a voice. This would be a glorious opportunity for educators to comment on, to highlight that Rahab had dialogue with the men, that she even made a pointed request of them. Rahab's position could be contrasted with the roles of Hagar, Zilpah, and Bilhah. Students could be challenged to understand the maturity of the matriarch Sarah who had *no* voice during the incidents with Pharaoh and Abimelech, yet was the female about whom God said to Abraham: 'Listen to her voice' (Gen. 21.12).

In a 'who am I' exercise, students must identify the comment 'I hid the spies' (Fish 1975: 6). Other exercises and drawings helped students interpret how Rahab hid the spies and helped them escape. She was described as having lied to the two soldiers and hidden 'the two spies under the bundles of flax' (Samuels 1989: 5). The examination of this vignette could engender a valuable exchange regarding the kinds of lies people tell in differing circumstances, and asking the students if lying is ever justified. So often children will see a moral/ethical dilemma when presented in a narrative or parable form and be able to extract a personal lesson and/or conclusion that is applicable to their own lives. A perceptive teacher will seize this moment and help students in their moral education.

When the king's soldiers demanded she give the spies to them, 'Rahab did not do what the king wanted' (Newman 1985: 13). She dissembled, saying the spies did not even stay at her inn, but had left the city at nightfall. She then hid them under a covering of flax on her roof. Another version of this scene was Rahab, when the soldiers came to her inn, telling the spies quickly to 'climb up to her roof and hide under the stalks of flax' (Daniel 1971: 12). An illustration of the roof scene appeared in this same text showing Rahab, hair covered, pointing to where the spies might have escaped. She holds flax in her hand, presumably with which to cover them.

Another book, presenting the Bible text and Rashi, had questions and exercises for the student to complete. The prepared summary highlighted Rahab's saving the spies, her request of them, and their plan to save her. In the lesson, pupils were asked what Rahab told the spies, and what she did to save their lives. Thought questions focused on why she safeguarded them, and why the spies commanded Rahab to gather her family at her house (Pollack 1934: 14).

Grishaver (1982: 12-13) asked students to pretend they were inter-viewing Rahab and to complete the blanks or circle answers Rahab would have given. The responses emphasized where Rahab's house was located, her motive for helping the spies, how she helped them, what deal she made with them, and what her future plans were after the destruction of Jericho. While some of the multiple choices were straightforward answers, others involved the pupils thinking about Rahab's position. She was spoken of as being 'one of many non-Jews in the Bible' (Grishaver 1982: 14); others were listed and students were asked to 'describe how each of these people treated the Jews' (1982: 14).

Rahab's Request

One Hebrew text, including a chapter emphasizing the covenant or pact between the spies and Rahab, presented her as a heroine in five terse sentences. A completion exercise asked what the spies had promised to do for her (Zielberman and Korach-Seger 1987: 21). Another source said that when the spies asked how they could reciprocate for Rahab, she responded: 'If you come and conquer our city, I beg of you to spare my family and me, and let this house stand' (Daniel 1971: 12). The red cord, to be placed in the window of her home, was recognized as a sign of her being saved 'when the Children of Israel march into Jericho' (Daniel 1971: 13). While God's role in leading the spies to Rahab's inn was acknowledged by them, the spies also said: 'If it had not been for that woman's kindness we would both be dead now' (Daniel 1971.13).

A section of workbook exercises was devoted to the pact between Rahab and the spies. Details highlighted what she must do to have the pact effectuated. Students had to complete two squares by writing what Rahab and the spies had done, that is, balancing their reciprocal good deeds. Students were asked how they knew Rahab was a wise woman, and had to respond when asked who saved Rahab and her family, and why she was saved. A dialogue was to be written between Rahab and the spies after they saved her (Yonay and Yonay 1989: 30-32). After having been saved along with her family, Rahab's fate was spoken about, and it was avowed 'they joined the Tribes of Israel' (Skulsky 1961: 47). A question was posed querying what the spies did following the fall of the wall (Pollack 1934: 29). The final page of another book stated God spared Rahab and her family to reward her for her good help (Okef n.d.: 47).

Art Images in Educational Materials
In examining and evaluating the content of children's educational materials, the inclusion of images significantly enriches the text(s). Early on pupils should learn about art as an important and revealing form of biblical interpretation. They should be challenged to look at the images to see how closely they mirror the *peshat* and ask a key question: are the images text-affiliated? (see Kramer 1998: 195-217). Students should be encouraged to express whether or not the image evokes emotion, and whether it has power and influence in enhancing the narrative. The following question can be posed which would focus the child upon the significance of the artist's interpretation: what do you think you will remember from your workbook—the written exercises or the pictures? This question could be a written assignment or a class discussion. The theme of art as biblical interpretation should then be pursued in future educational materials. Children might be asked if they can recollect any art that they have seen prior to the Rahab images.

Essentially, the Rahab images fall into four categories: (1) Rahab greeting the spies, (2) hiding the spies, (3) dissembling to the king's messengers, and (4) helping the spies escape. Some drawings have been found showing Rahab and her family being saved by the conquering Israelites. The images range from very simplistic drawings to more elaborate paintings. Most are seen in black and white.

One workbook showed three illustrations of her (Yonay and Yonay 1989: 26, 27, 33). In each she differed physically in terms of her attractiveness and hair color, thereby causing confusion to pupils. In the first drawing, she was blonde and pretty, meeting the spies for the first time out-of-doors! The second depiction showed an unattractive, dark-haired Rahab, covering the spies with flax, while image three was identical to the first of these three portrayals. A second pair of sources by another author did a similar presentation showing a blatant disparity between two successive presentations of Rahab peering through her window, watching the spies lowering themselves down from the roof (Samuels 1973: 5; Samuels 1989: 5). It would be difficult to rationalize to the pupils what the artists had in mind by drawing such differences.

A series of drawings was seen in another book (Okef n.d.: 6-8).

Rahab was first seen hiding a man on the roof of her house. Only her arm was visible as she pulled a blanket over the man. The area on which she stood was one of many such roof areas. The next two drawings showed her in a situation of protecting the hidden spies. In the first depiction, she had a lovely visage; in the second, she was quite unattractively portrayed as she told the king's messengers she did not know of the spies' whereabouts. The final of these pages had four scenes: 1 showed Rahab returning to the roof of her home; images 2 and 3 showed her directing the spies to escape, and 4 depicted her lowering the spies down a rope from a mountainside. This last was a unique picture in that Rahab was seen helping them down a mountain, rather than lowering them down a rope from a window. The text for this illustration described her home in the wall, but the picture did not seem in concert with the text.

Many wonderful images of Rahab (Figures 1 and 2) can be seen in a colorful storybook about Joshua. On facing pages (Levinger 1997: 8-9), two different sides of Rahab's personality are evident. In the first illustration, a very surprised Rahab tells the king's messenger that she does not know where the spies currently are. She confronts their anger by dissembling. There is a comical aspect to this image for above Rahab and the messengers can be seen the eyes of the hidden spies on the roof. This is a picture that will surely capture pupils' attention and should raise moral and ethical questions about dissembling/lying. On the facing page, Rahab the brave woman who has hidden the spies happily tells them that they are safe to leave. Simplistic in their depicting emotions of the characters, these illustrations are most effective in portraying the story.

A unique and very modern pictorial adaptation of Rahab's story presented her helping a young girl and boy on an archaeological dig. Depicted as a flirt, she tried to get information in order to assist the young people. 'She strolled along the top of the walls twirling her bright scarf...and approached a sentry... She flashed a friendly smile... She gave a playful flick with the end of her kerchief... Rahab stayed to flirt a while longer' (Benagh 1986: 28). Despite the simplicity of these drawings, Rahab is of a lovely visage and actively flirts with the guard, aiding and abetting the people on the archaeological dig. Could this image be construed as resembling the harlot interpretation of *zônâ*?

Figure 1. *The Beginner's Bible* (the story of Rahab).

A comical image depicts a very modestly dressed blonde Rahab looking quite surprised at the angry king as she denies having the spies in her home. At the same moment, however, the viewer sees the leg of one of the spies as he is hastening up the stairs! (Barr 1991: 74-75)

A concentration of images shows Rahab helping the spies escape. Interesting to note is that they do not always escape by means of the window, according to the *peshat*. In three images (Samuels 1989: 6; Samuels 1973: 5; Orenstein 1988: 10) they are lowering themselves down from the roof as Rahab watches them from her window. In the first of these pictures, she looks like a young girl. (Is this so that children might identify easily with her?)

The king's men went away. Rahab went to the roof and told the spies it was safe to come down.

Figure 2. *The Beginner's Bible* (the story of Rahab).

In the second (Figure 3), she is seen as a modestly dressed (young) woman who is very concerned with what is happening. With a concerned expression on her face, she gazes downward through her window in the wall, watching the spies escape. The area of the window is in brightness so the reader focuses on her first. And yet, the action in the image centers on the two men who are escaping. One has already reached the ground and is looking around the corner of the wall to check on their safety. The other is letting himself down from a rope attached to the roof. Clearly he is not coming from the window as the *peshat* indicates. The third image is a more sophisticated drawing showing the strength of the male body. These are heroes and the viewer can feel the excitement in their hasty departure. Rahab, portrayed from a partial side view, is standing on her roof as she observes them fleeing.

In examining the escape episode images, students should be encouraged to re-read the text and to comment on the disparity between the image and the *peshat*. How will students explain the lack of text-affiliation?

Figure 3. *Bible Stories for Jewish Children from Joshua to Queen Esther* (the story of Rahab). Reproduced by permission of Ktav Publishing House, Inc.

General Observations about Rahab in Jewish Educational Materials
Students learned that Rahab ran an inn and dispensed food and drink.
The semantic range of the word *zônâ* was absent from the materials;
rather her personality characteristics were inferred from her actions and
her suspenseful relationship with the spies, namely, how she hid them
and how they reciprocated by saving her family. Her personal risk in
saving the spies was appreciable. She and her family were saved
because of her goodness. Rahab was lauded as a heroine and praised by
the spies who recognized that her bravery and courage saved their lives.

No clear visual image emerged from the drawings because she was
not presented in a uniform way. Discrepancies in her appearance and
her age were evident. The illustrations stressed her concealing and
saving the spies, and her placing the rope in her window.

Conclusions

The portrait culled from Jewish interpreters mirrored the Hebrew Scriptures and glorified Rahab for her bravery. She was described as a
heroine who showed kindness without thought of gain, and saved not
only her own family from a warring nation, but also two members of
the hostile Israelites.

Rabbinic literature presented a balanced understanding of her, taking
into consideration the multiple definitions of *zônâ* and recognizing the
role she played with both negative and euphemistic explanations. Only
the Babylonian Talmud expanded on a theme of lust which arose
because of her beauty. She was lauded in midrashim for having become
a proselyte and praised because of her descendants.

The idea of Rahab's harlotry was downplayed and tempered with her
being an innkeeper, albeit one who might dispense sexual favors. She
was praised for her role in hiding the spies twice and later helping them
escape to safety. The expedient and cautious manner in which she hid
them occasioned favorable comments, as well as her care in placing the
scarlet thread out of her window. It became almost idyllic to speculate
on her having become a proselyte, and even the wife of Joshua, thereby
becoming the ancestress of prophets. To have praised her simply for her
acts of bravery might have been sufficient; to have conjectured she
became a proselyte added to her stature as an ideal person. To have
accorded all of these characteristics and qualities to a non-Israelite
female makes Rahab a biblical role model, a woman worthy of respect.

The educational resources presented a modified approach when depicting her, keeping in mind that young children might need a measure of protection when Rahab was described. The materials avoided any reference to the translation of *zônâ* as prostitute and defined the word as a seller of food. In other words, the spies went to her to get food and to be among others from whom they might learn if the men in Jericho were afraid of the Israelites. Her request of the spies to reciprocate and save her family was emphasized.

Perhaps more significance could have been laid on a non-*peshat* issue which is less likely to be presented in educational books, namely, Rahab's conversion and her subsequent lineage. Such information would reinforce a positive picture of her. Commentators stressed names of her descendants and it would be fruitful for this knowledge to be imparted to children. Not only did she successfully save her family, but she counted as her descendants many important individuals in Israel's history.

A summary of Rahab's personality may be seen in the following quote: 'When the spies left her, they told her how she would be safe from the Israelite soldiers when they would later march into Jericho. They said: "they will know that in this house lives a brave woman who helped Israel" ' (Samuels 1973: 4). On the basis of the educational materials, students will glean a narrower view of her than was presented in the Bible and in Jewish interpretation. Nevertheless, her heroism and self-sacrifice will surface and be remembered.

Part III
ON IDEOLOGY

TAMAR'S VEIL: IDEOLOGY AT THE ENTRANCE TO ENAIM

Jan William Tarlin

Genesis 38, the story of Judah and Tamar, is commonly cited in scholarly circles as a prime example of a Hebrew Bible text that can be both enjoyed and analyzed as a literary fiction. Indeed, Robert Alter made an analysis of this text the centerpiece of his now classic methodological polemic 'A Literary Approach to the Bible' (Alter 1981: 3-22). What has not been noted about Genesis 38, however, is that the sheer entertainment value, the sophisticated aesthetic pleasures, and the complex formal structures that can be read in it serve as ideological traps. These traps lure the reader into interpreting the text either as a seamless unity proclaiming the inevitability of patriarchy or as an equally tightly woven parable of the inevitable defeat of patriarchy by brave and clever women. The smoothness and coherence of both these readings constitute an ideological veil that obscures the messy, incoherent realities of patriarchy as lived, inhibiting the reader's ability to perceive and critique those realities, whether as they were in ancient Israel or as they are in a non-Israelite reader's own immediate context.

With the help of Slavoj Žižek's discourse on ideology (Žižek 1989 and especially 1994: 1-33), I will establish a wary distance from the inducements to holism that Genesis 38 provides and offer a reading that presents this text as a site of what Marc-Alain Ouaknin has called 'the "nonassemblage" of the unsynchronizable' (Ouaknin 1995: 169). By searching out the discontinuities in the seemingly smooth weave of the text, I will offer a glimpse of an exhilarating unpleasure that is simultaneously more uncanny and more politically productive than the pleasures provided by a totalizing interpretation (see Žižek 1989: 44-49, 68-84, 87-128). Rather than offering the satisfaction of viewing patriarchy as either a product of or an offense against a coherence inherent in human social relations, my reading of Genesis 38 will convey the eerie thrill of looking through the veil of ideology to discern patriarchy as an instance of the 'antagonism, splitting' that, paradoxically, both constitutes society and 'forever prevents its closure in a harmonious, transparent, rational Whole' (Žižek 1994: 22).

The crucial encounter between Judah and Tamar in Genesis 38 takes place at 'the entrance to Enaim' (38.14). David M. Gunn and Danna Nolan Fewell have noted that this place name, *petaḥ 'ênayim*, may also be translated as 'the opening of the eyes' (Gunn and Fewell 1993: 39). And, indeed, the encounter at the entrance to Enaim sets in motion a line of plot development that culminates in a classical 'recognition scene'. Yet, I want to suggest that some ironic interpretive questions are in order concerning whether the literary attractions of Genesis 38 open the reader's eyes to patriarchy as a tangle of antagonistic gender relations or whether, on the contrary, they seduce the reader into misrecognizing patriarchy as a rational system whose structure renders it either permanently fixed or intrinsically doomed. Only if these questions are asked and answered carefully can this text become an occasion for an opening of the reader's eyes to the uncanny territory beyond ideology.

At first glance, Genesis 38 might well seem to have deployed irony so thoroughly and precisely in the articulation of its own content, significance, and implications as to leave no foothold for ironic interpretive questioning. Tamar had been married to two of Judah's sons, Er and Onan. Er displeased Yahweh in some unspecified way and Yahweh killed him before he could produce a child with Tamar. Onan formally accepted the responsibilities of levirate marriage by taking Tamar as his wife but, disinclined to father children who would be reckoned as the offspring of his dead brother for purposes of descent and inheritance, he violated the primary obligation of such a marriage by 'spilling [his semen] on the ground' (Gen. 38.9) rather than allowing Tamar the possibility of pregnancy. When Yahweh punished Onan by death, Judah assumed that some lethal fault in Tamar was responsible for the tragedies inflicted on his family, and consequently withheld his third, and last, son, Shelah, from her on the pretext that the boy was too young for marriage. Tamar was to wait as a childless widow in her father's house until Shelah reached marriageable age: a wait that Judah intended to be endless.

Enough time passed to allow Tamar to see through Judah's ruse. One day she heard that the recently widowed Judah would be passing nearby. Tamar removed her widow's clothing, veiled herself, and sat by the road at the entrance to Enaim waiting for Judah.

Judah understood the veiled woman he saw at the roadside to be a 'wild woman' issuing a sexual invitation; he responded by soliciting sex from her. She asked him what he was prepared to pay, and he promised a kid goat from his flock. Since the kid was not presently available, the woman demanded Judah's seal, cord, and staff—in Robert Alter's words, 'a kind of ancient Near Eastern equivalent of all a person's major credit cards' (Alter 1981: 9)—as a pledge. Judah agreed; they had sex; he left; she conceived.

Judah sent a friend, Hirah the Adullamite, back to Enaim with the kid to retrieve his valuables. The Adullamite made discreet inquiries to try to locate the woman, but to no avail. Judah decided to let well enough alone, resigned himself to the loss of his personal effects, and hoped he had heard the last of the incident.

Three months later, Judah was informed that his daughter-in-law had 'been a wild woman' (Gen. 38.24) and, moreover, had become pregnant as a result of her 'wildness'. (For an explanation of these admittedly experimental translations see below.) He demanded that she be burned alive publicly for her transgression. As she was being led to her execution, Tamar produced Judah's seal, cord, and staff, and demanded that he identify their owner. Judah recognized not only his effects and the true identity of the 'wild woman' that he had encountered, but also the fact that his daughter-in-law's 'wildness' had done more to preserve and perpetuate Israelite patriarchal values than had his own ungainly and foolish pursuit of patriarchal privileges. Tamar was granted her life; Judah had no further sexual relations with her; and she became the mother of twin boys, one of whom, Perez, was a direct ancestor of King David.

To the naked eye, then, Genesis 38 can appear as an elegantly ironic tale in which a canny and courageous woman risks dishonor and death to uphold the value system of Israelite patriarchy when the patriarchs most concerned have proved incapable of doing so. Judah recognizes both his own failure and Tamar's righteousness and bravery. Yahweh recognizes Tamar's superlative virtue by giving her not one son but two, and making one of them a link in one of Israel's most important patriarchal lineages. All's well that ends well.

Or, alternatively:

Genesis 38 can easily appear to the naked eye as an elegantly ironic tale in which a canny and courageous woman risks death and dishonor to expose the foolishness and fragility of Israelite patriarchy even while appearing to perpetuate it. The knowing reader recognizes what neither Judah nor Yahweh seem able to: namely, that a system that can be so effectively manipulated by those who it purports to subjugate is ultimately doomed. It isn't over 'til it's over; change is gonna come.

Yet it is precisely the kind of recognition produced by these readings of Genesis 38 that, in Žižek's view, demands a very careful second look. According to Žižek an act of recognition that conveys a vision of social reality so elegant, complex, and coherent that it appears capable of weaving any amount of irony, audacity, failure, or direct assault into its own smooth texture, is, in fact, an act of misrecognition *par excellence*. Such visions, according to Žižek, misrecognize the fundamentally conflictual, contradictory, and irrational character of social reality, distorting it so that it appears to be a unified ensemble of coherent and rational systems. A discourse that induces this form of faulty vision is precisely what Žižek means by an ideology (1989: 28-33; 1994: 1-7). In the light of this definition, it becomes clear that the two readings of Genesis 38 sketched above are equally ideological.

Now, Žižek never argues that ideology is dispensable; he is quite clear that any attempt to live continuously in the brute reality of society without ideology's illusions would lead to individual madness and communal catastrophe (1989: 161-73; 1994: 4-7). However, Žižek is equally clear that effective politics is only possible through the cultivation of the ability to see through the ideological veil to the abyss in and around which it is woven, where, after all, the real affects of political action are registered (1989: 71-84; 1994: 17-18). Such cultivation can best be pursued through learning how to ask and answer ironic interpretive questions that expose the holes and tears in discourses that the quest for aesthetic pleasure would lead us to view as flawless unities.

Illustrating Žižek's oft-repeated principle that the only secret any surface hides is the fact there are no depths under it in which anything might be concealed (see, for example, Žižek 1989: 28-29), all the material needed to frame the questions that will reveal the gaps in the fabric of Genesis 38 is in plain view on the face of the text. For example, the action at the entrance to Enaim, the place of the opening of the eyes, is entirely controlled by the way that the veil that separates Tamar and Judah distorts both her perception of herself and his perception of her. She cannot see beyond it; he cannot see through it. The veil constrains both Tamar's presentation of herself to Judah and what Judah makes of that self-presentation. The question invited by the text but discouraged by ideological readings of it is: 'What quality of recognition is likely to result from this kind of opening of the eyes?'

What kind of vision does the veil induce at the entrance to Enaim? The standard answer to this question is that Tamar's veil is the medium through which she manipulates a spectacle in which Judah is unknowingly seduced into playing the role demanded of him by Israelite patriarchy: provider of offspring for his dead sons. In this reading the veil is understood to be the uniform of a professional prostitute and Tamar's use of it an act of deliberate, clever, audacious disguise. However, bearing in mind Žižek's insight that ideologies are produced and maintained by things that we do that are not of our doing (Žižek 1989: 30-33, 36-43), it is possible to discern that rather than being the manipulator of the veil, and through it of Judah and of their entire interaction, Tamar is actually manipulated by the veil (see Žižek 1989: 33-35 on things as agents of ideology).

Fewell and Gunn have provided the basis for such a reading by showing that *ṣā'îp*, the Hebrew word for 'veil' used in Gen. 38.14 and 38.19, is never used elsewhere in the Hebrew Bible in connection with prostitutes; in fact, they point out, its only other use is in connection with a bride: Rebekah veiling herself before first meeting Isaac in Gen. 24.65 (Fewell and Gunn 1993: 87-89). According to Fewell and Gunn, then, Tamar presents herself to Judah as a bride to remind him of his obligation to provide her with a husband from his family to raise up children for his dead sons. However, since Judah has repressed all consciousness of such an obligation, he simply sees an anonymous woman at a public roadside without a male escort as a woman announcing her sexual availability.

An extension of Fewell and Gunn's reading yields an intricate set of variations on Tamar's identity played upon her by the veil. That full set of variations is as follows:

Tamar presents herself to Judah as a bride having claims upon his lineage under the norms of Israelite patriarchy; Judah sees something quite different. Genesis 38.15 says that 'Judah saw her and thought her to be a *zônâ* because her face was covered'. Having rejected the sense of obligation that would have sensitized him to the symbolism of Tamar's gesture, unable to recognize her as his daughter-in-law because her facial features are obscured, Judah sees only her anonymity and her unattached condition. Any woman who would present herself in such a state, he reasons, must be a *zônâ* (38.15).

Zônâ is usually translated as prostitute or whore, but in the light of Phyllis Bird's ground-breaking essay, ' "To Play The Harlot" ' (Bird 1997: 219-36) other translations become possible. Bird has convincingly demonstrated that the verbal forms of the Hebrew root *znh,* from which the noun *zônâ* also derives, cover a wide range of behaviors that have as their common denominator the fact that those who engage in them have refused to submit their persons and/or sexuality to the norms of Israelite patriarchy. Moreover, Bird shows that even when these verbs are masculine in form they retain a 'female orientation' (Bird 1997: 236); the men whose actions they describe are being compared to misbehaving women. Bird herself maintains a strict separation between the wide range of meanings available for the verbal forms of *znh* and the univocal meaning that she attributes to what she construes as the 'professional noun' *zônâ*: a prostitute for hire (Bird 1997: 236). Yet it is hard to see why this separation is required, particularly since Bird is willing to go so far as to argue that *'ēset zᵉnûnîm* in Hos. 1.2 describes 'a woman of loose sexual morals', not a professional prostitute (Bird 1997: 226). Therefore, building on Bird's work, I experimentally translate *zônâ* in Gen. 38.15 colloquially as 'wild woman' (and, for the same reasons, I translate *zānᵉtâ* and *zᵉnûnîm* in 38.24 as 'been a wild woman' and 'wildness' respectively).

That Judah does not necessarily see the woman before him as a professional prostitute is confirmed by the fact that he does not approach her with a business proposition, but with an unadorned sexual request *hābâ nā ' 'abô' ēlayik*—'permit me to come (in) to you'. Tamar, choosing from among the options offered her by her newly established identity as a wild woman picks the one that gives her the most power in this situation: she becomes a prostitute by demanding payment or pledge of payment in exchange for fulfilling Judah's request.

The pledge that Tamar extracts from her father-in-law (his seal, cord, and staff) enables Judah to construct one final variation on her identity in the climactic recognition scene that occurs three months after their encounter at the entrance to Enaim. When Tamar saves her life by producing Judah's pledge, he perceives that the illicitly pregnant woman holding his tokens of patriarchal identity, authority and value deserves them more than he does. She has succeeded in upholding the structure of Israelite patriarchy where he and his sons have failed miserably to do so. To use Žižek's vocabulary, borrowed via Jacques Lacan from Freud, Judah perceives Tamar to have a bigger, better, and more effective phallus than his own (Žižek 1989: 222-24). It is important to note here that in this Freudian and Neo-Freudian vocabulary the phallus is not the penis but, rather, the penis-like signifier of wholeness, coherence and power (see Lacan 1977: 281-91), here materialized by the ensemble of staff, seal, and cord. In this final variation on Tamar's identity, then, she becomes quite literally a phallic mother, and the climactic recognition scene of Genesis 38 becomes a classic case of the phenomenon of fetishistic misrecognition described by Freud (Freud 1953: 152-57). How did this happen? What kind of vision has Tamar's veil induced?

By donning the veil at the entrance to Enaim, Tamar set in motion a series of transformations that reconfigured her from abandoned widowed daughter-in-law, to bride, to wild woman, to prostitute, to phallic mother. In short, Tamar's veil turns her into what Žižek calls a spectre: an obscenely enjoyable fantasy object that gives the illusion of holding together an ideological fabric at precisely the point where there is a gap in it that no amount of weaving over will close (Žižek 1994: 15-30). Whether the ideology in question is patriarchal or anti-patriarchal the name of the spectre that appears to hold it together at its weakest point is 'woman'. Her ghostly faces are the ones through which Tamar must be misrecognized to secure her existence in an ideological discourse.

Yet there is also another aspect to Žižek's spectre in addition to the one that supplies illusory cover for the hole in the ideological fabric. This second aspect disappears into the hole, and in so doing sends a tremor through the fabric, momentarily materializing the negative space woven into it (Žižek 1994: 22-23). The embodiment of this second aspect of the spectre 'woman' in Genesis 38 might be called the vanishing *qᵉdēšâ*, and, ironically, she is produced precisely by a patriarchal discourse that attempts to put the best, most euphemistic, possible face on Judah's misadventure at the entrance to Enaim.

As both Gunn and Fewell (1993: 40-41) and Alter (1981: 9) have noted, there is a slippage in the words used to describe the woman to whom Judah tries to send the kid from his flock in order to redeem his pledged items. In Gen. 38.20 the narrator says that Judah sends his friend the Adullamite to redeem his pledge from *hā 'iššâ*, the woman, not the *zônâ*. In 38.21, when the friend actually speaks to the people in the area around Enaim, he raises euphemism to the level of the honorific by asking not for a *zônâ* or an *'iššâ*, but for a *qᵉdēšâ*: an ambiguous word that literally means holy woman, but may also mean sanctuary woman, or temple prostitute (see Bird 1997: 206-208, 233-35; also Oden 1987: 131-53). This figure has been formed from the creative, face-saving, patriarchal refiguration of an abandoned widowed daughter-in-law whose veil has turned her into a spectral prostitute. The people of Enaim quite rightly respond that no such person exists.

Yet her image with its traces of the sacred, the sexy, and the uncanny lingers on. This mysterious figure is not illicitly pregnant. She will not have to produce Judah's seal, cord and staff to save her life. She will not have to produce heirs for her dead husbands and ancestors for King David to secure her existence. She is just gone, and she has taken both the external material supports of Judah's patriarchal identity, authority, and value and all ideological certainties about patriarchy's inevitable downfall with her.

The vanishing $q^e d\bar{e}\check{s}\bar{a}$ sends only the slightest tremor through the story world of Genesis 38. No one will ever think of her again after pregnant, spectre-haunted Tamar turns up with Judah's pledged items. Yet the reader who ponders the $q^e d\bar{e}\check{s}\bar{a}$'s vanishing will be reminded that she made her exit through a hole that is a permanent feature of any ideological reading of this text. The hole does not exist as result of the systemic inadequacy of patriarchy or as function of the contingent errors made by a specific set of fallible characters in materializing the structures of a fundamentally sound patriarchal system. Rather this reader would see that the hole exists as the place from which all the figures in the fabric emerge and to which they return.

All these figures—men, women, and spectres are created just as the $q^e d\bar{e}\check{s}\bar{a}$ was: out of pure negativity, the irresolvable antagonism that is the substance of our social existence before we begin the impossible but necessary attempt to weave it into a unified, coherent, rational fabric. Both Žižek's discourse on ideology and the vanishing $q^e d\bar{e}\check{s}\bar{a}$ of Genesis 38, therefore, point us toward the conclusion that the unpleasurable, uncanny world of the spectre is a more promising site for constructing politically progressive readings of the Bible than is the ideological world of aesthetically pleasing heroines and heroes who will seduce and abandon us.

HYSTERICAL PHALLI: NUMBERS 16, TWO CONTEMPORARY PARALLELS, AND THE LOGIC OF COLONIZATION

Erin Runions

This paper began as I was being arrested. I was sitting on the floor, half under a table, crowded and tense, with 70 other students. Riot squad surrounded us, their hefty batons thudding, fondly, into leather gloves to the menacingly irregular beat of intent police dogs fretting somewhere out of sight. Our offense was an act of civil disobedience in protest at the ongoing demolition of social programs (including education) under the seemingly invincible wheels of corporate globalization. We were occupying the offices of le Conseil du patronat du Québec, a very influential right-wing business lobby group in Quebec, a group that has constantly lobbied for business interests, to the explicit detriment of the poor. We had blockaded ourselves inside for 12 hours before the police burst through a wall into the office complex. They came in with over 20 riot squad and (as it turned out, only) one dog, herding us all into two rooms to subdue us there. As we sat and chanted slogans or tried to debate, a police officer came in periodically and pointed with a big gloved hand at the person he wanted next. As I looked up at the enormous, dare I say phallic, finger pointing down at us, I faded into a slow-motion academic moment, thinking, 'Hmm, what does it mean to resist interpellation, to resist the "Hey you!" of Althusser's metaphoric police officer?'[1] Then coming out of that moment the phallic finger pointed at me, and when like others, I refused the interpellation, I was dragged off and submitted to violent physical and verbal treatment.

After this encounter, and after learning more of police brutality through other community involvements, I began to consider the relation

1.   I am referring here to the theory of Marxist critic Louis Althusser that human subjectivity is formed in response to the 'hey you' of ideology. Althusser likens the hailing of ideology to the 'hey you' of a police officer to which a person responds as 'you' and turns around, as if guilty (Althusser 1984: 48-49).

between violence and resistance to ideological interpellation. I concluded with the fairly straightforward observation that resistance to dominant ideology consistently provokes excessive violence,[2] but the why and how of the *excess* were less self-evident. After some consideration, I found that Slavoj Žižek's Lacanian reformulation of Althusser's ideological interpellation provided the framework I needed to think through the more complex details of this process. In this paper then, I would like to use Žižek's work to explore the relation between violence and resistance to ideological interpellation, with reference to the biblical story of 'Korah's rebellion' in Numbers 16,[3] and to two contemporary accounts of resistance to colonization. These are: one, the Royal Canadian Mounted Police's brutal siege and attack on 18 aboriginal traditionalists on their sundance grounds in 'British Columbia', and two, the violence and intimidation used by police in response to an action in Montreal protesting the Multilateral Agreement on Investment (MAI). My purpose is to show that the logic of the violence in Numbers 16 toward 'rebellion' on the verge of the colonization of Canaan also

2.   For instance, about a week after the student occupation, several Montreal activists were arrested in their homes without warrants and held for over 24 hours in isolation. This was just extra harassment for them, as they had already been arrested and charged for the symbolic action of stealing food from an expensive hotel buffet and taking it outside to eat on the street.

Since then, police brutality at demonstrations in Montreal has become more and more intense, particularly if the demonstrations pass by, or stop in front of the American consulate. During the bombing in Iraq and Kosovo, it seemed the Montreal police force had been employed to tame anti-American dissent of any kind at a time when American patriotism, even in Québec, was crucial. For example, at a demonstration outside the US consulate protesting the impending execution of the innocent former Black Panther member Mumia Abu-Jamal, riot cops in full riot gear surrounded the crowd without warning, seizing placards and signs and ripping them up (see Runions and Williams 1999). In this incident several demonstrators were roughed up, and one was arrested, then charged with 'assaulting' a police officer after he finally pushed away an undercover police officer who had repeatedly elbowed him without cause, and held in prison for 24 hours.

In addition, the mistreatment of activists in Canada by police has become an object of a fair amount of media attention over the last year with what has come to be known as sprAyPEC (the indiscriminate use of pepper spray at close range and without warning to dislodge protesters from eyesight or earshot of Indonesian dictator Suharto at the 1997 Asia Pacific Economic Conference in Vancouver).

3.   For Žižek and readings of other biblical texts see Boer 1999, forthcoming a, forthcoming b.

operates in these two current instances of resistance to the interpellation of colonization. Without going as far as making the argument that this story in particular is *causal* for contemporary responses to colonial ideology[4] I would like to point out that the ideological operation provoking violence is remarkably similar in all three accounts. This observation is at the very least interesting, and perhaps also significant, given

---

4.   Such an argument would require tracing the history of interpretation for Numbers 16, which would be an extremely interesting project, but beyond the scope of this paper. Of course the story is mentioned in both testaments as a deterrent for disloyalty (Deut. 11.6; Ps. 106.16-18, Jude 11). The story was also used at Qumran, as evidenced in 4Q423 5 (see Scott forthcoming). James Scott argues that the story may be used to condemn leaders within the Qumran community who spoke out against the Teacher of Righteousness. For other uses of the story in early Jewish and Christian writing, see Scott (forthcoming: n. 36). Later in the early period of the Christian tradition, Gregory of Nyssa, in his *Life of Moses*, relates Moses' conflict with the Levites to his own conflict with some of his followers (Olson 1996: 100). The story is still used to today to fortify leadership. In the preliminaries to this paper, I did a web search—prompted by David Gunn's recent look at the politics of Zion on the web (Gunn 1999)—to get a sense of how the story is used politically today. It seems often to be used to forestall 'backsliding' (e.g. 'Christian Newsletter of Bible Believers Fellowship: Cain, Balaam, and Korah', where the story is an exhortation to prisoners not to backslide). The story is also used frequently to speak about church government (e.g. 'Avoiding Congregational Gangrene'), and as a support for capital punishment (see: 'Probe Ministries: Capital Punishment').

Most interesting of these websites (and I did not get through all 324 hits on the 'Rebellion of Korah') was the website, 'On Doctrine, Correction, and Getting Along', a website with an address curiously symptomatic of the kinds of colonial undertones both in the story and in its possible applications. The text on this website expectedly invokes Korah as an example of doctrinal heresy, but it also contains the following frightening 'example [of right doctrine] from history' lumping colonialism, sexism and capitalism all in together: *'When the Puritans set out to establish a new nation, a city set on a hill, men and women alike sailed off to live their faith and to take dominion in a new world.* Some of these women no doubt had harsh parents, were not given the same opportunities as their husbands and brothers, and experienced great hardship. Imagine their starvation, or giving birth on the sea or in the wilderness, or holding dying children in their arms. Did these women invoke the psychological ghosts of an imperfect abusive past, or the injustice of it all? Or were they so grounded in victorious (postmillennial, Calvinistic) eschatology, *convinced that they were instruments of dominion*, part of Christ's specific purposes to advance His kingdom on the earth (before His return), that they forged ahead with gratitude? Journals show that the latter case is true' (emphasis mine).

that the Bible has been used as tool of colonization, and that the narrative of the promised land has authorized more than one conquest.

Figure 1. Protester being arrested in Opération SalAMI, video still, permission of Me Myself und I Productions, Montreal.

I will suggest that for each of these stories the having or not having of land and resources generates an antagonism which is overlooked in the official records by an appeal to a higher order (Yahweh's will, property rights, *la loi*)—an antagonism which the ideological master signifiers (Moses, 'crown land' and capitalism) try to mediate. However, the violence incurred when these ideological master signifiers are not successful in interpellating protesters can be read as a result of a set of complex relations taking place in what Žižek calls the 'realm beyond interpellation': in refusing to be interpellated by the master signifiers (Moses, 'crown land', and capitalism) protesters *recognize* these master signifiers as symptoms of the social order, symptoms which stand in for a central lack or antagonism. The recognition of these master signifiers as symptoms has the effect of putting into question another set of master signifiers (holiness, justice, and democracy) with which protesters *have been* interpellated and which motivate their protest. And finally, this questioning results in what I will call the hysterical phallus, that is, the ugly irruption of the Real, uncontrollable *jouissance*, or, in simple terms, violence. With the last of these arguments, I take a playful turn—guided by these stories—away from some of the more misogynist notions Žižek builds on (many of them inherited from Lacan): the hysterical woman, the unifying phallus, the vagina as wound, 'lack' as the (feminine) object of desire.

Repression in the Paran Desert

Numbers 16 has come to be a classic tale of dissidence crushed, with Korah figuring as 'an archetypal heretic' (Wenham 1981: 134). In this story, Korah the Levite along with Reubenites Dathan, Abiram, and On accuse Moses and Aaron of setting themselves up as exclusively holy amongst the people of Israel, arguing instead that all the people of the assembly should be recognized as holy. Moses responds by telling them to appear before Yahweh the next day, with their fire censors so that Yahweh might demonstrate to the assembly who was truly holy. Moses then calls a meeting with Dathan and Abiram, but they refuse to meet with him saying, 'We will not go. Is it too little that you have brought us up from the land of milk and honey to die in the desert, that you must set yourself up over us as a prince?' (Num. 16.13-14). With this response first Moses becomes furious, asking Yahweh not to pay any attention to their smoke offerings the next day, and then Yahweh becomes furious. Moses again commands Korah to assemble the people the next day with their smoke offerings, Yahweh threatens to destroy the whole assembly, and Moses negotiates the destruction of only the leading rebellious parties. When the contest with divine wrath finally takes place, Korah, Dathan and Abiram (On is not mentioned after Num. 16.1) are swallowed up by an earthquake, with their whole families and all of their possessions descending to Sheol as a demonstration of Moses' holiness (although the text leaves some question as to whether Korah is swallowed up with the rest of them, since only his tent and his men are mentioned).[5] Their 250 followers, offering incense, are burned up in a fire coming from Yahweh. Here too the violence is excessive. The rebels are consumed by an earthquake *and* a fire, when surely one would do.

---

5. Milgrom uses this discrepancy as a means of sorting out the various recensions of the text (1990: 414-19), suggesting that the 'tent of Yahweh' (the tabernacle) becomes the 'tents of Korah, Dathan and Abiram' in a late recension in order to associate Korah with Dathan and Abiram.

In trying to understand perturbing details like the doubled work of earthquake and fire, and whether Korah died in the earthquake or fire, many scholars have concluded that this story is a composite text (Noth 1968: 121-31; Coats 1968: 174-84; Milgrom 1990: 414-20; Wenham 1981: 141-42; Snaith 1967: 255; Levine 1993: 54-55, 405; Budd 1984: 184) dealing with two issues, land and cultic practice (Levine 1993: 412, 418; Budd 1984: 189-91; Magonet 1982: 6-9). Because the story follows another rebellion (Num. 13–14) in which the people do not want to take possession of the land of Canaan—nearly stoning Caleb and Joshua for their recommendation to do so—it has been argued that the original issue in this story was controversy over the conquest of Canaan. Further, it has been suggested (Levine 1993: 424-25; Budd 1984: 191) that for the Reubenites, Dathan and Abiram, the bone of contention was Moses' insistence that the Reubenites cross the Jordan to fight along with the rest of the tribes of Israel (Num. 32), even though their land was allocated east of the Jordan (Josh. 13.14-23).[6] This is considered to be an earlier strand of the tradition, which is later merged into a story about cultic and Levitical authority, a story which occludes the original settlement issue. It has been suggested that in this later story the question of cultic leadership is twofold: Korah, as noticed by the Rabbis, was Aaron's first cousin, and may have been slighted when his (hierarchically) younger cousin Elizaphan (Korah's father's younger brother's son) was chosen over him to be the prince of his clan (Magonet 1982: 5, 24: Milgrom 1990: 130). Further, the Korahites, it seems from archaeological and textual evidence,[7] were skilled in cultic arts, making Moses' proclamation of Aaron's unique status all the more insulting (Levine 1993: 430).

While my concern is not to understand the textual, source or tradition history of this passage, I would like to frame the issues raised by the hypothesis of a composite text in slightly different terms. First, the

6. That land is an underlying issue in this story is perhaps corroborated by, or carried on in, the Qumran tradition with the reference to Korah in what seems to be a farming manual, or a wisdom book that makes extensive use of the farming metaphor (see Scott forthcoming).

7. Textual evidence is found in 1 Chron. 6; and also in the superscriptions on Pss. 42; 44–49; 84; 85; 87; 88 attributing them to the sons of Korah. Levine notes archaeological evidence for the Korahites' cultic skill is found at Arad. There archaeologists found an eighth-century BCE jar base which listed names of cultic personnel including the Korahites (Levine 1993: 429).

connection through the Reubenites of this story to the issue of land settlement, along with the story's placement in the book, following the rejected reconnaissance mission, at the very least places this kind of divine disciplinary action for rebellion alongside, if not at the heart of, the colonial impulse. The violent punishment insures Moses against further rebellion, during the colonization process, or at least it tries. In addition, it is interesting that if conflict over colonization is an issue, even the central issue, it is nowhere given in this story. If the composite text hypothesis is accepted, the issue of holiness comes to replace, or stand in for the conflict over settlement, and this I will argue fits with Žižek's understanding of *objet petit a*—a fantasy that stands in for, and smoothes over a fundamental social antagonism. Lastly, if colonization is an underlying issue in this story, then the excess violence (fire and earthquake) is doubly so, because in Numbers 14 Israel has already been violently punished through defeat in battle, for rebelling against colonization and not conforming to Yahweh's plan of conquest (Num. 14.36-45). For me the troubling issue in the doubled (tripled) instance of divine wrath (military defeat, earthquake and fire) is not a question of source, but of excess, especially because the excess is specifically related to resistance. All of these issues raised by the suggestion that this story contains a less obvious strand contesting 'settlement policy', correspond with the way I read Žižek, but before turning to his work, I would like to look at two other stories of excess violence in response to refused interpellation in the context of colonization.

RCMP Siege at Gustafsen Lake

During the time of my own unpleasant encounters with the police, I became aware of a vastly more violent police operation that took place from August 19 to September 17, 1995, on the other side of Canada, in Northern British Columbia at Gustafsen Lake.[8] There the Royal Canadian Mounted Police (RCMP) surrounded 18 aboriginal traditionalists preparing for their annual sundance. The RCMP moved in 400 police with 'dog teams, airplanes, helicopters, Armoured Personel Carriers, grenades, landmines, M16 and C7 assault rifles, hollow point bullets—prohibited by the Geneva Convention—and fifty-calibre machine guns' (ABC 1997: 5).

---

8.   For a range of material on the RCMP siege at Gustafsen lake, from Ts'Peten Defenders' account of the events, to mainstream media reports to a record of court proceedings, see: 'Ts'Peten (Gustafsen Lake) Standoff'.

Figure 2.   Police tank at Gustafsen Lake, video still M. Brown,
permission of John Splitting the Sky Hill.

The reason for this excess, this barrage of artillery? The traditionalists, now known as the Ts'Peten Defenders, were camping out on unceded territory, which had been claimed as 'crown land', and which was being leased out to an American rancher (though court testimonies showed that it was not certain the land they were camping on was included in his lease). Earlier in the year some of those among this group had had their lawyer, Bruce Clark, petition the queen of England (who is still the queen of Canada) to convene a long disused 'special constitutional court in Britain mandated to hear…disputes between indigenous nations and the colonies' (ABC 1997: 6). The aboriginal people making the petition were confident that this British court would recognize that no treaty had ever been signed for this land, nor indeed for much of the land in British Columbia, and that it was therefore rightfully aboriginal peoples' land.[9] The queen however, responded to their petition by dis-

9.   Their confidence in the monarch was based on two things: first, the queen's administrative obligation under the British constitution to convene this court; and second, more historically, a 1763 proclamation by King George III recognizing 'right of aboriginal peoples to maintain control of their territories unmolested and

missing her constitutional duty on the grounds of 'political convention' saying that it was not her practice to meddle in the affairs of the colonies (Dr Bruce Clark, in Brown 1997).

It was later that year that the RCMP put into violent action what their own records called, 'giving the Natives stress out there' (ABC 1997: 7). 'Deception at Gustafsen Lake' The 'crisis' began when the RCMP escorted a local rancher and a number of ranch hands with rifles to the camp. As they delivered a hand-written eviction notice, one of the ranchers cracked a bullwhip and threatened, 'to string up some red niggers'. About a month later six men, who were later revealed to be RCMP, in camouflage, with assault rifles, were seen creeping up on the camp, so a warning shot was fired from the camp (ABC 1997: 7). This warning shot justified the RCMP's siege. During the month that followed more than 400 RCMP officers were deployed to 'secure' the area. The aboriginal defenders refused to leave, arguing that they had a right to the land, and to the sundance grounds; they did not however aggress the police encircling them. Conversely, they endured continual provocation by the RCMP, including numerous shots into agreed safe zones, and accusations of aggression. When the defenders finally agreed to leave the camp, because the danger of police violence was escalating, they were all arrested and charged with attempted murder and mischief endangering lives.

Interestingly, from the start of the siege till the finish of the trial, government and legal officials[10] denied the land issue as a cause for the siege, arguing instead that the issue was one of terrorism and lawlessness. The siege was wholeheartedly supported by the ('progressive' New Democratic Party) provincial government at the time, with the hopes of winning support for being tough with terrorists. The media coverage for the 'crisis' corroborated this point of view, portraying the defenders as fringe, fanatical, and terrorists, though as court testimonies

undisturbed, within the protection of the British Crown' (Splitting the Sky Hill, in Brown 1997).

10. In the trial too, the crown lawyer and judge argued that this was not a land claims issue, in spite of the defenders statements to the contrary (see: Cernetig 1997; Canadian Press 1997). British Columbia attorney general Ujjal Dosanjh, made the same argument at the start of the crisis: 'Gustafsen Lake has nothing to do with aboriginal land-claim issues. It's purely to do with the weapons there and the shots that have been fired' (Hume 1995).

revealed, this was engineered by the RCMP in what they called a 'smear and misinformation campaign', made up of fabricated shootings and aggressions from the camp. Their campaign was successful, as evidenced by the following national newspaper report of the trial:

'[I]t was camp occupants who introduced weapons and violence to the standoff at Gustafsen Lake,' [Judge Josephson] wrote. 'It was that, not an act of trespass that required a massive response by police which strained their resources to the limit.' The sentencing ends a 10-month trial that followed the occupation of ranch land in the BC Interior by a small, fringe group of natives and their supporters. Claiming the land was sacred and had never been ceded to the Crown, members of the group fired at police who tried to remove them.

The RCMP spent 5.5 million and brought in more than 400 officers to bring the protesters to justice. It was the largest such operation in RCMP history (Cernetig 1997).

This report, oblivious, it would seem, to the perverse irony here, indicates that the chief contention in the eyes of the justice system and the media was the right of the crown and its tenants to property, free of harassment or violence.

The police offensive, with all its gross injustices, was thoroughly documented by RCMP testimony in the ensuing court case and by the RCMP's own video tapes, including 24 hour overhead surveillance tapes. Yet, in spite of all the clear evidence against the RCMP, after a year-long trial (July 1996–July 1997), the court found the defenders guilty. In a shocking display of the racism within the legal system, the judge 'prohibited the jury from considering all the major pillars of the defense… He took an unheard of 4 days to instruct the jury before they retired, telling them which testimony they could consider and insisting repeatedly that they had to accept the law as he explained it to them without question' (ABC 1997: 8).

Les maudits flics à Montréal

The final account of forceful suppression of dissidence that I would like to treat took place in Montreal when over 100 activists blockaded the beginning of a meeting of the Organization of Economic Cooperation and Development (OECD) being held in a downtown hotel. Like the student occupation in which I was arrested four months before, this civil disobedience was in protest of the MAI, the Multilateral Agreement on Investment,[11] an international free-trade deal, which the OECD had been trying to negotiate for several years, behind closed doors, without public consultation or awareness. If ratified, the MAI would establish a new set of legally binding rules for investment, granting transnational corporations the unrestricted 'right' to buy, sell, and move their operations whenever and wherever they want around the world, unfettered by government regulation. It would curtail nations' abilities to regulate investors or the behaviour of corporations within their borders. Regulations such as environmental standards, labour standards, or cultural protection laws would be considered to violate the 'right-to-profit' granted by the MAI, and companies could sue governments for enforcing standards or regulations (Anonymous 1998).[12]

The blockade of the OECD conference was called Opération salAMI, a play on AMI, the French acronym for the MAI, and the adjective *sale*, meaning dirty, nasty, or low. The action was a planned non-violent civil disobedience, whereby protesters physically blocked the doors and did not move when asked. The police, reacting violently, first verbally threatened pain (*ça va faire mal!*), and then removed protesters, seizing them by the neck, jaw or between the eyes. One protester was taken to hospital with a (fortunately temporarily) paralyzed jaw, several were bloodied up. Those arrested were detained in prison for up to 28 hours (four hours over the legal 24-hour limit), enduring very cramped and cold quarters, insults and intimidation tactics by police officers.[13]

11. The demands for the student occupation were twofold: (1) to the Québec government that education be free for students; and (2) to the Canadian government that the negotiation of the MAI become accountable to the public. With these demands and this action, we were focusing on the links between big business lobbies, free trade deals like the MAI, and the decimation of social programs.

12. The MAI was due to be signed in May 1998 (which is when the civil disobedience action took place), but owing to pressure from the European Union and public protest, negotiations were delayed. In October of 1998, France pulled out of MAI negotiations entirely, effectively killing it for the time; however it is not dead yet: an MAI clone is currently being discussed in the World Trade Organization, alternately called the TEP (Transatlantic Economic Partnership) or TAFTA (Transatlantic Free Trade Agreement). There is a fair amount of resistance to, and concern over, this new manifestation of the MAI, especially in less economically powerful southern countries.

13. For a range of mainstream media accounts of the protest see: Sweet and Cherry (1998); Canadian Press (1998); Alarie (1998).

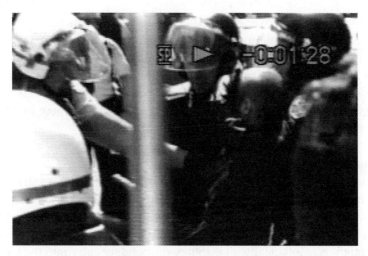

Figure 3. Point de pression, Opération SalAMI, video still,
permission of Me Myself und I Productions, Montreal.

Protesters were charged, convicted, criminalized on four counts, the
constitutionally granted freedom to protest in 'Canada' notwithstand-
ing: troubling the peace, mischief (criminal code), obstructing the work
of an officer of 'the peace', and unlawful assembly. In the trial, the
defendants pleaded a 'defense of necessity', arguing that this was the
only recourse left to them, having already tried letters, popular education, other protests etc. The judge threw out the defense of necessity,
ruling that the threat posed by *le mal appréhendé* was not 'immediate
or direct' (La Reine c. Bouchard 1999: 26). His judgment turned around
his worry, which he articulated several times and through recourse to
other judgments and opinions about civil disobedience (including Martin Luther King Jr) that such a ruling would lead to 'anarchy' (in his
terms, complete inability to enforce the laws of the land), apparently
overlooking the very same 'anarchy' (in his terms) that the MAI would
produce (La Reine c. Bouchard 1999: 24-27).

Here too the issue at stake was not acknowledged by the judge in any
serious way. In the 38-page judgment, l'AMI is mentioned a mere five
times by name (two or three more times as *ce traité*), and these mainly
in the summary of the facts, prior to the judgment per se (La Reine c.
Bouchard 1999: 5-6). In the judge's five-page consideration of the
defense of necessity—the protesters' major pillar of defense—the name
of *le mal* they were obliged to protest (l'AMI) is only given twice,
whereas the term *la loi*, in its general sense (i.e. not referring to a

specific law) occurs over twelve times (La Reine c. Bouchard 1999: 23-27). This scarce mention of the MAI is significant, given that the action was in protest of the MAI, that the eight-day trial was a 'political trial' which attempted to put the MAI itself on the stand, and that two full days of the trial were devoted to expert witnesses on the MAI. As might be expected, for the judge, the primacy of *la loi* was far more important that the political import and necessity of the action.

Parallels
These contemporary events have (at least) three things immediately in common with Numbers 16. First they deal in some way or another with colonialism, and resistance to it. As already mentioned, the story Korah, Abiram and Dathan takes place on the verge of colonization, and might possibly deal with disputes surrounding entry into the land of Canaan. The events at Gustafsen Lake, too, take place as a result of continued disputes over land settlements and treaties in 'Canada'. And the MAI too can be seen as a new kind of colonialism, with corporations, rather than nations vying for control of yet uncharted (and if they have their way, unregulated) resources.[14]

Second, in the public records of these events (Bible, media, legal proceedings), the specific issue generating the antagonism—i.e. the having or not having of land and resources—is either not made directly present, or denied. Korah, Dathan and Abiram are portrayed as rebels, angry with Moses and Aaron for setting themselves as uniquely holy, but there is no mention of land in the story. The aboriginal peoples are portrayed as renegade terrorists in media reports and by government and legal officials; the land issue is denied. The protesters of the MAI are portrayed as those advocating lawlessness, and the judge refuses to acknowledge the issue at the heart of the MAI which provoked the protest, focusing instead on the primacy of the law. In all three cases then, an appeal to the ideals of a higher order (Yahweh's will, right to property unharassed, *la loi*), and an accusation that this order has been breached obscure the very concrete issues at stake (the having or not

14. Christa Wichterich shows that globalization is actually being conceived by its promoters as colonization. She gives an example of an advocate for corporate transnationalism using the decidedly colonial metaphor of a ship moving from place to place, stopping where it finds cheap labour: 'Le président de l'industrie textile de Rhénanie du Nord, Dirk Busse, imagine l'usine de l'an 2000 comme un navire qui jettera l'ancre partout où les salaires sont bas' (1999: 20).

having access to and control over land and resources). Interestingly, this 'higher' (other) order is, in each case, precisely the one that the protesters have questioned: Korah, Dathan and Abiram argue that Yahweh's will is not only made known to Moses and Aaron but that Yahweh is among all the people (Num. 16.3), the Ts'Peten Defenders argue that they have a right to property without being violated, and the MAI protesters argue that nations' laws will not be defendable under the MAI.

Finally, all three stories demonstrate more violence than possibly necessary to deal with the 'threat' to colonialism. As noted, earthquake *and* fire are Korah's fate for questioning Moses. The RCMP pull a full-scale military operation on 18 peaceful sundancers, some of whom have inquired into legal processes around land treaties, emptying 20,000 rounds of bullets onto the site (clear-cutting the trees later, to eliminate the evidence). And finally, the police in Montreal are excessively violent to 100 protesters who could by no means, on their own, seriously threaten the process of globalization.

Why in each case the slippage between land and law? Why in each case the excess in violence? Mapping these stories alongside Žižek's reformulation of Althusser's theory of ideological interpellation highlights the ideological operations occurring on a number of levels in these stories. Looking at the stories through this lens provides me with an interesting possible response to my questions: the protesters' refusal to be interpellated into the symbolic order (Yahweh's will, right to property, *la loi*) brings into view and questions the ideological processes at work, and this causes the irruption of the hysterical phallus. So I turn to Žižek.

Žižek, Ideology and Social Antagonism

Žižek develops the Lacanian underpinnings of Althusser's account of interpellation. For Althusser, ideology is the imaginary relation that people have with the material relations of production; individuals are formed as subjects through recognizing, or rather misrecognizing, themselves in ideological discourses, or in other words, through responding to the hailing of ideology. A number of critics (e.g. Eagleton 1994: 214; Smith 1988: 18-22) have noticed that Althusser is drawing here on Lacan's notion of imaginary identification: individuals recognize themselves in ideology in a manner similar to the way that infants, according to Lacan, misrecognize their reflection in the mirror as a unified whole which they do not necessarily experience in their small toddling bodies. Thus persons interpellated by ideology recognize themselves in, or identify with, the image presented to them in ideology and so behave accordingly. Žižek, in building on Althusser, argues that Althusser does not adequately account for the process by which the external apparatuses of ideology (schools, family, religion) become internalized. Žižek suggests that the Lacanian account of the subject's passage through the symbolic order (Lacan's Other) fills in this gap in Althusser (Žižek 1989: 43-44).

For Žižek, ideological interpellation is not just a moment of imaginary identification with ideological discourse, but is the moment that Lacan describes as the subject's entry into language, the symbolic order, the Other (all coterminous and, significantly, gendered as female). For Lacan (simplifying somewhat) the subject is formed, on entry into the symbolic order, as it is pinned to a master signifier. For Žižek, this pinning is the moment of ideological interpellation. The master signifier ideologically positions the subject and encodes the subject's subsequent relations in the symbolic order. As Žižek puts it, the subject is 'fastened, pinned to a signifier which represents [it] for the Other, and through this pinning [it] is loaded with a symbolic mandate, [it] is given a place in the...network of symbolic relations' (1989: 113). This pinning that gives the subject its mandate takes place through a process of identification with the symbolic order (the Other), what Žižek calls an identification with the *lack* in the Other.

For Žižek the lack in the Other is that which is non-symbolizable (1989: 162-63), that 'strange traumatic element which cannot be symbolized, [or] integrated into the symbolic order' (1989: 133). This traumatic element is the Lacanian Real (to be distinguished from 'reality'): it is 'the non-symbolizable traumatic kernel' (Žižek 1994: 26) which 'gives rise to ever-new symbolizations [including fantasy] by means of which one endeavours to integrate and domesticate it' (1994: 22). The only way the subject can identify with this unrepresentable lack in the Other is through fantasy. Thus for Žižek ideology is reality: the fantasy-construction which masks this troubling 'hard kernel of the Real' and which structures social *reality* around it; we can only gain access to this traumatic element through ideology—ideology is, in a sense, a support for the Real, but hides its functioning as such (1989: 45-49; 1994: 19-22).

But, influenced by Ernesto Laclau and Chantal Mouffe, Žižek reads the Real, the non-symbolizable lack in the Other, as a fundamental social antagonism. It is an antagonism which 'is *nowhere directly given as a positive entity yet which none the less functions*' (Žižek 1994: 22, emphasis mine) giving rise to all other kinds of antagonism. Žižek gives the example of class struggle as this kind of non-locatable antagonism, which both generates other antagonisms and 'functions as the point of enabling us to locate every social phenomenon'. Social reality is structured around this fundamental 'hard kernel' and is the fantasy which smoothes it over and with which people identify.

Žižek's combination of 'lack' and antagonism is useful, it seems to me, in thinking about the antagonisms that arise in colonial contexts. The struggle is always—at least in these stories—framed in terms of some kind of entitlement (to land, to cult, to resources), but it gets played out in terms of a contestation over power, on a level where power is ethereal, nebulous (Yahweh's will, unwritten/settled property rights and *la loi*). But this fits with the now commonplace Foucauldian line, that power is nowhere given in the social order, it is always somewhere else, that hard traumatic kernel of lack that generates all other struggles.[15] Thus in the contest over land and leadership, the struggle manifests itself over who has Yahweh's will, who is holy. In the contest over land, the struggle manifests itself over who has uninhibited right to the land. In the contest over the MAI, the struggle manifests itself over who will make and enforce laws. The Real (power) that is operative here does not reside within these specific polarities, but is rather the fundamental 'imbalance in social relations that prevent[s] the community from stabilizing itself into a harmonious whole' (Žižek 1994: 26).

Point de capiton and objet petit a
In interpellation into ideology then, the subject identifies with this lack in the Other, this antagonism, by way of what Žižek, following Lacan, terms the *point de capiton* (or in English, the less alluring 'upholstery button'). The *point de capiton* pins the subject to the symbolic order. For Lacan, the *point de capiton* is the 'pure signifier', the master signifier with no signified, the signifier of a lack in the Other: we might say the signifier whose signified does not exist because it is lack.[16] The

15. Žižek uses Claude Lefort's discussion of democracy to argue this point with respect to democracy. Lefort argues that democracy can only operate if the locus of power remains empty (Žižek 1993: 190; Lefort 1988: 228-30).

16. Thus, *points de capiton* are interchangeable. Žižek gives the example of

point de capiton, or master signifier, steps in self-referentially to 'unify a given field' (Žižek 1989: 95), representing the lack of the Other as itself. Lacan describes this pure signifier with the metaphor of the phallus, coming to fill the lack of phallus in the Other (metaphorically speaking, the woman). Žižek thinks of the pure (phallic) signifier in terms of ideology: the pure signifier is the ideological *point de capiton* which is successful in its *capitonnage* as 'only in so far as it effaces its own traces' (Žižek 1989: 102).

This ideological operation occurs through fantasy, or what Lacan and Žižek term the *objet petit a*. The *objet petit a* is what Žižek calls the 'real-impossible correlative' to the *point de capiton* (1989: 95); it is a little piece of the Real 'which persists as a surplus' (1989: 71), and which, through fantasy, is elevated to the position of pure signifier or *point de capiton*. The *objet petit a* steps in to fill the lack of the Other, as if it were the *point de capiton*. The *objet petit a,* stands in for lack (Lacan 1977: 320). Žižek describes this *objet petit a* as an ordinary object that 'as soon as it is "elevated to the status of Thing [*point de capiton*]", starts to function as a kind of screen, and empty space on which the subject projects the fantasies that support [its] desire' (1991: 133). It is therefore termed by Žižek (following Lacan) 'the object-cause of desire' (1989: 180-97). Elsewhere, Žižek describes it as part of the antagonism of the Real that takes on extraordinary fantasy proportions (1997: 26-27). The *objet petit a* is always a symptom, and like all symptoms it 'stands in' for the Real; it is a little piece of the Real standing in for the central antagonism of the Real; it is a symptom that has become an ideological *point de capiton*, hiding its role as symptom from those pinned to it in interpellation. The ideological operation *par excellence,* then, occurs when through fantasy the *objet petit a* steps in to fill the lack as *point de capiton*.

Turning to the three accounts at hand, I would say that each has an ideological *point de capiton*, a little piece of the real which has been elevated to unify or mask the antagonism of the social order. The figure

communism which could just as easily be inserted, as capitalism, in place of the lack of the Other; but each has a quite different effect on the signification of the same terms (1989: 102). His point is that this is how ideology functions. See Butler (1993: 208-22) for a critique of Žižek's view of the *point de capiton*. She questions whether his consideration of *points de capiton* as rigid designators allows for 'the kind of variation and rearticulation required for an anti-essentialist radical democratic project' (1993: 211).

of Moses as the holy leader comes as the bearer of Yahweh's will to regulate the difference between those who have power and those who do not in the newly formed social organization of the tribes of Israel.[17] In the antagonism played out at Gustafsen Lake, the fantasy of 'British Columbia' (or crown land) fills in the disputes over right to property: 'crown land' poses as an originary entity, as if it, as a legal body with its own jurisdiction, had always been there as some kind of binding authority. The *point de capiton* 'capitalism'[18] unifies the antagonism played out in the questions of legal jurisdiction surrounding the protest of the MAI: capitalism is a fantasy which smoothes over worries of jurisdiction by arguing that the MAI and other nasty trade deals like it are all part of an inexorable global market economy, and therefore both necessary and beyond national laws.

But in each case, protesters refuse to identify with these *points de capiton* which mask the social antagonism, thus they refuse interpellation: Dathan and Abiram refuse to meet with Moses, when he calls them; aboriginal people refuse to respond to the eviction notice in the name of the crown and its tenant; and MAI protesters refuse the call of the capitalist state to let the market take its course. By refusing interpellation the resisters recognize these *points de capiton* (Moses, crown land, and capitalism) as symptoms; that is, as *objets petits a,* little pieces of the Real, which as fantasy formations mask or fill out the central lack (Žižek 1989: 74), the antagonism of the protesters' social orders.

Symptoms Displacing Symptoms

What is interesting though, is how it is that these *points de capiton* are recognized as symptoms. It is clear that for the protesters each of these so-called master signifiers is a poor substitute for what the protesters themselves invoke as ideal, or in other words, as poor substitutes for the master signifiers with which they themselves have been interpellated. Korah, Dathan and the others call for an ideal non-mediated relationship with God in the assembly of Israel (understood as holiness). The Ts'Peten Defenders appeal to the queen's ruling in favour of aboriginal land claims (understood as justice). And MAI protesters appeal to an

17. Cf. Žižek, following Hegel, on holiness/divinity as master signifier (1989: 194), or following Schelling, substituting the symbolic order for God (1997: 64-65).

18. Cf. Žižek (1989: 50-53) on capitalism, surplus value, and the logic of *objet petit a.*

ideal of shared wealth and decision-making (understood as democracy). Thus, if Moses, crown land and capitalism are recognized as symptoms, it is only in relation to these other master signifiers: Moses in relation to the chosen and holy assembly, crown land in relation to justice, and capitalism in relation to democracy. Thus it is the recognition of Moses, crown land and capitalism as symptoms that *brings into view* the ideological *points de capiton* holiness, justice or democracy with which the protesters have themselves been interpellated. The first set of inadequate master signifiers can only be recognized as such against the second set of ideal master signifiers, revealing the ideological positioning of protesters.

But if Žižek is to be taken seriously, Moses, crown land and capitalism, as recognizable symptoms, stand in for the central antagonism, the fundamental imbalance in power relations which is *still at work* within the ideals of holiness, justice and democracy. Once holiness, justice and democracy are *recognized* as ideological *points de capiton*, they too must be understood as symptoms, ideals which smooth over unrecognized problems within the social order. Thus refusal to be interpellated by one set of signifiers (Moses, crown land and capitalism) necessarily questions the master signifiers by which they are refused in the first place (holiness, justice, democracy). So Korah, Dathan and Abiram ask where holiness resides; the Ts'Peten Defenders petition the courts, and MAI protesters question government proceedings.

Beyond Interpellation

This, I would argue, is precisely the set of interactions that brings on violence; but to understand this, I need to look more closely at the details in Žižek's description of this realm beyond interpellation. According to Žižek, in the process of the subject's identification with the lack in the Other, the Other addresses the subject with the question, 'What do you want from me?' (*Che vuoi?*)[19] (Lacan 1977: 312). The question is asked as if the subject knows why it has the symbolic mandate conferred upon it by the master signifier (Žižek 1989: 113). Since the subject does not know why it has this symbolic mandate, it internalizes and reformulates the question as 'What does the Other want of me?' (Lacan 1977: 316), thereby also internalizing the desire of the Other. The interaction goes something like this: the subject desires what

19. Loris Mirella, in commenting on a draft, asked the pointed question, 'Why does the Other always speak in Italian instead of French or English?'

the Other desires (Lacan 1977: 312; 1978: 214-15), the Other desires what it itself lacks, and so, because it is lacking, the subject can never really know what the Other desires. Turning to fantasy as recourse, the subject desires and identifies with the *objet petit a*, that object of fantasy that stands in for the Other's lack (and to reiterate, for Lacan this is the phallus). 'Fantasy appears, then, as an answer to *"Che vuoi?"* to the unbearable enigma of the desire of the Other, of the lack in the Other' (Žižek 1989: 118).

For Žižek, like Lacan, failure of this process results in hysteria (which has typically been associated with women).[20] Hysteria is the 'incapacity of the subject to fulfill the symbolic identification, to assume fully and without restraint' the identification with the lack in the Other, by internalizing the desire of the Other. The hysteric, instead of posing the question, 'What does the Other want of me' and then com-plying, asks 'Why am I what you [the big Other] are telling me that I am?' (Žižek 1989: 113, 187). 'Why are you calling me with this master signifier?'

Hysterical Phalli
But, and this is where I would like to play with Žižek's phallus, what if, in the recognition that takes place in resisting interpellation, the subject *does know* why it is taking the position it does within the symbolic order and this sends the question in the other direction: instead of ask-ing the Other, 'Why am I what you are telling me that I am?' it asks, and 'What are you really? Why are you *not* what you are telling me that you are? Why are you—holiness, justice, democracy—really just a fan-tasy standing in to hide the central lack, the central antagonism of the social order?' The question it seems, sends the phallus into hysterics. Although Žižek never speaks of a hysterical phallus per se (for that would surely contravene his Lacanian legacy), he describes it when he says that the demonstration of power confirms impotence. 'The more violent [the] reaction [of power] the more it confirms its fundamental impotence,' he says, or in other words, the more it confirms its funda-mental lack (Žižek 1989: 157-58). It is the unveiling of the lack sup-porting it that provokes the frenzy of the phallus.

Thus, when protesters refuse interpellation by the master signifiers Moses, crown land and capitalism, there is a chain effect whereby the

20. For historical examples of this association see Veith (1965); for examples in Žižek, see 1989: 113; 1991: 65-66.

master signifiers which represent the big Other for protesters are also questioned: holiness, justice and democracy are caught and questioned in the act of being symptoms, of merely standing in for lack, phantas-mically covering it over. In response, to this 'unmasking' the antago-nism that makes up that lack explodes in ugly *jouissance* (another way that Žižek speaks of the Real). Thus Yahweh, the Holy One, causes the earth to swallow up insurgent Israelites and their families,[21] the justice system in British Columbia employs 400 police to try to blow up 18 aboriginal sundancers, while democracy sends the police to rough up MAI protesters.

Thinking of the violent response to resisted interpellation as the *jouissance* of the hysterical phallus explains, in Žižekian terms, why the police are always so ugly (or the equally unpleasant figure of Sheol which gapes in the mouth of the earth). For Žižek the Real is *jouis-sance*, and *jouissance* is ugly, and 'always traumatic' (Žižek 1997: 25). Ugliness is 'a *topological* category' designating an object that is 'larger than itself'. It is something that spills out from the inside. Žižek uses the unfortunate (but telling) illustration of menstruation as 'the exem-plary case of such an ugly inside spilling out' (Žižek 1997: 24). As non-symbolizable, the Real fits this topological description of ugliness. The Real is ugly because it cannot be symbolized, because its 'existence is larger than its representation' (Žižek 1997: 21). It seems to me that the phallus, rather than the vagina and its fluid, is the exemplary case, the hysterical phallus produces *jouissance* par excellence: the lack which the phallus hides explodes in ugly violence. The antagonism produced by the lack of power in the social order explodes, turning the phallus inside out: the ugliness of military force and police brutality spills out of capitalist colonial order, and Sheol gapes its mouth in the midst of holy colonizing order. The logic is always the same: when dissidents recognize that the guarantors of the social order are not what they seem, and unmask it through questioning—it explodes: the legal and demo-cratic orders wield batons or firing arms; the Holy One spits out fire.

Land as Object Cause of Desire
But what of the land and resources, the site of all these struggles? I would suggest that, in fact, it is the land that is the *objet petit a*, the 'real' little piece of the Real that persists as a surplus and that causes

---

21. Cf. Žižek on Schelling and divine fury (1997: 16-17).

RUNIONS *Hysterical Phalli* 203

desire ('the object-cause of desire' in Žižek's terms). The land is that bit of material relations around which the having or not having of power plays, and creates antagonism. The land, and its resources, is that screen[22] over which all of these various ideological fantasies are projected: Yahweh's command, Moses, holiness; uninhibited property rights, 'crown land', justice, *la loi*, capitalism, democracy.

The materiality and substantiality of the land as object-cause of desire is, as I see it, where these accounts of colonial antagonism and violence differ slightly from Žižek's description of lack, *objet petit a*, and ideology. For Žižek the only thing that has any real substance is fantasy, ideology, the phallus. The *objet petit a* is pure semblance, devoid of any substantial support (Žižek 1993: 35-36). But, in these stories at least, the land (traditionally gendered as feminine) is the material support for these other ideological configurations (recalling the theory's Marxist roots). The land, the object-cause of colonial desire, is not lack, but self-sufficient plenitude. Indeed, perhaps the plenitude of the land is too difficult to bear and this is what provokes antagonism, requiring fantasy to smooth it over. This is certainly the case in Numbers. The spies tell the people, 'The land...it flows with milk and honey...yet...it is a land that devours its inhabitants' (Num. 13.27, 32); the people revolt; and the nebulous, nowhere-present of Yahweh's will must be invoked to calm the fear. The fantasy/phallus is only needed at the point that the desire for the land produces antagonism. Ironically, the antagonism which the fantasy/phallus stands in for can only be seen as 'lack' after the imposition of the fantasy/phallus, thus justifying its presence after the fact. This is not to say that the imposition of this fantasy does not have material effects (i.e. I am not returning here to a vulgar Marxism in which ideology is merely false consciousness): it does smooth over the antagonism, and it does affect the land. But, when the fantasy/phallus is pulled—through the questioning of those resisting interpellation—back from this scene of 'lack', this scene of the antagonism produced by desire for the land, it can no longer contain itself; it explodes hysterically.

Jouissance par excellence
I would like to climax, so to speak, by exhibiting an almost prototypic example of the hysterical phallus through reference to the RCMP's

22. For an interesting reading of the land as the screen on which desire is played out see Long (1999); Gunn (1999) too deals with this issue.

narcissistic, and I might say onanistic, records of their own violent *jouissance*. Throughout their 'operation' at Gustafsen Lake the RCMP video-taped their activities, and the activities within the camp, including 24-hour overhead surveillance taping. These tapes record RCMP personnel making comments like: 'Kill this Clark and smear the prick and everyone with him' (Horwood 1997a, 1997b), or, 'This is not the first time we've had to take flak-jackets to the firing range' (this just before a press conference reporting that RCMP officers had been fired upon from the camp) (tape transcriptions, ABC 1997: 47). Further, the overhead surveillance tapes show RCMP firing at several people in the camp as they walked, unarmed, through 'safe' zones. In one of the most extreme instances, the overhead surveillance tape for 11 September 1995 shows the RCMP setting the land mine which explodes a truck driving over it on its way to get water, it shows a tank come out of the woods and ram the truck several times, and it shows a dog, which jumped out of the back of the truck to run away, fall dead on the side of the road, shot eight times (Ogilvie 1997).

These RCMP records, I might say, are homage to the ideals we call holiness, justice and democracy—and of course, a tribute to the phallus.

Figure 4. Truck at Gustafsen Lake, video still, M. Brown, permission of
John Splitting the Sky Hill.

Figure 5. *Violent Jouissance*, video still, M. Brown, permission of
John Splitting the Sky Hill.

BIBLIOGRAPHY

ABC (Montreal Anarchist Black Cross)
    1997   *The Gustafsen Lake Crisis: Statements from Ts'Peten Defenders* (Montreal: McGill and Concordia Québec Public Interest Research Groups).

Advertisement
    1997a   'Legendary BIBLE HERBS™ —Now Available in a Convenient, Easy-Swallow, No-Taste PILL!', *Weekly World News*, 11 November: 22.
    1997b   'God's Amazing Gift to the World. How You Can Get Love, Money and Good Luck with the Only Crosses on Earth Actually Created by the Mighty Hands of God', *Weekly World News*, 11 November: 42.

Aichele, G.
    1997   *Sign, Text, Scripture: Semiotics and the Bible* (Sheffield: Sheffield Academic Press).
    1999   'An Apology for the Madman', *Paradoxa* 5.12: 117-31.

Alarie, S.
    1998   '100 arrestations: Manif contre la dictature de l'argent', *Le journal de Montréal*, 26 May: A1-2.

Albright, W.F., and C.S. Mann.
    1971   *Matthew* (Anchor Bible, 26; Garden City, NY: Doubleday).

Alter, R.
    1981   *The Art of Biblical Narrative* (New York: Basic Books).

Alternate Bris Support Group
        http://www.fathermag.com/htmlmodules/circ/xbris.html.

Althusser, L.
    1984   'Ideological State Apparatuses (Notes toward an Investigation)', in *Essays on Ideology* (London and New York: Verso): 1-60.

Anonymous
    1998   *Popular Action to Free Education* (Pamphlet on 11 February 1998 student occupation and demonstration).

Armstrong, K.
    1994   *A History of God: The 4000-Year Quest of Judaism, Christianity and Islam* (New York: Alfred A. Knopf).

Arnold, K., and R. Palmer
    1952   *The Coming of the Saucers* (Amherst).

Auerbach, N.
    1995   *Our Vampire, Ourselves* (Chicago: University of Chicago Press).

Avoiding Congregational Gangrene
        http://www.pbc.org/dp/stedman/timothy/3786.html.

Bach, A.
 1990 *The Pleasure of her Text: Feminist Readings of Biblical and Historical Texts* (Philadelphia: Trinity Press International).

Bailey, R.
 1990 *David in Love and War: The Pursuit of Power in II Samuel 10–12* (Sheffield: JSOT Press).

Bal, M.
 1987 *Lethal Love: Feminist Literary Readings of Biblical Love Stories* (Bloomington: Indiana University Press).
 1988 *Death and Dissymetry: The Politics of Coherence in the Book of Judges* (Chicago: University of Chicago Press).

Balfour, G.
 1997 'Fear Silences Ham Radio Witness: "Men in Black" Riddle of US Jet Buzzed by UFO', *Sun*, December 30: 3.

Barbour, P.L. (ed.)
 1986 *The Complete Works of Captain John Smith (1580–1631)*, II and III (Chapel Hill, NC: University of North Carolina Press).

Barr, M.
 1991 *Children's Bible Stories: Old Testament* (n.p.: P.S.I. and Associates).

Barrett, Charles K.
 1994 *A Critical and Exegetical Commentary on the Acts of the Apostles*, I (ICC, 31; Edinburgh: T. & T. Clark).

Barthes, R.
 1988 *The Semiotic Challenge* (trans. Richard Howard; New York: Hill and Wang).

Bartlett, J.
 1951 *Familiar Quotations* (12th edn rev. and enlarged; Boston: Little, Brown).

Basevi, C.
 1990 'El Salmo 29. Algunas observaciones filologicas sobre el texto hebreo y griego', *Scripta Theologica* 22: 13-47.

Beidelman, T.O.
 1986 'Circumcision', in M. Eliade (ed.), *The Encyclopedia of Religion*, III (16 vols.; New York: Macmillan): 511-14.

Bellah, R.N, *et al.*
 1985 *Habits of the Heart: Individualism and Commitment in American Life* (San Francisco: Harper & Row).

Benagh, C.L.
 1986 *Joshua and the Battle of Jericho* (Nashville: Abingdon Press).

Bender, A.K.
 1963 *The Flying Saucers and the Three Men* (London: Neville Spearman).

Benjamin, W.
 1968 *Illuminations* (trans. Harry Zohn; New York: Schocken Books).

Berger, J.
 1998 'A Tiger Chewed My Arm Off and Swallowed it Like a Hot Dog with Ketchup!', *Weekly World News*, 7 April: 2-3.

Berger, P.
 1969 *The Sacred Canopy* (Garden City: Anchor).

Berlin, A.
    1994   *Poetics and Interpretation of Biblical Narrative* (Indiana: Eisenbrauns).
Bird, P.
    1997   *Missing Persons and Mistaken Identities: Women and Gender in Ancient Israel* (Minneapolis: Fortress Press).
Blake, W.
    1979   *The Works of William Blake* (New York: A.M.S. Press).
Bluestone, G.
    1957   *Novels into Film* (Berkeley: University of California Press).
Boer, R.
    1999   'David is a Thing', in F.C. Black, R. Boer and E. Runions (eds.), *The Labour of Reading: Desire, Alienation, and Biblical Interpretation* (Semeia Studies, 36; Atlanta: Scholars Press): 163-76.
    Forthcoming a   'The Second Coming: Repetition and Insatiable Desire in the Song of Songs', *Biblical Interpretation* 8.3.
    Forthcoming b   'King Solomon Meets Annie Sprinkle', in Stephen Moore (ed.), *Semeia* (Atlanta: Scholars Press).
Boling, R.
    1975   *Anchor Bible: Judges* (New York: Doubleday).
Borges, J.L.
    1964   'Kafka and His Precursors', in D.A. Yates and J.E. Irby (eds.), *Labyrinths* (trans. J.E. Irby; New York: New Directions): 199-201.
Boyarin, D.
    1992   ' "This We Know to Be the Carnal Israel": Circumcision and the Erotic Life of God and Israel', *Critical Inquiry* 18.3: 474-505.
    1993   *Carnal Israel: Reading Sex in Talmudic Culture* (Berkeley: University of California Press).
    1994   *A Radical Jew: Paul and the Politics of Identity* (Berkeley and Los Angeles: University of California Press).
    1995   'Homotopia: The *Fem*inized Jewish Man and the Lives of Women in Late Antiquity', *differences: A Journal of Cultural Studies* 7.2: 41-81.
Braude, W.G. (trans.)
    1968   *Pesikta Rabbati: Discourses for Feasts, Fasts, and Special Sabbaths* (2 vols.; New Haven: Yale University Press).
Braude, W.G., and I.J. Kapstein (trans.)
    1975   *Pesikta de-Rab Kahana: R. Kahana's Compilation of Discourses for Sabbaths and Festal Days* (Philadelphia: Jewish Publication Society of America).
    1981   *Tanna debe Eliyyahu: The Lore of the School of Elijah* (Philadelphia: Jewish Publication Society of America).
Brenner, A. (ed.)
    1998   *A Feminist Companion to Ruth and Esther* (Feminist Companion to the Bible, Second Series; Sheffield: Sheffield Academic Press).
Broder, T.
    1997   'Gaze upon This Image of Paradise and You Can…Visit Heaven Anytime You Want!', *Weekly World News*, 11 November: 6.

Bronner, L.
    1968   *The Stories of Elijah and Elisha* (Pretoria Oriental Series, 6; Leiden: E.J. Brill).

Brown, M. (producer and director)
    1997   *Above the Law: Part 1, Deception at Gustafsen Lake* (Videotape. Vancouver, BC: Ts'Peten Defenders and their Supporters).

Brown, R.E.
    1978   *The Birth of the Messiah: A Commentary on the Infancy Narratives in Matthew and Luke* (London: Geoffrey Chapman).

Budd, P.J.
    1984   *Numbers* (WBC; Waco: Word Books).

Burns, R.J.
    1992   'Zipporah', in *The Anchor Bible Dictionary* (CD-ROM edn, 1997; D.N. Freedman, editor-in-chief; New York: Doubleday).

Butler, J.
    1993   *Bodies that Matter: On the Discursive Limits of 'Sex'* (New York and London: Routledge).

Buonaventura, W.
    1998   *Serpent of the Nile: Women and Dance in the Arab World* (London: Saqi Books).

Calvino, I.
    1979   *If On a Winter's Night a Traveler* (trans. W. Weaver; New York: Harcourt Brace Jovanovich).

Camus, A.
    1991   *The Myth of Sisyphus and Other Essays* (trans. J. O'Brien; New York: Vintage International).

Canadian Press
    1997   'Gustafsen Lake Case not Land-claims Issue, Crown Tells Jurors', *The Vancouver Sun*, 1 May (http://kafka.uvic.ca/~vipirg/SISIS/court/may01cli.html).
    1998   'OECD head unfazed by MAI protests', *The Globe and Mail*, 26 May: B4.

Caputo, J.D.
    1997   *The Prayers and Tears of Jacques Derrida: Religion without Religion* (Bloomington: Indiana University Press).

Carlton, D.
    1998   'Florida Woman's Horrifying Encounter: "A Space Alien Ate My Dog!" ', *Weekly World News*, 4 August: 7.

Caron, M. (ed.)
    1988   *Helse en hemelse vrouwen. Schrikbeelden en voorbeelden van de vrouw in de christelijke cultuur* (Utrecht: Rijksmuseum Het Catharijneconvent).

Castelli, E.
    1991   *Imitating Paul: A Discourse of Power* (Louisville: Westminster/John Knox Press).

Cernetig, M.   1997 'Judge Tough on Native Protesters: Gustafsen Standoff Hurt Democracy', *Toronto Globe and Mail*, 31 July, A1 (http://kafka.uvic.ca/~vipirg/SISIS/court/jul31cli.html).

Charlesworth, J.H.
    1983   *The Old Testament Pseudepigrapha* (New York: Doubleday).
Christian Newsletter of Bible Believers Fellowship: Cain, Balaam, and Korah
                http://www.prisonministry.org/newsletters/cain.htm.
Church of England Newspaper
    1998   'Phew! It's a Scorcher! Author Nick's 'Bible' is a Super, Soaraway Suc-
                cess', 13 November: 6.
Coats, G.W.
    1968   *Rebellion in the Wilderness: The Murmuring Motif in the Wilderness*
                (Nashville: Abingdon Press).
Cohen, J.J. (ed.)
    1996   *Monster Theory: Reading Culture* (Minneapolis: University of Minnesota
                Press).
Cohen, L.
    1936   *Bible Tales for Very Young Children*, Book 2 (New York: UAHC).
Cossé, L.
    1999   *A Corner of the Veil* (New York: Scribner).
Craigie, P.C.
    1983   *Ugarit and the Old Testament* (Grand Rapids: Eerdmans).
Creed, K.
    1997a   'Virgin Mary's Toothbrush and Sandals Found...Buried Near Rock
                Where She Rested on the Way to Bethlehem!', *Weekly World News*,
                23 December: 37.
    1997b   'Missing Text from New Testament Found', *Weekly World News*,
                30 December: 24-25.
    1998   'Space Alien Baby! UFO Crash Survivor Baby Is Alive and Well—and
                Living at a Secret New Mexico Military Base!', *Weekly World News*,
                1 September: 18-19.
Cunningham, R.
    1998   'Bible's Burning Bush Found in Holy Land!', *Weekly World News*, 10
                March: 35.
Daniel, D.
    1971   *The Jewish Beginning from Joshua to Judah Maccabee*, Part 2 (New
                York: Ktav).
Debray, R.
    1996   *Media Manifestos* (trans. Eric Rauth, London: Verso).
Declaration of the First International Symposium on Circumcision
                http://www.cirp.org/pages/intactivist/declaration.html.
Dennis, T.
    1994   *Sarah Laughed: Women's Voices in the Old Testament* (Nashville:
                Abingdon Press).
Derrida, J.
    1979   *Spurs: Nietzsche's Styles* (trans. B. Harlow; Chicago: University of Chic-
                ago Press).
    1986   'Shibboleth', in G.H. Hartman and S. Budick (eds.), *Midrash and Litera-
                ture* (New Haven: Yale University Press): 307-47.

Dexter, B.
 1997   'Simple 12-Point Plan That Will Get You into Heaven!', *Weekly World News*, 30 December: 13.
 1998   ' "Weekly World News" T-Shirts Bringing Miracles to Thousands!', *Weekly World News*, 4 August: 51.
Dijkstra, B.
 1986   *Idols of Perversity. Fantasies of Feminine Evil in Fin-de-Siècle Culture* (New York/Oxford: Oxford University Press).
 1996   *Evil Sisters: The Threat of Female Sexuality in Twentieth-Century Culture* (New York: Owl Books).
Donaldson, L.E.
 1999   'The Sign of Orpah: Reading Ruth through Native Eyes', in A. Brenner, (ed.), *A Feminist Companion to Ruth*, II (Sheffield: Sheffield Academic Press, 1999): 130-44.
Eagleton, T.
 1994   'Ideology and its Vicissitudes in Western Marxism', in S. Žižek (ed.), *Mapping Ideology* (London and New York: Verso): 179-226.
Eco, U.
 1979   *The Role of the Reader* (Bloomington, IN: Indiana University Press).
Edgerton, G., and K.M. Jackson
 1996   'Redesigning Pocahontas: Disney, the "White Man's Indian" and the Marketing of Dreams', *Journal of Popular Film and Television* 24.2: 90-98.
Eilberg-Schwartz, H.
 1994   *God's Phallus, and Other Problems for Men and Monotheism* (Boston: Beacon Press).
Eissfeldt, O.
 1965   *The Old Testament: An Introduction* (trans. P.R. Ackroyd; New York: Harper and Row).
Elwell, W. (ed.)
 1989   *Evangelical Commentary on the Bible* (Grand Rapids: Baker Book House).
Exum, J.C.
 1993   *Fragmented Women: Feminist (Sub)versions of Biblical Narrative* (Valley Forge: Trinity Press International).
 1996   *Plotted, Shot and Painted: Cultural Representations of Biblical Women* (Sheffield: Sheffield Academic Press).
Exum, J.C., and S.D. Moore (eds.)
 1998   *Biblical Studies/Cultural Studies: The Third Sheffield Colloquium* (Gender, Culture, Theory, 7; Sheffield: Sheffield Academic Press).
Featherstone, M.
 1991   *Consumer Culture and Postmodernism* (London: Sage).
Ferrucci, F.
 1996   *The Life of God (As Told by Himself)* (Chicago: University of Chicago Press).
Fewell, D.N., and D.M. Gunn
 1993   *Gender, Power, and Promise: The Subject of the Bible's First Story* (Nashville: Abingdon).

Fish, T.
   1975   *Hufshah Ne'imah*, Workbook 4 (Jerusalem: S. Zak).
Fishbane, M.
   1979   *Text and Texture: Close Reading of Selected Biblical Texts* (New York:
                 Schocken Books).
Fokkelman, J.P.
   1981   *Narrative Art and Poetry in the Books of Samuel. I. King David (II
                 Samuel 9–20 & I Kings 1–2* (Assen: Van Gorcum).
Foster, M.
   1998a   'Hitler Was the Anti-Christ and the End Times Are Already Over!',
                 Weekly World News, 12 May: 21.
   1998b   'Tower of Babel Found on Mars!', *Weekly World News*, 19 May: 19.
Fraser, G.M.
   1988   *The Hollywood History of the World: From One Million Years B.C. to
                 Apocalypse Now* (New York: Fawcett Columbine).
Freedman, D.N.
   1987   'Yahweh of Samaria and His Asherah', *BA* 50. Reprinted in J.R. Huddle-
                 stun (ed.), *Divine Commitment and Human Obligation: Selected Writings
                 of David Noel Freedman* (Grand Rapids: Eerdmans, 1997): 403-408.
Frege, G.
   1952   'On Sense and Meaning', in P.T. Geach and M. Black (trans. and eds.),
                 Translations From the Writings of Gottlob Frege (Totowa, NJ: Rowman
                 and Littlefield): 56-78.
French, M.
   1985   *Beyond Power: On Women, Men, and Morals* (New York: Ballantine
                 Books).
Freud, S.
   1953   *The Standard Edition of the Complete Psychological Works*, XXI (trans.
                 Strachey *et al.*; London: Hogarth Press).
Friedman, R.E.
   1995   *The Hidden Face of God* (Harper San Francisco).
Frymer-Kensky, T.
   1992   *In the Wake of the Goddesses* (New York: Fawcett Columbine).
Gelder, K.
   1994   *Reading the Vampire* (London/New York: Routledge).
Ginzberg, L.
   1955   *Legends of the Jews: Notes to Vols I and II* (Philadelphia: The Jewish
                 Publication Society of America).
Grant, R.M.
   1986   *Gods and the One God* (Library of Early Christianity, 1; Philadelphia:
                 Westminster).
Grishaver, J.L.
   1982   *Bible People*. Book 3. *Prophets and Writings* (Denver: Alternatives in
                 Religious Education).
Gunn, D.M.
   1999   'Yearning for Jerusalem: Reading Myth on the Web', in F.C. Black,
                 R. Boer and E. Runions (eds.), *The Labour of Reading: Desire, Alienation,*

and Biblical Interpretation (Semeia Studies, 36; Atlanta: Scholars Press): 123-40.

Gunn, D.M., and D.N. Fewell
1993   *Narrative in the Hebrew Bible* (Oxford: Oxford University Press).

Handelman, S.A.
1982   *The Slayers of Moses: The Emergence of Rabbinic Interpretation in Modern Literary Theory* (Albany: State University of New York Press).

Harrington, M.
1983   *The Politics at God's Funeral* (New York: Holt, Rinehart and Winston).

Hertzberg, H.
1964   *I & II Samuel: A Commentary* (trans. J.S. Bowden; Old Testament Library; London: SCM Press).

Herzog, M. (director)
1997   *The Making of the Men in Black* (produced by J. Cvengros, M. Herzog, and K. Gill; Burbank City, CA: Columbia Pictures).

Hoenig, S.B. (ed.)
1969   *The Book of Joshua: A New English Translation of the Text and Rashi, with a Commentary Digest* (New York: The Judaica Press).

Hoffman, L.A.
1996   *Covenant of Blood: Circumcision and Gender in Rabbinic Judaism* (Chicago: University of Chicago Press).

Horwood, H.
1997a   'Mountie Regrets "Smear" Remark', *The Province*, 21 January (http://kafka.uvic.ca/~vipirg/SISIS/court/jan2197.html).
1997b   'Sgt. Cites Boss: "Kill this Clark" ', *The Province*, 4 February (http://kafka.uvic.ca/~vipirg/SISIS/court/feb0497.html).

Houtman, C.
1983   'Exodus 4:24-26 and Its Interpretation', *Journal of Northwest Semitic Languages* 11: 81-105.

Hudson, C.
1976   *The Southeastern Indians* (Knoxville: The University of Tennessee Press).

Hume, M.
1995   'Standoff at Gustafsen Lake Preceded by a Vision', *The Vancouver Sun*, 12 September (http://kafka.uvic.ca/~vipirg/SISIS/GustLake/sep1295c.html).

Huss, R., and N. Silverstein
1968   *The Film Experience: Elements of Motion Picture Art*. New York: Dell.

Hyland, D.A.
1973   *The Origins of Philosophy: From Myth to Meaning* (New York: G.P. Putnam's Sons).

Irwin, W.R.
1976   *The Game of the Impossible: A Rhetoric of Fantasy* (Urbana: University of Illinois).

Jackson, R.
1981   *Fantasy: The Literature of Subversion* (London and New York: Methuen).

Jeffries, R.
1997a   'Captured Space Alien's Grim Prophecy: God Will Destroy Earth in the Year 2000!', *Weekly World News*, 18 November: 2-3.

1997b   'Mystery over Holy Land! Sky Turns a Strange Shade of Green from Jerusalem to Bethlehem and the People are Terrified!', *Weekly World News*, 16 December: 8-9.

1997c   'Star of Bethlehem Was Really a UFO...Sent to Earth by God Himself, Says Expert', *Weekly World News*, 23 December: 7.

1998a   'The Great Tribulation Has Begun!', *Weekly World News*, 27 January: 46-47.

1998b   'Miracle Discovery in the Holy Land! Stone Tablet Containing 7 Ancient Prophecies Found in Jesus' Tomb!', *Weekly World News*, 14 April: 8-9.

Jeffries, R., and V. Sardi
1998   'Are We on the Eve of Destruction? Five Top Experts Say Yes!', *Weekly World News*, 24 February: 2-3.

Jenkins, G., R. Allen and A. Roberts
1951   'David and Bathsheba' (New York: New York Lion Music Corp., Twentieth Century Music Corp.).

Jewish Publication Society
1962   *Torah* (Philadelphia: Jewish Publication Society).

Johnson, A.R.
1955   *Sacral Kingship in Ancient Israel* (Cardiff: University of Wales Press).

Kaai, A.
1997   *Openbaring in beeld* (Zoetermeer, The Netherlands: Boekencentrum, 3rd edn. English edn: *Apocalypse, Meditations on the Revelation of John in Word and Picture* [Zoetermeer, The Netherlands: Boekencentrum, 1992]).

Kafka, F.
1948   'In the Penal Colony', in *The Penal Colony* (trans. W. Muir and E. Muir; New York: Schocken Books): 191-227.

1956   *The Trial* (trans. W. Muir and E. Muir; rev. E.M. Butler; New York: Vintage Books).

1958   *Parables and Paradoxes* (trans. C. Greenberg, E. Kaiser, E. Wilkins, W. Muir, E. Muir, T. Stern and J. Stern; New York: Schocken Books).

Kapelrud, A.S.
1952   *Baal in the Ras Shamra Texts* (Copenhagen: G.E.C. Cad).

Kaufman, S.
1990   'Zipporah', *Tikkun* 5 (September–October): 69.

Keller, C.
1996   *Apocalypse Now and Then: A Feminist Guide to the End of the World* (Boston: Beacon Press).

Klein, L.
1993   'The Book of Judges: Paradigm and Deviation in Images of Women', in A. Brenner (ed.), *A Feminist Companion to Judges* (Sheffield: Sheffield Academic Press): 55-72.

Kramer, P.S.
1998   'The Dismissal of Hagar in Five Art Works of the Sixteenth and Seventeenth Centuries', in A. Brenner (ed.), *Genesis: A Feminist Companion to the Bible. Second Series* (Sheffield: Sheffield Academic Press): 195-217.

Kristeva, J.
1982   *Powers of Horror: An Essay on Abjection* (trans. L.S. Roudiez; New York: Columbia University Press).

1989   *Language: The Unknown* (trans. A.M. Menke; New York: Columbia University Press).

Kunin, S.D.
1996   'The Bridegroom of Blood: A Structuralist Analysis', *JSOT* 70: 3-16.

Lacan, J.
1977   *Écrits: A Selection* (trans. A. Sheridan; New York: W.W. Norton and Company).
1978   *The Four Fundamental Concepts of Psycho-Analysis* (ed. J.-A. Miller, trans. A. Sheridan; New York: W.W. Norton and Company).

Laclau, E., and C. Mouffe
1985   *Hegemony and Socialist Strategy: Toward a Radical Democratic Politics* (London and New York: Verso).

Landy, F.
1997   'Do We Want Our Children to Read this Book?', in D.N. Fewell and G.A. Phillip (eds.), *Bible and the Ethics of Reading* (*Semeia*, 77; Atlanta: Scholars Press): 157-76.

Lauterbach, J.Z. (trans.)
1933   *Mekilta de-Rabbi Ishmael* (3 vols.; Philadelphia: Jewish Publication Society of America).

Lefort, C.
1988   *Democracy and Political Theory* (trans. D. Macey; Cambridge: Polity Press).

Levinger, J.R.
1997   *The Beginners Bible: Joshua in Jericho* (Brentwook, TN: Performance Unlimited, Inc.).

Leven, J.
1982   *Satan: His Psychotherapy and Cure by the Unfortunate Dr. Kassler, J.S.P.S.* (New York: Ballantine).

Levine, B.A.
1993   *Numbers 1–20: A New Translation with Introduction and Commentary* (Anchor Bible; New York: Doubleday).

Lind, R.N.
1997   'War Hero Faced a Life of Loneliness after His Face Was Burned Off in 1982—But Then He Found the Woman of His Dreams!', *Weekly World News*, 4 November: 2-3.

Livingston, J.C.
1998   *Anatomy of the Sacred: An Introduction to Religion* (Upper Saddle River: Prentice Hall, 3rd edn).

Long, B.O.
1999   'Reading the Land: Holy Land as Text of Witness', in F.C. Black, R. Boer and E. Runions (eds.), *The Labour of Reading: Desire, Alienation, and Biblical Interpretation* (Semeia Studies, 36; Atlanta: Scholars Press): 141-59.

Lyotard, J.-F.
1988   *The Differend* (trans. G. Van Den Abbeele; Minneapolis: University of Minnesota Press).

Magonet, J.
1982   'The Korah Rebellion', *JSOT* 24: 3-25.

Margulis, B.
    1970   'The Canaanite Origin of Psalm 29 Reconsidered', *Biblica* 51: 332-48.
Matthews, J.
    1998   *The Winter Solstice* (Wheaton: Quest Books).
Merideth, B.
    1989   'Desire and Danger: The Drama of Betrayal in Judges and Judith', in
                M. Bal (ed.), *Anti-Covenant: Counter-Reading Women's Lives in the
                Hebrew Bible* (Sheffield: Almond Press): 63-78.
Mesnard, J.
    1969   *Pascal* (trans. C. Abraham and M. Abraham; Tuscaloosa, AL: University
                of Alabama Press).
Metz, Christian
    1974   *Film Language: A Semiotics of the Cinema* (trans. M. Taylor; New York:
                Oxford University Press).
Miles, J.
    1995   *God: A Biography* (New York: Alfred A. Knopf).
Milgrom, J.
    1990   *Numbers: The Traditional Hebrew Text with the New JPS Translation
                Commentary* (JPS Torah Commentary; Philadelphia: The Jewish Publica-
                tion Society).
Milhaud, D.
    1954   *David* (text by A. Lunel; Tel Aviv: Israeli Music Publishers).
Milton, J.
    1974   *Samson Agonistes* (London: University Tutorial Press).
Mirella, L.
    1987   'Kidlat Tahimik's PERFUMED NIGHTMARE: Interview and Article',
                Polygraph 1: 57-66.
Molloy, M.
    1999   *Experiencing the World's Religions: Tradition, Challenge, and Change*
                (Mountain View, CA: Mayfield).
Monaco, J.
    1981   *How to Read a Film: The Art, Technology, Language, History, and
                Theory of Film and Media* (New York and Oxford: Oxford University
                Press, rev. edn).
Moore, E.
    1888   *Delilah, A Tale of Olden Times* (Washington, DC: T. McGill & Co.).
Moore, G.F.
    1949   *International Critical Commentary* (Edinburgh: T. & T. Clark).
Morgan, A.
    1998   'Not Tonight Dear, I Have a Headache!', *Weekly World News* 7 April: 37.
Morgenstern, J.
    1966   *Rites of Birth, Marriage, Death, and Kindred Occasions among the Sem-
                ites* (Cincinnati: Hebrew Union College Press).
Morrow, J.
    1984   *Bible Stories for Adults* (San Diego: Harcourt Brace).
    1990   *Only Begotten Daughter* (San Diego: Harcourt Brace).
    1994   *Towing Jehovah* (San Diego: Harcourt Brace).
    1996   *Blameless in Abaddon* (San Diego: Harcourt Brace).

    1999   *The Eternal Footman* (San Diego: Harcourt Brace).

Mulvey, L.
    1975   'Visual Pleasure and Narrative Cinema', *Screen* 16.3: 6-18.

National Organization of Circumcision Information Resource Centers
                http://www.nocirc.org/.

National Organization to Halt the Abuse and Routine Mutilation of Males: A Health and Human Rights Organization
                http://www.noharmm.org/.

Neale, S.
    1993   'Prologue: Masculinity as Spectacle', in S. Cohan and I.R. Hark (eds.), *Screening the Male: Exploring Masculinities in Hollywood Cinema* (London and New York: Routledge): 9-20.

Newman, S.
    1985   *A Child's Introduction to the Early Prophets* (New York: Behrman).

Niebuhr, H.R.
    1970   *Radical Monotheism and Western Culture* (New York: Harper Torchbook).

Nietzsche, F.
    1961   *Thus Spake Zarathustra* (New York: Penguin).

Nohrnberg, J.
    1995   *Like unto Moses: The Constituting of an Interruption* (Bloomington, IN: Indiana University Press).

Noth, M.
    1962   *Exodus* (OTL;. London: SCM Press).
    1968   *Numbers: A Commentary* (Philadelphia: Westminster).

Oden, R.A., Jr
    1987   *The Bible Without Theology: The Theological Tradition and Alternatives to It* (Cambridge: Harper & Row).

Ogilvie, C.
    1997   'Up in Smoke and All on Video', *The Province*, 31 January (http://kafka.uvic.ca/~vipirg/SISIS/court/jan3197.html).

Okef, U.
    n.d.   *Ha-Tanakh Sheli Be-temunot: Yehoshua Kovesh Yeriho*, XIII (Ramat Gan: Revivim).

Olson, D.T.
    1996   *Numbers* (Louisville: John Knox Press).

On Doctrine, Correction, and Getting Along
                http://forerunner.com/puritan/PS.Doctrine.html.

Orenstein, J.
    1988   *Sipurey HaTanakh LeYeladim* (Racine, WI: Western Publishing).

Otto, R.
    1958   *The Idea of the Holy* (New York: Oxford).

Ouaknin, M.-A.
    1995   *The Burnt Book: Reading the Talmud* (trans. Ll. Brown; Princeton: Princeton University Press).

Oursel, R.
    1975   *Haut-Poitou Roman* (La nuit des temps, 42; Yonne [France]: Zodiaque).

Page, N.
    1998   *The Tabloid Bible* (London: HarperCollins).

Patrick, D.
    1981   *The Rending of God in the Old Testament* (Philadelphia: Fortress).
Patterson, J.T.
    1996   *Grand Expectations: The United States, 1945–1974* (The Oxford History
                of the United States, X; Oxford and New York: Oxford University Press).
Peirce, C.S.
    1992   *The Essential Peirce: Selected Philosophical Writings*. I. *(1867–1893)*
                (N. Houser and C. Kloesel [eds.]; Bloomington, IN: Indiana University
                Press).
Perry, S.
    1997   *Men in Black* (London: Penguin).
Pike, F.B.
    1992   *The United States and Latin America: Myths and Stereotypes of Civiliza-
                tion and Nature* (Austin: University of Texas Press).
Pinski, D.
    1923   *King David and his Wives* (trans. I. Goldberg; New York: B.W. Huebsch).
Pinsky, M.L.
    1995   'In Walt's World, No Churches on Main Street or on Screen', *The
                Orlando Sentinel*, 16 July, A1 and A11.
Pippin, T.
    1992   *Death and Desire. The Rhetoric of Gender in the Apocalypse of John*
                (Literary Currents in Biblical Interpretation; Louisville, KY: Westminster/
                John Knox Press).
Plato
    1973   *Phaedrus* (trans. W. Hamilton; Middlesex, England: Penguin Books).
Pollack, Y.C.
    1934   *Nevi'im Rishonim La-talmidim: Yehoshua* (New York: Hebrew
                Publishing).
Pottle, S.
    1974   *Samson and Delilah* (words by G. Hawthorne, ASCAP; Nashville: Trigon
                Music, Inc.).
Pritchard, J.B. (ed.)
    1958   *The Ancient Near East: An Anthology of Texts and Pictures* (Princeton:
                Princeton University Press).
Probe Ministries: Capital Punishment
                http://www.leaderu.com/orgs/probe/docs/cap-pun.html.
Rad, G. von
    1961   *Genesis* (rev. edn; trans. J.H. Marks; London: SCM Press).
Randles, J.
    1997   *MIB: Investigating the Truth Behind the Men in Black Phenomenon*
                (London: Piatkus).
Rasmussen, W., and R. Tilton
    1994   *Pocahontas: Her Life and Legend* (Richmond: Virginia Historical
                Society).
La Reine c. Bouchard, *et al.*
    1999   Québec, Canada, cour municipal de la ville de Montréal, province de
                Québec, district de Montréal, sous la présidence de M. le juge Denis Bois-
                vert; No. 198-082-455, le 18 juin.

Rice, A.
    1995   *Memmoch the Devil: The Vampire Chronicles* (New York: Alfred A. Knopf).

Robinson, B.P.
    1986   'Zipporah to the Rescue: A Contextual Study of Exodus IV 24-6', *Vetus Testamentum* 36.4: 447-61.

Roller, P.
    1998   'Amazing Archaeology Triumph...Noah's Ark Discovery!', *Sun*, 11 August: 20-21.

Rollins, P.C.
    1983a   'Film, Television, and American Studies', in P.C. Rollins (ed.), *Hollywood As Historian: American Film in a Cultural Context* (Lexington: The University Press of Kentucky): 246-68.
    1983b   'Ideology and Film Rhetoric: Three Documentaries of the New Deal Era (1936–1941)', in P.C. Rollins (ed.), *Hollywood As Historian: American Film in a Cultural Context* (Lexington: The University Press of Kentucky): 32-48.

Rosenberg, D.
    1994   *World Mythology* (Lincolnwood: NTC Publishing Group, 2nd edn).

Rowlett, L.
    1992   'Inclusion, Exclusion and Marginality in the Book of Joshua', *JSOT* 55: 15-23.
    1996a   'Coopting the Female Body: Rahab, Pocahontas and Malantzin', Paper, American Academy of Religion annual meeting, New Orleans, November 1996.
    1996b   *Joshua and the Rhetoric of Violence* (Sheffield: Sheffield Academic Press).

Runions, E., and B. Williams
    1999   'Noisy Choppers Just the Start', *Montréal Hour,* 6–12 May: 3.

Rutledge, D.
    1998   'Demon Lover: Epistemology in the Flesh', *Body & Society* 4.2: 1-17.

Said, E.W.
    1991   *Orientalism. Western Conceptions of the Orient* (London: Penguin Books [1978]).

Sakenfeld, K.D.
    1995   *Journeying with God: A Commentary on the Book of Numbers* (Grand Rapids: Eerdmans).

Salten, F.
    1931   *Samson and Delilah: A Novel* (New York: Simon & Schuster).

Samuels, R.
    1973   *Bible Stories for Jewish Children from Joshua to Queen Esther* (New York: Ktav).
    1989   *Prophets, Writings, and You: A Value Clarification Text* (New York: Ktav).

Sanford, G.
    1997   'Is Bizarre Christmas Weather a Sign of Christ's Second Coming?', *Weekly World News*, 23 December: 40-41.

1998a   'Holy Moses! Did President Clinton Meet Jesus?', *Weekly World News*, 7 April: 38.

1998b   'Weather Disasters Are a Sure Sign Christ Will Return to Earth Soon!', *Weekly World News*, 26 May: 40-41.

1998c   'Jesus Is Back on Earth—The End of the World Is Near!', *Weekly World News*, 2 June: 8-9.

Scarry, E.
1985   *The Body in Pain: The Making and Unmaking of the World* (New York: Oxford University Press).

Schäfer, P.
1997   *Judeophobia: Attitudes toward the Jews in the Ancient World* (Cambridge, MA: Harvard University Press).

Schweitzer, A.
1961   *The Quest of the Historical Jesus* (trans. W. Montgomery; New York: Macmillan).

Scott, J.M.
forthcoming   'Korah and Qumran', in P.W. Flint (ed.), *The Bible at Qumran: Text, Shape and Interpretation* (SDSRL, 3; Grand Rapids: Eerdmans).

Segal, A.F.
1995   'The Ten Commandments', in M.C. Carnes *et al.* (eds.), *Past Imperfect: History According to the Movies* (New York: Henry Holt): 36-39.

Seidman, N.
1994   'Carnal Knowledge: Sex and the Body in Jewish Studies', *Jewish Social Studies: History, Culture, and Society* 1.1: 115-46.

Selvidge, M.
1992   'Powerful and Powerless Women in the Apocalypse', *Neotestamentica* 26.1: 157-67.

Serres, M.
1995   *Angels. A Modern Myth* (Paris and New York: Flammarion).

Shalev, M.
1985   *The Bible Now* (Tel Aviv: Schocken).

Shevell, C.D.
1953   *Joshua: Workbook* (New York: Jewish Education Committee).

Silva, J.
1998   'Couple Describe First Interstellar Wedding! "We Were Married on a UFO!" ', *Weekly World News*, 4 August: 31.

Skulsky, S.
1961   *Legends of Joshua. Retold for Jewish Youth* (trans. I.M. Lask; New York: Shulsinger Brothers).

Smelik, K.A.D., and J. Naftaniel-Joéls
1986a   *Daniel* (Kampen: Kok).
1986b   *Esther* (Kampen: Kok).
1987   *Jona* (Kampen: Kok).

Smith, M.S.
1994   *The Ugaritic Baal Cycle.* I. *Introduction with Text, Translation, and Commentary of KTU 1.1–1.2* (VTSup, 55; Leiden: E.J. Brill).

Smith, P.
    1988   *Discerning the Subject* (foreword by J. Mowitt; Theory and History of
            Literature, 55; Minneapolis: University of Minnesota Press).
Snaith, N.H.
    1967   *Leviticus and Numbers* (The Century Bible; London: Nelson).
Sobchack, V.C.
    1983   '*The Grapes of Wrath* (1940): Thematic Emphasis through Visual Style',
            in P.C. Rollins (ed.), *Hollywood As Historian: American Film in a Cul-
            tural Context* (Lexington: The University Press of Kentucky): 68-87.
Solomon, E.
    1997   *Men in Black: The Script and the Story behind the Film* (Forewords by
            B. Sonnenfeld, W.F. Parkes and L. MacDonald; London: Penguin).
Sonnenfeld, B. (director)
    1997   *Men in Black* (Burbank City, CA: Columbia Pictures).
Splitting the Sky Hill, J.
    1998   Public Lecture. Montreal, Québec, 14 February.
Splitting the Sky Hill, J., and S. Bruderer
            Unpublished MS, 'The Autobiography of Dacajeweiah (Splitting the Sky)
            with Sandra Bruderer'.
Stern, D.
    1984   'Moses-cide; Midrash and Contemporary Literary Criticism', *Prooftexts*
            4: 193-204.
Sternberg, M.
    1987   *The Poetics of Biblical Narrative* (Bloomington: Indiana University
            Press).
Sun
    1997   'Jesus Was Son of Rich Architect—New Revelation from Top Priest', 2
            December: 23.
Sweet, D., and P. Cherry
    1998   'Protesters Block Hotel', *Montreal Gazette,* 26 May: A1-2.
Talmud
    1948, 1952   *The Babylonian Talmud* (ed. I. Epstein; London: Soncino Press).
Terrien, S.
    1978   *The Elusive Presence* (San Francisco: Harper and Row).
Toombs, L.E.
    1995   'When Religions Collide: The Yahweh/Baal Confrontation', in J.M.
            O'Brien and F.L. Horton Jr (eds.), *The Yahweh/Baal Confrontation and
            Other Studies in Biblical Literature and Archaeology: Essays in Honour
            of Emmett Willard Hamrick* (Studies in the Bible and Early Christianity,
            35; Lewiston: Mellen): 13-46.
Toulmin, S.
    1985   *The Return to Cosmology: Postmodern Science and the Theology of
            Nature* (Berkeley: University of California).
Ts'Peten (Gustafsen Lake) Standoff
            http://kafka.uvic.ca/~vipirg/SISIS/gustmain.html.

Van der Meer, F.
    1978   *Apocalypse. Visioenen uit het boek der Openbaring in de kunst* (Antwerpen: Mercatorfonds. English edn: *Apocalypse. Visions from the Book of Revelation in Western Art* [London: Thames & Hudson]).

Veith, I.
    1965   *Hysteria: The History of a Disease* (Phoenix Books; Chicago: University of Chicago Press).

Victoria, A.
    1997   'Are We in the Biblical Last Days? More Than 1,500 Scientists, Clergymen and Scholars Say Yes—That the End of the World Is upon Us!', *Weekly World News*, 2 December: 8-9.
    1998   'End of the World Rumors Are Sweeping through Washington!', *Weekly World News*, 19 May: 1, 46-47.

Walsh, R.
    1997a   'Ancient Biblical Worlds and Recent Magical Realism: Affirming and Denying Reality', in G. Aichele and T. Pippen (eds.), *The Monstrous and the Unspeakable: The Bible as Fantastic Literature* (Sheffield: Sheffield Academic Press): 135-47.
    1997b   *Reading the Bible: An Introduction* (Notre Dame: Cross Cultural).

Weiser, A.
    1962   *The Psalms* (trans. H. Hartwell; Old Testament Library; Philadelphia: Westminster).

Weissman, Y.
    1995   *The Little Midrash Says: The Story of Yehoshua* (New York: Benei Yakov).

Wenham, G.J.
    1981   *Numbers: An Introduction and Commentary* (TynOTC; Downers Grove, IL: Inter-Varsity Press).

White, S.
    1993   'Split Skins: Female Agency and Bodily Mutilation in *The Little Mermaid*', in J. Collins, H. Radner and A.P. Collins (eds.), *Film Theory Goes to the Movies* (New York and London: Routledge): 182-95.

Wichterich, C.
    1999   *La femme mondialisée* (trans. Olivier Mannoni; Solin: Actes Sud).

Williams, P.
    1980   *Symbolic Change and the Modernization Process in Historical Perspective* (Englewood Cliffs: Prentice–Hall).

Wills, G.
    1998   'Eve Would Have Flipped Her Wig over This! "Fig Leaf" Swimsuits for Men!', *Weekly World News*, 26 May: 46-47.

Weekly World News
    1997a   'Weekly World News Fans Flocking to Florida's Lake Okeechobee to Await the End of the World!', 4 November: 41.
    1997b   'REPENT! 12 Top Clergymen Tell Why the World Must End by the Year 2000!', 18 November: 8-9.
    1998a   'Gal with 36-Inch-Long Fingernails Kills Herself—WHILE PICKING HER NOSE!', 27 January: 47.
    1998b   'Is This Man the Anti-Christ? First Interview!', 14 April: 19.

Yonay, S. and R. Yonay
    1989   *Sefer Yehoshua* (New York: Shai).

Young, F.
    1982   *Can These Dry Bones Live?* (London: SCM).

Zielberman, Y., and D. Korach-Seger
    1987   *Bereshit Sheli: Student Workbook* (Jerusalem: Office of Education and Culture).

Zink, J.
    1988   *Visionen* (Diabücherei Christliche Kunst. Bd. 24/Text. Eschbach: Verlag am Eschbach).

Žižek, S.
    1989   *The Sublime Object of Ideology* (Phronesis; London: Verso).
    1991   *Looking Awry: An Introduction to Jacques Lacan through Popular Culture* (October Books; Cambridge, MA: MIT Press).
    1993   *Tarrying with the Negative: Kant, Hegel and the Critique of Ideology* (Durham: Duke University Press).
    1997   *The Abyss of Freedom/Ages of the Word: An Essay by Slavoj Žižek with the Text of Schelling's Die Weltalter (second draft, 1813) in English Translation by Judith Norman* (Ann Arbor: University of Michigan Press).

Žižek, S. (ed.)
    1994   *Mapping Ideology* (London and New York: Verso).

INDEXES

INDEX OF REFERENCES

OLD TESTAMENT

OTHER ANCIENT SOURCES

INDEX OF AUTHORS

JOURNAL FOR THE STUDY OF THE OLD TESTAMENT
SUPPLEMENT SERIES